Cover Photos

1. Thrilled with my new 500cc Enfield Bullet as I leave Marikar Motors' showroom in Chennai. March 2000
2. Lazing on a beach on an island off the coast near Cartagena, Colombia with a fellow traveller from Manchester
3. Macho Mexican man. He was selling goat burritos but really should be in films!
4. Pretending to be Zenobia in Palmyra, Syria
5. I was kidnapped in Colombia by a member of a motorcycle club and kept for a week of sightseeing that ended with a party before I was allowed to leave!
6. Volcanoes in Java, Indonesia. They are everywhere!
7. Having my spokes finely tuned in Rawalpindi, Pakistan
8. Man fishing on the Mekong River, Cambodia
9. Riding the bike up a plank onto the catamaran prior to the first of two voyages from Hell!
10. Preparations for the Lae Festival. Papua, New Guinea
11. A young jockey at a dodgy horserace in Honduras
12. A bike drop in Colombia
13. A greasy-pole competition for presents at the top. Java, Indonesia
14. A Thai lady packing fish into boxes at a market
15. Ignominious descent with a dislocated elbow from the ski-slopes in New Zealand
16. A peaceful scene in northern Pakistan

I really like this book!

I'm not often inclined to start comments about a book with words such as, what a phenomenal read! *Hit The Road, Jac!* more that deserves the description . . . It's very easy to give it 5★.

—Sam Manicom, author of *Into Africa, Under Asian Skies, Distant Suns,* and *Tortillas to Totems,* and Jupiter's Travellers Advisor to the Ted Simon Foundation

HIT THE ROAD, JAC!

Road Dog Publications was formed in 2010 as an imprint of Lost Classics Book Company and is dedicated to publishing the best in books on motorcycling, motorsports, and adventure travel. Visit us at www.roaddogpub.com.

Hit the Road, Jac!; Seven Years, Twenty Countries, No Plan

Maps by the author
Edited by Thérèse Wayman (UK Edition) and
Michael Fitterling (North American Edition)
Proofing by Nich Brown (UK Edition) and
Randy Mayes (North American Edition)

ISBN 978-1-890623-64-7
Library of Congress Control Number: 2018946991

Follow the author at her website at www.jacquifurneaux.com
on Facebook at Jacqui Furneaux Travels
and on Instagram at jacqui.furneaux

An Imprint of Lost Classics Book Company
This book also available in eBook format at online booksellers. ISBN 978-1-890623-65-4

HIT THE ROAD, JAC!

SEVEN YEARS, TWENTY COUNTRIES, NO PLAN

by

Jacqui Furneaux

Publisher
Lake Wales, Florida

Dedicated to my parents, May and Roy, who never told me to be careful.

Photo courtesy of Hilary Galea

ABOUT THE AUTHOR

Seven years, twenty countries, no plan.
How it started . . .

In 1998, after bringing up a family and enjoying a lifetime career as a nurse and health visitor in the UK, I set out on a year's journey, on my own for the first time ever, having always been someone's daughter, little sister, or wife. I started backpacking in Thailand and explored many South East Asian countries armed only with wide-open eyes and a guide book. Six months into the trip and feeling quite the adventurous explorer, I went to Pakistan and then to Rajasthan, India, where I met a Dutchman who was travelling on an Enfield Bullet motorbike. He fired my imagination with tales of the open road.

I returned to the UK, but I found it hard to settle down, as I really liked travelling, and although at my age I really should have known better, I set off again, this time combining my love of travel with my other passion . . . motorcycling. I'd owned various Japanese motorbikes over the years since passing my test at the age of twenty-four but had never had an Enfield!

Hit the Road, Jac!

**Picking up my brand new Enfield from the
showroom in Chennai, India.**

Exchanging guide books for road maps, for my fiftieth birthday I bought a brand new 500cc Enfield Bullet in India and rode it, initially alongside the Dutchman who had suggested the idea. He was seventeen years younger than me, and I thought the adventure might last six months, at most. None of it was planned. I would not have dreamed I'd be having this chance of a lifetime when I should have been saving for my retirement. But life's too short not to take a chance.

TABLE OF CONTENTS

1

Sikkim, India, 2000

The Kissing Tarmac Days

"Look—they're getting out!"

As soon as we pulled the leeches off and deposited them in the toilet (not knowing what else to do with them) they emerged over the rim, heading towards us more quickly than I'd imagined a leech could move. Some of the black slug-like creatures were already bloated with our blood; others wanted to be. It was like a horror film.

I'd encountered a leech a couple of years before when backpacking in Laos and had pulled it off my arm, so I knew they weren't dangerous. In fact, I knew them to have a long and noble history in medicine, relieving people considered to have an excess of blood. Besides, I'd been brought up to wonder at nature, not to be revolted by it. So our horror film turned to comedy as we laughed at each other and the bloody state we were in.

We weren't on a dangerous mission in deepest Africa but just back from a walk only a kilometre from the road we'd arrived on

1

the day before, the latest stop during our meandering motorcycle ride round India. It was the 24th of June 2000, not that the time or the date mattered to me. I had six whole gloriously unplanned months on my visa.

Starting in Chennai in southern Indiam we had got as far north as the state of Sikkim, bordering with Nepal, Tibet, and Bhutan, and were now staying in a Buddhist monastery. Our room was so vast we often played badminton in it. The monastery was near remote Pemayangtse, a warm and humid region during the rainy season. The Himalayan mist occasionally cleared, allowing views of the magnificent Kanchenjunga, the third highest mountain in the world.

The lush, mossy ground was like a sponge, the trees dripping with moisture. A cheeky leech had burrowed painlessly into my skin and dangled from my forehead, having ambushed me from a tree. When he'd recovered from a fit of laughter, Hendrikus pulled it off.

Back in our room, we removed our boots and found our socks soggy with blood and containing engorged leeches. Some fell to the tiled bathroom floor, but dozens more were still attached. Skinny when empty, they'd been able to wriggle through our socks. We'd prised them off each other with pliers and cleared our feet and legs of them, then thought we'd better have a complete search, so removed all our clothes.

Now it was my turn to laugh. I was entrusted with the task of pulling them off the nether regions of my boyfriend from the Netherlands. He'd been wearing shorts, and several bloodsuckers were attached where he least wanted them. Shrieks of disbelief echoed round the bathroom walls. With blood dripping from each puncture, we looked so hideous all we could do was laugh until, horrified, we saw them climbing out of the toilet. Adding shampoo to the toilet bowl made it too slippery to climb; the leeches couldn't get a grip on the porcelain and were flushed away. We were safe.

I looked at myself and smiled. How had I, Jacqui Furneaux, age fifty, become covered in leeches, in this remote place in a country I'd never imagined I'd visit, with a man I'd known for only a few months? Strangest of all was that outside the old monastery was a black 500cc Enfield Bullet, and I'd ridden it here. Next to it was Hendrikus's greyish-green one. Whatever would my parents have said?

Feminism hadn't really hit the Somerset coastal town of Weston-super-Mare when I was leaving school in the late 1960s. The Secondary Girls' School I attended through failing my 11+ exam didn't inspire me to do anything academically outstanding. The huge school was overwhelming; my class size went from three at my little primary school to thirty-six pupils. Disgraced since failing the exam, there I began to believe what I'd been told: I'd never make anything of myself. Although my mother, the family breadwinner, should have been an example to me to work hard so I could provide for myself, I was far more inclined towards outdoor activities.

I had been called a tomboy all my life, being adventurous, fearless, and happiest outdoors, preferring to climb trees and make dens with my older brother, Roger, in the woodland behind our home than do school work. I wasn't treated like a delicate doll and, if injured, was inspected, dusted off, and told I'd live. I bore injuries and bruises with pride. Nobody expected much of me, and I didn't expect much from myself, either. Having such low expectations gave me freedom. I was happy with that.

Adults asked me from the age of six what I was going to do when I grew up. I didn't know then and didn't know at sixteen, either. Doris Day's song, *Que Sera Sera, Whatever Will Be Will Be*, was often on the radio and sung by my family throughout my childhood years. It must have had an effect on me, because I waited to see what would happen, believing I had very little choice in the matter of my own future. Roles for women and girls were shifting, but it was still the norm to get a job until marriage and children and then be supported by one's husband. I was confused. Was I meant to conform to the marriage and children role or support myself?

An ability to identify and climb trees didn't automatically point me towards any particular career. Always disappointed by my school reports, "Jacqueline must try harder," my mother repeatedly pleaded, "Why can't you be like your brother?" Four years older than me, he was her golden boy, possibly as difficult a role for him as it was for me. He worked hard at school and didn't break things around the house like I did. I adored him and accompanied him and his adventurous friends everywhere in those happy days, when we could stay out all day, our parents never knowing where we were.

We enjoyed unrestricted outdoor freedom and were never told, "Be careful; you might hurt yourself."

My constant presence must have been wearisome for him, but he never complained. So that I could remain in the gang with him and his friends, I was every bit as tough, with my own sheath-knife for making spears or prising limpets from rock-pools. I was better at climbing trees than any of them and was the best at lighting campfires too.

When he and his friends reached fourteen and left me and their childish ways behind, I was stuck as a ten-year-old outsider. Fortunately, my love of the outdoors was catered for when I discovered Girl Guides. I thrived and put endless effort into gaining proficiency badges like Pioneer, Camp Leader, and Boatswain but sniffed at Homemaker, Cook, or anything of a domestic nature. My fictional heroes were Beryl the Peril and George from Enid Blyton's *Famous Five*.

Despite knowing the world had more to offer me than working in the local Clarks shoe factory, I had no idea what to do with my reasonable collection of GCE "O" level and GCSE passes. Careers advice was limited to nursing, secretarial work, or making shoes, so to please my father, I started nurse training at Bristol Royal Infirmary. Ironically, despite my 11+ failure, a classmate from my little private school, who had passed her exam and gone to the grammar school, arrived to start her training on the same day I did. Suddenly, I didn't feel as dim as I had been told I was when compared unfavourably with her all those years before.

"Going with the flow" was the theme in the hippy 1970s, and I happily conformed to family and societal expectations, managing a family and career and adding community nursing qualifications to my nurse registration. At the age of forty-eight, when my marriage came to an end due to my having an affair, I was forced to make a decision about my future, something I did not find easy. Disappointed and ashamed, accepting all the blame, I ran off to backpack in Asia for a year.

I'd missed out on this sort of thing when I was younger and it seemed a good time to make myself scarce. I flew to Thailand, where I was surprised to find lots of other people doing the same thing. I teamed up with a young Swiss woman and travelled with her for two months in Laos until I'd got the hang of it and then carried on through Vietnam, Cambodia, Malaysia, and Singapore. When I felt really confident, I went to Pakistan and India.

Nine months into my sojourn, I reached Jaiselmer, in the Indian state of Rajasthan. I'd collected information about local camel safaris into the nearby Thar Desert and was on my way for lunch to read through them and pick the best. As I approached a restaurant away from the tourist area, I saw a big, dusty man with red hair get off a dirty old-fashioned motorbike and enter the restaurant. I had an interest in motorcycles, owning several since my twenties, and gave it a look-over before going inside. It was unlike any of the modern Japanese bikes I had owned, and I assumed it was an old British model.

The rider was seated at a table in the fan-cooled gloom inside the restaurant. I asked him if he would mind if I joined him for lunch apologeticly, as he looked hot and weary and perhaps wanted to be alone.

Happy to have company, Hendrikus told me about his bike, an Enfield Bullet, bought new in Chennai only a few months before. These bikes were originally English-made but proved so suitable for all-terrain use in India that the Indian Army and Police used them, until eventually, the entire factory was shipped from Redditch to Madras (now Chennai), where they have been made ever since. Production has never ceased since their design in the 1950s. It didn't look very new then, and I wondered what on earth he'd been doing with it.

We spent the rest of that day together, and before I retired to my crumbling hotel inside the walls of this sandcastle city in the desert, he had invited me to explore the area as pillion.

It was March 1999. I was forty-nine and, after nine months, had been backpacking in Asia long enough to abandon commonly held concerns about protocol and personal safety. So when this dashing Dutchman invited me to accompany him into the restricted zone between India and Pakistan, it seemed perfectly normal to forget about the camel safari and go with him. There's something about India that makes the bizarre quite acceptable, and I had not the least hesitation to go with him.

We spent four surreal days together, blagging our way through security posts and camping in the desert, letting the tyres down to ride across the sand. We camped unobserved in sand dunes and watched the sunrise, talking about our travels and our lives. He was great fun to be with and not averse to taking risks. He told me enthralling stories about riding the bike across deserts, over mountains, and through rivers.

We were both upset at parting, but I had been through this heartache many times with backpackers I'd met; so many wonderful people going their own ways. In those days before social media and when even emails were new, I don't know why, but we exchanged postal, not email addresses. I travelled to Goa to meet my younger daughter, Abby, who was joining me for a three-week holiday. Hendrikus headed towards Pakistan.

On my return to Bristol, England, three months later, after a full year away, there was a letter from him waiting at my mother's address (I had no home). I replied to the Dutch address he had given me. We said things like, "Wasn't it great! Where are you and what are you doing?" and that, I thought, was that.

He turned up in Bristol four months after that and asked me to return to India, buy my own Enfield, and travel with him. It didn't take more than a minute or two for me to decide. He was a handsome ex-lifeguard, seventeen years younger than me, and had an optimistic outlook. I had been happily helping my friend, Martin, set up Bristol's first backpackers' hostel (my investment in this business provided me with an income of £300 per month) but was not cured of the yearning to travel since my own backpacking experience. And anyway, I still hadn't decided what to do when I grew up.

We spent a month or so getting to know each other whilst he built websites, earning some money to continue travelling—this time with me! He called me "Every man's dream," and he was my dream man. But acutely aware of our age difference, I thought it might last a maximum of six months before he tired of me, then I'd return and be normal. In the meantime, I would ride this miracle for however long it lasted.

When I left the showroom and my shiny new Enfield stalled for the umpteenth time in the chaotic Chennai traffic amidst honking and choking buses, lorries, and motor rickshaws in the midday heat, I wondered if I'd made the right decision to spend £1,000 on this machine for my fiftieth birthday. Why had I let Hendrikus's Enfield travel-tales inspire me and not listened to friends who'd urged caution? Still on a five-year unpaid career break, I could always return to health visiting in Stoke-on-Trent if this escapade didn't work out. But my father had told me to "Travel, my dear," and anyway, I was committed now I'd bought this motorbike.

I'd had various motorbikes since the hot summer of 1976, when my husband returned from work one afternoon to find me and our two little daughters, Claire and Abby, in a plastic paddling pool in the garden, trying to keep cool. "Why don't you have a ride on this?" He pointed to the Honda 90 step-through motorcycle he used for getting to work. I looked at it with distaste. As a nurse, I had cared for patients in A&E, brought in by ambulance after accidents.

To me, motorbikes were dangerous, dirty, noisy things, and I hesitated. "Go on. It'll cool you down." I had a car licence and a helmet, so after he showed me how to go and stop, I went. And that was it. I was hooked and thereafter always had a motorbike. Women riders were not so common then, and some people thought me strange, but I've never let that stop me doing anything.

Now, in India, I had to unlearn modern bike foot controls. Not only was the Enfield's gear-change lever on the side where the back brake was on my previously-owned Japanese bikes, but the gears were "first is up, all the rest are down" instead of "first is down, all the rest are up." I liked not having an electric start button, feeling that at last I had a proper motorbike like my father's BSA.

Kick-starting the bike successfully was an achievement in itself. The technique involved watching the compressor dial to tell me when the piston was in the right position to fire up the engine. I had a lot of practice whilst following Hendrikus and adapted to the "flowing like water" way of riding in Indian traffic.

Vehicles inched themselves into the stream, and everyone shuffled to make room. Those in the middle manoeuvre to the edge to leave. By the time we left the city, I had mixed feelings about this birthday treat to myself.

"What do you mean, I've got to change the oil?" I retorted when Hendrikus told me about maintaining this relic of a past age. I'd never so much as picked up a spanner before, taking my Suzuki GS500 for an annual service only when it was warm enough to emerge from the garage. I thought the little tool kit in the side box of the Enfield was for someone else to use, along with the manuals.

Sorting out documents had been a lengthy, frustrating obstacle race round Chennai. I needed to go with the dealer to get a letter from the British Embassy, which would enable me to apply for an Indian driving licence. It was necessary to use a false address supplied by the dealer for this, as non-residents of India are not allowed to buy motor vehicles. I also had to provide proof that the money I had brought with me in travellers' cheques was really mine. A "No Objections Certificate" was required to prove the Enfield was not stolen, but I was told at the office I would have to get a different form first from the AA. Then I had to go to the Police Crime Records office and the Regional Transport Office.

Each of these offices was staffed by people dedicated to their section of bureaucracy who wrote meticulously in accounts and record books. From floor to ceiling, rooms were lined with ancient ledgers, probably dating back to the Raj. In the end, fifteen signatures from five different departments had been required to take possession of my Enfield.

All this had taken many days to achieve, but finally all the documents had been scrutinised, stamped, and signed. The bike was mine, and I was free to ride it away, after it had received a Hindu blessing and was graced with a jasmine-flower garland.

Included with the bike was lifelong road tax for the state of Tamil Nadu; insurance was not necessary. It also came with "ladies' handles" to enable a side-saddle, sari-clad woman pillion to hold on with one hand whilst holding a child on her lap with the other. It was not unusual to see families of up to five on one motorcycle. Unlikely to have a side-saddle pillion, the handles were invaluable for tying on my luggage.

Whilst my bike was being prepared, and Hendrikus's bike was undergoing major repairs, we sailed to the Andaman Islands, in the Bay of Bengal, to celebrate our March birthdays, within days of each other. The ship left from Chennai but after our trip, returned us to Calcutta. Sleeping on deck, we expected mosquitoes, but a seafaring spider in my sleeping bag was quite a shock. I was left with tiny fang marks on my leg and the feeling that a cigarette had been stubbed on it.

Arriving in Calcutta late in the evening and unable to find a hotel that would accept foreigners, we did what other people were doing and slept on the pavement. I awoke in the night to the sound of rustling plastic bags and found a man in a loincloth trying on my glasses. When I objected, he took them off, shrugged, and shuffled away, seemingly dissatisfied with the fit or magnification.

From Calcutta, we returned by train to collect our bikes from Chennai, where I had a crash bar and luggage racks fitted. Two large car horns attached to the front forks would herald my approach to pedestrians and animals on the road.

We left Chennai, heading north out of Tamil Nadu into Andhra Pradesh towards Hyderabad, where Hendrikus wanted to do an IT course to enable him to work as we travelled. It was good to be in the countryside. We wore black jeans, long-sleeved T-shirts and fingerless gloves, all of which soon turned brown from road dust and diesel. Then they faded to grey after soaking in caustic washing powder that almost took my skin off. My mother, who had no wrinkles on her face at ninety, had never let the sun spoil her skin so I tied a thin scarf over my nose and mouth to protect me from burning.

Being on tight budgets, we ate street food and stayed in cheap hotels; some once plush but now faded, others concrete boxes containing just beds and a squat toilet. Most had posters on the walls, and one of these delighted us particularly. With a background of a country scene with a waterfall frozen in time were the words: *We are made for higher timings.* This nonsensical statement was oft repeated at times when words of wisdom were required in the forthcoming months.

To my delight, we went off-road and slept outside by rivers and in orchards. Twice my bike fell on me during the night, soaking me in petrol as I slept beside it in mango groves with soft ground, so I tied it to a tree like a rancher securing a horse at a corral. In the hills of the Eastern Ghats we slept on a huge, flat rock overlooking the vast plain below. It was big enough for us both and the petrol camping stove and food. Because the rock held the day's heat all night, we didn't need bedding.

At dawn, as we drank mugs of tea, we watched the light reveal the tranquil, hazy view for miles around as India woke up. It was so quiet we could hear the wheels of ox-drawn carts before we could pick them out in the distance.

Sometimes, to wangle overnight stops in old colonial houses with beautiful grounds, Hendrikus told the wardens of Government resthouses that we were employed by the government to assess the road conditions. Nobody seemed to mind, and we paid them whatever they asked.

I was getting used to the Enfield, finding it comfortable to ride all day, but it gradually dawned on me that a huge part of travelling with this bike was the bike itself. Keeping it happy took up a good deal of the time. I'm an "If it ain't broke, don't fix it" woman. Hendrikus was an avid, if not obsessive, maintenance man. Even when I knew I'd only run out of petrol he wanted to strip the carburettor. Petrol stations were plentiful, but I hadn't yet developed my mental petrol gauge.

The work of identifying and fixing problems was interesting and challenging, and I enjoyed working together. It was a good way to learn, even though I often wailed: "Oh -what's wrong with it NOW?" Timing maladjustments meant poor starting and running, the carburettor caused fuel problems, the clutch cable could be too slack or too tight, causing either forward creeping or gearbox crunching. It was never-ending. Just when I thought it was all done, the next bout of stalling or spluttering would start.

Then I realised that I was expecting it to behave like one of the modern motorbikes I'd owned. It just couldn't hurry, especially in temperatures of over 104 degrees Fahrenheit on these roads, using petrol of dubious quality, and with a rider yet to learn to know and love it. Once I saw it as a new antique and adjusted my own mental pace to match it, I began to feel differently. But at first I really didn't like my Enfield.

The sitting position enabled good all-round vision, but I had my first fall when a rickshaw darted out in front of me at Nellore. According to the registration document, the bike weighed 370 pounds, but with spare parts and all my luggage, it was too heavy for me to pick up. My five feet two inches height and hundred and ten pounds in weight weren't enough. Hendrikus had to help me.

Before I rode the Enfield in India, I used to think I knew how to ride a motorcycle, but I'd only ever ridden on tarmac in the UK. Here, on the back roads of India, there was precious little of that. I learned about dodging potholes, riding on tracks across fields and through streams. Although I resented the amount of time it took to maintain it, I tolerated the bike but fell in love with India.

After fifty years of Western life and living by the clock, I fell in love, too, with this blissfully unstructured and aimless life. I developed a "travel grin" of childish contentment. Nobody made me feel wicked for not doing anything useful. On quiet roads, I could ride side-saddle or stand on the saddle with one leg out behind me, or cross my hands on the handlebars, operating the throttle with my left hand, enabling hand-holding with Hendrikus, whichever side of me he was. He held sweets out for me to grab as I chugged past. Sometimes the throttle cable became clogged with dirt and stuck as if on cruise control. Riding with arms folded, I steered with my body-weight as I'd done on my bicycle in my youth.

We rode without helmets, allowing us to chat as we tootled along, rarely going faster than 30 mph, the road conditions conducive to this relaxed pace. I could feel the warm wind in my hair, hear the confidently thumping engine, smell the aromas, taste the dust of rural India, and see all around the open countryside. Riding with no helmet was worth the risk.

We rode into villages made of mud houses with thatched roofs and, on approaching one, thought a tornado was brewing in a dry and dusty field. As we got nearer, we saw it was a wrestling competition. Two men, dressed only in underpants, flew at each other. Dust filled the air, covering the spectators. Furious fighting between the fit, wiry men resulted in victory to the man who forced his opponent's shoulders onto the ground. The competitors stood side by side for a chummy photograph afterwards. We didn't wrestle but did join roadside cricket games with schoolboys or farm-workers.

Markets provided food and entertainment. I had my silver ring turned into "gold" when it was dipped in some "magic potion," and my fortune was told by a parrot that picked a card with its beak. I learned to enjoy chai, the sweet, milky tea that I'd refused in Pakistani homes when a health visitor. We saw women in beautiful saris carrying heavy loads of gravel on their heads on building sites. We heard jingly Indian music coming from the shops when we rode through towns and ate freshly cooked food and drank tap or well water as Indians did.

Sometimes, we would travel as little as twenty miles before finding a place we couldn't bear to pass. Other times, we'd ride all day, stopping only for refreshment from stalls when we saw them.

Juice extracted by feeding lengths of sugar cane through a mangle was my favourite, or mango lassi made from yoghurt. We'd always stop to see what people were selling.

The days stretched endlessly, and nobody was checking their watch to tell me there wasn't time and we should hurry on, although Hendrikus got impatient with me sometimes. I wasn't always sure why, but I loved being with him and tried not to be a nuisance.

It was so hot that whenever we had the opportunity we cooled off fully-dressed in village ponds, joining local children with their water buffalo or camels. We'd strip off and swim in pristine rivers if nobody was about. My contact lenses felt welded to my eyeballs with the heat. Returning to the bike after lunch in a blissfully air-conditioned restaurant, the heat from my clutch lever seared my fingers, leaving a lasting brown stripe across them. The little tarmac there was on the roads was of limited use, as it melted and studded the tyres with loose gravel.

People waved as we rode on country roads strewn with millet drying in the heat. We must have been an unusual sight. One terrified small boy ran away when we stopped at the roadside to buy fresh coconuts, opened for us with a machete by his father. He disappeared into the distance, scared by these two strange beings on overloaded motorbikes, one of them a big, bearded, red-haired man, the other a small woman.

Rural India made me smile with utter contentment. Away from the cities, traffic conditions were quite different, with tractors or carts carrying huge hay loads. Herds of goats would be on the roads, and once, thousands of ducks were being shepherded to a small lake for their daily swim; we stopped to watch them hurry along, quacking with delight as they approached the water.

We were often tempted by rocky tracks, heading we knew not where, and I realised why Hendrikus's bike didn't look new. Neither did mine by then, because I dropped it, fell off it, scraped it through narrow gullies and dented it, and dirt stuck to every crevice.

I didn't feel unsafe in India. Yes, curious men would surround us when we stopped for a fruit juice or for fuel and fiddle with the Enfield's levers, but luggage was left untouched on the bikes for hours, whilst we went to find somewhere to stay or to explore.

Day after day of quiet country roads took us through magnificent scenery from the Nallamala Hills. "Perhaps we'll see a tiger," I said excitedly, as we stopped in the Nagarjunasgar National Park to enjoy a roadside brew, keeping a hopeful but nervous look-out.

It took us ten days to go from Chennai to Hyderabad. We had ridden a distance of only 620 miles. We stayed there for a month in a very cheap hotel that provided us with our own en-suite river every time it rained, but for fifty pence a night, we felt it churlish to complain.

Every day for breakfast I gorged on delicious mango and yoghurt, then masala dosa (a crisp pancake made from rice and lentil flour, stuffed with spiced potato and herbs).

Whilst Hendrikus attended his IT course, I rode my bike on my own for the first time, through crowded streets, avoiding speed bumps, chickens, cows, and people. I did some solo mechanic work too, as my throttle was sticking. It seemed free at the handlebar, so I explored the carburettor end. The cable was forced into too much of an angle as it passed under the tank and wasn't pulling the barrel up and down freely. A bit of tinkering and repositioning sorted that problem out.

Flushed with success, I found a bit of inner tube on the road outside our hotel and padded the battery inside its box to cushion it. Then I removed the grip rail from the seat-back, so I could shift my luggage further back for greater comfort. Hey—I was a mechanical genius and had the dirty fingernails to prove it. However, just scratching my skin led to black fingernails, the dirt sticking to the sweat dripping from me, even when I wasn't doing anything.

Such a contrast was this life to the one I had as a health visitor. I couldn't handle new-born babies with rough, dirt-engrained hands like this. Much as I'd enjoyed my job, I didn't now want to be doing anything else. I was loving life in Hyderabad, living in a cheap dump of a hotel behind the station with my boyfriend.

I kept myself busy, exploring the museum and local temples. I went to the health clinic and found nutritional advice displays like those we'd had at my health centre in Burslem, Stoke-on-Trent, except that the recommended food included mangos and coconut instead of broccoli and apples.

There was plenty to keep me occupied. One evening a calf got loose in the traffic by our hotel. I acted like a cowgirl, leaping off my bike to grab the rope around its neck. It was stronger, heavier, and more desperate than me, and it tore off dragging me behind it for a while before I had to let go and watch it disappear into the traffic rather than be run over myself. After all, it was sacred; I wasn't.

Soon after, some naan bread was crunchier than it should have been. A large piece of a tooth had broken off. For a relatively small amount, a local dentist did a major rebuild that has been entirely satisfactory ever since.

By then, we'd been travelling for a few months, and I needed a haircut. With some trepidation, in case I wasn't welcome, I opened the door of a beauty parlour I had noticed being used by women in burkas. I was beckoned in. Inside, women had discarded their burkas, revealing fashionable, feminine clothes.

They were animatedly chatting as their finger and toe-nails were painted and their hair was styled. I watched, intrigued, when a procedure called "threading" was performed to remove unwanted facial hair. Skilful use of twisted threads whisked it away. This is now common in the UK, but I had never seen it before. Using sign-language to indicate my needs, I was a given an excellent shampoo, head-massage, and trim.

It wasn't all work and study for Hendrikus. One evening, we went to the cinema to see *The Beach*. The manager, who was also the ticket vendor, ice-cream seller, and projectionist, was thrilled that two foreigners were visiting his cinema and treated us like royalty, showing us to the best seats and not starting the film until we were comfortable.

At the interval, he collected us for a "Thumbs Up" Indian cola drink in the projection room. Sad to say, the twenty year-old British-made sound system he was so proud of was unbearably loud and muffled, necessitating fingers in ears for most of the visually poor film, but the brightness of our host more than made up for the film quality.

Hendrikus finished his IT course, and having a vague idea to go to Nepal, we continued north to explore Orissa (now called Odisha). A rickshaw darting out in front of me made me wobble and fall off. I landed in something foul-smelling that stank all day, until I doused myself in one of the plentiful rivers we had to cross.

The map indicated an abrupt end to the road before one river. "There must be a bridge . . . the road wouldn't just end there, would it?" We carried on, but end there it did, and after struggling along sections of thick sand, the river was up to my knees. Hendrikus explained that, provided I keep the bike going fairly quickly, I would create a shallow bow-wave, and no water would go up the exhaust pipe and stall the engine. Grumbling that nurses and Enfields were not designed to do this, I managed to keep the bike going over rocks as big and round as footballs.

On the other side, there was more hateful sand and an awkward track. My triumph at managing to cross the river and negotiate the track was short-lived as I hit a patch of sand on the road, stopping me dead and sending me flying into a hedge.

"Today we won't use the map. We'll use the compass to keep us going north," announced Hendrikus one morning. Somehow though, by the end of the day, we ended up where we'd started in the morning. It had been a great day on narrow tracks, so it didn't matter. Strangely, the same thing happened when we used his GPS, so we went back to using maps and asking directions, a much better way to travel, we decided.

Hendrikus was not at all afflicted by a feeling of failure at asking directions; he relished it as a means of having more contact with the people whose country we had come to see. They were only too pleased to be helpful, even if they didn't always understand where we wanted to go and all pointed in different directions. Everyone enjoyed the contact, and there were smiles all round.

At last, Hendrikus had his wish to dismantle the carburettor on my bike. On investigation, we found that a rubber stopper in the choke had perished. A bit of old inner tube did well as a replacement. Unfortunately, my first puncture wasn't so easily dealt with.

The previous night had been spent in the corner of a field under a thatched shelter that we shared with an enormous and vocal frog. Tractors had been working all night, and we hadn't had much sleep in the sticky heat. We were tired when we left at dawn. My puncture couldn't have happened at a worse time. It was at midday in 104 degrees heat in a place with no shade.

I must have run over a branch of the ubiquitous Indian thorn-tree, because there were two thorns looking like nails stuck in the tyre, necessitating two patches on the inner tube. We carried air-compressors, and after an hour's work, the wheel was back in. I went to ride off, but the tyre was flat and had to come off again; the tube had got pinched by the tyre lever during refitting. Tempers were frayed, poor Hendrikus doing most of the hard physical work.

That night, after three nights sleeping out, we treated ourselves to a cheap hotel. Whatever hotels had meant to me in the past, they bore little resemblance to the ones we used now; the only thing they had in common was that a bed, of sorts, was in the room.

We entered Puri during preparations for the holy Ratha Yatra festival, when a wooden doll-like representation of the deity Jagannath, and two lesser gods, normally kept in the temple, are paraded around the town on three separate massive wooden, elaborately decorated chariots. Made afresh each year and then burnt, the word *juggernaut* originates from these impressive chariots. They were being built in the street and were so big that my head just reached the wheel-hub.

As we observed the preparations, we saw a little "hole-in-the-wall" shop, where customers were furtively buying hash. This was, after all, a former hippy outpost.

The festival was still weeks away, so we moved on. Internet cafés were numerous in towns, so sending and receiving emails was a regular activity. I missed my daughters and relished any news.

At one session, Hendrikus learnt that his best friend's wife had left him. He immediately decided that what Theo needed more than anything at the height of his distress was a month in India riding pillion on bumpy dirt tracks, sleeping in cheap hotels, or camping wild, eating street food containing heaven-knows-what, suffering the relentless attentions of mosquitoes, washing in streams (if at all), and sweltering in heat from which there is no escape. "He'll love it," he declared. It would mean Theo riding pillion with Hendrikus while I carried his luggage on my bike.

By this time, we were fazed at nothing, taking each day as it came and dealing with everything as it happened. We increased our pace in order to be in Delhi to meet Theo in a month's time. My bike had a full service in the Enfield-mad city of Cuttack in a brand new workshop that was blessed with incense sticks and prayers. Beautifully kept Enfields were everywhere there, so the future of the new workshop looked promising.

We were on the border between West Bengal and Bihar. The vista was less pretty as we rode across the plains. After a hot and sticky ride all day along the frantic National Highway 5, dusk was approaching. We chose a dhaba, a roadside restaurant truck stop where we could eat and stay the night outside under a canopy on

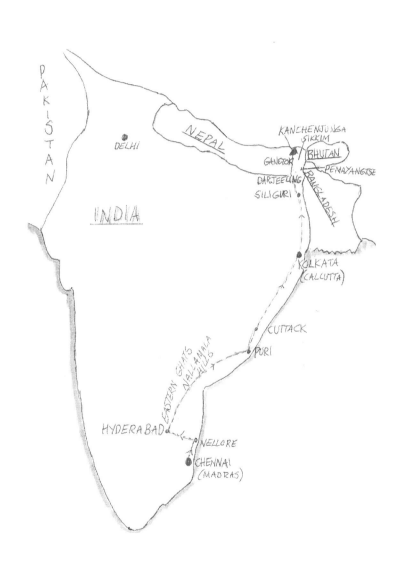

charpoys (wooden beds with woven string instead of springs or a mattress). We'd been looking forward to a cold beer, but our dhaba had none. We were directed to a nearby off-licence across the state border in Bihar.

By then it was dark and the road badly pot-holed and rough. I had all my luggage on the bike and Hendrikus as pillion. I overtook a long queue of lorries as we approached the checkpoint. The police officer demanded an astronomical amount for letting us through, even though we explained we'd be returning in a few minutes, so I naughtily rode round the barrier and went on, planning to do the same on the way back.

After we'd bought our beer, there was a sudden downpour, causing reduced visibility and slowing me as the heavy rain splashed on the road and on my glasses in the dark. The bike decided to stall at the barrier. The angry policeman approached. I kicked and kicked the starter, an awkward manoeuvre with the additional weight. Finally, I was successful and rode past him and his raised fist.

Feeling like Bonnie and Clyde, we enjoyed the beer all the more for the adventure. The rain was torrential that night, but in the morning as the bright sun dried them, the friendly manager said, "God has washed your motorcycles!"

We left the plains and this dismal area with its numerous overturned lorries and dead roadside goats and dogs. I collided with a dog, but it ran off, unhurt. We made our way up towards Darjeeling, famous for its tea. The scenery improved.

Passing green pastoral fields from Siligiri, we began a steep ascent up a long, narrow zigzag road. Apart from the labouring of our engines, it was serene, as no lorries could climb it. So alarming was the gradient, I worried that my heavily rear-loaded bike would tip over backwards. I couldn't find second gear on a few occasions and had to quickly engage first gear again to prevent a rapid backwards decent.

We calculated that we'd climbed 5,900 feet in twenty-four miles. As we climbed, it was like being in a different country. We had frequent stops for a brew and to cool the bikes after steep climbing in low gears.

Women in colourful saris worked in the terraced fields picking leaves, looking just as they do on packets of PG Tips tea. I liked Darjeeling. The people and the food were different, with oriental influences as we were so close to Nepal and China. Actually, it was hard to feel we were still in India. Steamed savoury Nepalese dumplings, called momo, were a favourite treat. I bought packets of local tea and sent them to Claire and Abby.

Our last push north was to Sikkim, and it was there that I not only discovered leeches but also what happens when the Enfield's neutral-finder doesn't work. Leaving the mountainous capital, Gangtok, a long road descended into the distance. Perfect for some freewheeling.

Already accumulating quite some speed, I kicked the neutral lever with my heel and released the clutch. I almost went over the handlebar but had the wit to pull the clutch in quickly as I snaked down the road. From fourth gear, it had gone into second instead of neutral, and was like jamming on the brakes. I never trusted it after that, always letting out the clutch very gingerly.

I learned something else in Gangtok, too. Hendrikus had made it clear he was tired of doing all the maintenance, so I had the brilliant idea of doing the overdue oil-changes on both bikes. While he rested in our hotel, I did mine perfectly, and overconfidently set to on his Enfield. But instead of loosening one of the plugs under the oil tank on his bike to drain out the old oil, I mistakenly over-tightened it and ruined the thread.

It was a stupid mistake, and he was justifiably cross. Multiple washers plugged the leak and sufficed as a temporary repair until we found somewhere where a new thread could be cut and a bigger plug fitted. Subsequently, I always double, no, triple-check each time I approach a nut with a spanner.

After Sikkim, the time for Theo's arrival was approaching, and all of a sudden we had to hurry. I wasn't used to this! We were on our way to Nepal, and I had no Carnet de Passage. Hendrikus already had such a document, essential in many countries. It acts as a vehicle passport and is a guarantee for customs purposes to ensure that the owner of the vehicle will not sell it in that country. It is a laborious and expensive procedure to obtain, and I was going to try to get into Nepal without one.

2

NEPAL, INDIA AGAIN, AND THEO

THAT'S WHAT FRIENDS ARE FOR

I held my breath at the border, but all it took was some form-filling and a small fee before I was issued with a temporary importation document and allowed to ride the Enfield excitedly into Nepal, my first border-crossing.

Nepal, separating north-east India from China, has a reputation for being slightly less offbeat than India, but just across the border, near Bagdogra, I saw a naked woman walking along a road as if it were quite the normal thing to do. We were in Nepal for only ten days. There were mountains, there must have been mountains, but what I remember most about Nepal is the variety of the places we slept.

There was unrest there. Dissatisfied with the power of the monarchy, Moaist insurgents were attempting to enforce communism. Rebels were at large, but in hiding. We decided they wouldn't be interested in us, so continued to sleep outside.

Our first night was spent in the rain, torrential enough to put off any terrorist but not would-be campers like us. Hendrikus had picked the spot. I'll never know why, but he chose to set up camp under a pylon situated in a dip. Even before we'd erected the tent we were soaked. The sudden downpour trickled down each pylon support and started to fill the hollow where the tent was. It was a most uncomfortable night, and every time I shifted my position, I could feel and hear the water sloshing underneath like a water bed.

Hendrikus's little tent was not entirely waterproof, so by the morning we were soggy, and packed up in tight-lipped silence. He'd stopped calling me "Every man's dream" and started to call me "Beauty," but not that morning. However, the two not very happy campers had survived the night unmolested by Maoists. It stopped raining, and the winding uphill ride to Kathmandu (one of my favourite riding roads ever) was just thrilling.

The sun came out, wet-weather gear was stowed away, and I was warm and laughing with sheer joy as I swung from left to right on the bends, up and down mountains, and speeding away from dogs who ran with fury for my ankles. I bonded with my bike and felt part of it like I'd never felt before.

We should have had helmets in the capital city but didn't. Kathmandu policemen tried to catch us but couldn't. We discovered Hotel Bluebird, an old hotel with beautifully carved wooden lintels. One night wasn't long enough to form an impression of Kathmandu; we arrived, slept, and left. I was disappointed that there wasn't time to absorb its spiritual aura, but by the morning, the tent and clothes that we had draped over the woodcarvings were dry, and Delhi was still over a thousand kilometres away.

Hendrikus's friend would be packing by then. I didn't worry about having a third person travelling with us. I'd heard how adventurous and tough he was so didn't worry that he might find our way of travelling too extreme. "Theo would LOVE this," Hendrikus would exclaim as we disappeared up inviting tracks just to see where they led, usually rewarded with a view or ideal camping spot. If anything, I worried I might not be able to keep up with the combined zaniness of not just one, but two daring Dutchmen.

A half-built petrol station on a quiet road near Pokhara was our next bedroom as we travelled west. We set up home in a roofed part (at dusk, it had started to pour with rain again) with plenty of room to garage us and the Enfields. Unobserved, we cooked noodles and drank Nepalese brandy that I'd just had time to buy before leaving Kathmandu. We felt like millionaires until reminded of our lowly surroundings by a mouse scampering over us in the night.

Keeping camping equipment to a bare minimum in preference to spare bike parts and tools, we didn't have sleeping mats, but I've always been able to sleep on the hardest of surfaces since being a keen Girl Guide in the days before such luxuries. To me, even a sewn-in tent groundsheet is a miracle.

Due to the rain, next day the roads were muddy and winding. I was going too fast when approaching a bend, braked, and performed a perfect sideways pirouette, thus wiping off the speedometer attached to the front fork. Travelling about 125 miles per day, the next two nights were spent in perfect camping spots (chosen by me and not under pylons) amongst trees next to rivers. I washed some clothes and swam with water buffalo, definitely the most idyllic way to do the laundry.

We read our books by the light of campfires, hardly discreet, but no Maoists bothered us. Our only visitors bore not firearms but a basket of truffles. A man and his sons had been foraging in the forest with their dog. Too stunned to ask them to sell us some, we each calculated how much the large basket-full would fetch in London or Amsterdam.

Ten days after entering Nepal at the eastern-most point, we left it at Banbasa, the most western. Hello again, India. One of the first things we saw was an overloaded passenger truck with so many people hanging on at the back, it tipped backwards on the rear wheels with the headlights in the air. It was one of those "if only I'd had my camera" moments.

On the road towards Delhi we had to wait at a level crossing. As other vehicles drew up to the barrier, drivers started to fill the right-hand side of the road, as well as the left on both sides. When the train had gone through and the barriers were raised, both sides charged at each other as if in battle. Horns and shouts accompanied the mayhem. We joined in the fun, blaring our horns too, squeezing between rickshaws, carts, and lorries, eventually getting through and out the other side. India!

It was inevitable that at some point Hendrikus and I would lose each other. On the two-day ride to Delhi from Rudrapur, we each thought the other was in front. Without mobile phones, we had no way of contacting each other. Fortunately, we had already chosen a guesthouse in Delhi and knew that whoever got there first would wait until the other turned up.

At Moradabad, about halfway, my clutch cable snapped. I'd just started to replace it with my spare when two men approached. They snatched the spanners from me saying, "No Madam, we cannot allow you to do this." They sent another man to a local mechanic, who arrived within minutes and did the job for some gratefully-given rupees. The men invited me to stay with them when I explained I had lost my partner. They treated me to a meal and gave me the best bedroom. How staggeringly kind people are to strangers in need. I wondered if this would happen if an Indian person was stranded with a problem in a British city.

I found Hendrikus the next day at the Sunny Guest House in Delhi. My first experience of travelling alone had been most enjoyable. I had stopped wherever and whenever I wanted, enjoying lemon tea and toast at a pleasant café that Hendrikus would never have stopped at; he always chose cheap truck stops. I'd not got lost and even had an adventure. I felt confidence growing and chuckled.

Not so long ago I'd been working where not all my clients were pleased to see me approach the door. "Oh bloody hell, it's the f***ing health visitor!" But now Hendrikus was complimentary about my ability to travel and ride a motorbike. I was appreciated for what I did, rather than being disapproved of for what I didn't.

NHS Management bullied us to reach impossible targets. You try telling people with little money or hope that they should stop smoking or take an unpaid day off to get the kids immunised or wean their babies on puréed fresh vegetables rather than putting mashed baked beans in a baby's bottle with the top of the teat cut off.

Hendrikus was in charge, but I was ready for anything, happy to sit back and enjoy the show. By being able to cope with the situation on finding myself alone in Moradabad, I realised that if the time ever came I would be fine on my own. Then I remembered how often I had to be helped to pick the bike up and how difficult bike maintenance was and reconsidered.

Poor Theo. He must have wished he'd stayed in Holland. Before coming to India, the furthest he'd been away from home was a package holiday in Spain. Now he was staying in a crowded dormitory in a rickety guesthouse with two people who had been travelling rough on motorbikes for months. No longer the smartly-dressed health professional, I kept myself clean, but my clothes looked well-travelled.

I left Hendrikus and Theo to exchange their news in Dutch whilst I had the Enfield serviced. I returned to a sorry tale. Poor Theo had his wallet and passport stolen when they'd gone for a bus-ride. I felt so sorry for him. He didn't seem the rufty-tufty explorer Hendrikus had made him out to be.

Arranging money transfers, replacement return air tickets, and a new passport took many days. He didn't like Indian food and would eat only at Delhi's one and only McDonald's (lamb instead of sacred cow) and drink cola. Hendrikus told him that outside the city we would find nicer food so, rather overloaded, we set off for Amritsar, favouring the quiet country roads of Haryana, rather than the frenetic Grand Trunk Road. Hendrikus and I loved sleeping under the stars near Hisar and bathing in streams in the Punjab. Poor, uncomfortable Theo was homesick.

If the dormitory at the Sunny Guest House had been a shock, he must have thought we were making him undergo some sort of cruel endurance test at Amritsar's Golden Temple. Budget travellers like us slept on mattresses on the floor in the foreigners' section of the pilgrims' hostel. Motorbikes were also welcome. I had been to the temple on a couple of occasions whilst backpacking and was used to sleeping shoulder-to-shoulder with strangers in a long row. Turbaned Sikh guards were on duty at all times, keeping an eye on the Enfields.

The Golden Temple is one of my favourite buildings; a place of calm, despite its violent history and the war-scenes depicted on the walls surrounding the huge holy water tank. A painting showed a martyr carrying his own severed head, fighting on valiantly for the Sikh cause.

Hendrikus's bike showed similar endurance despite all the extra weight, needing only to have the rear mudguard lifted clear of the back tyre to prevent it rubbing. The same could not be said for Theo, who said he hated India. Hendrikus wanted to show him an adventurous time and decided we would go to Kashmir.

Naïvely unconcerned about going into the area of dispute between India and Pakistan, we rode to Jammu and Kashmir state. We should have expected trouble as we passed soldiers behind sandbags on road bends, exchanging cheery waves with them as we climbed steeply north.

They let us pass; after all, we must have looked comedic rather than threatening. None of us wore helmets, our features clearly visible; burly Hendrikus with long, red hair, Theo tall and pale, and me, a small woman on another motorbike almost buried amongst luggage with tied-on bags flying wildly with every bump in the road.

After a few days, I started to worry about Theo's health. He wouldn't eat anything except packet noodles. He'd sip only carbonated drinks, whilst Hendrikus and I drank tap water and heartily tucked into lentil dhal and rice, omelettes, chapattis, kebabs, yoghurt, and all manner of roadside fare.

Theo was sick that night. Hendrikus took him to sit outside our delightful riverside hotel in the moonlight for some fresh air. As they sat talking, they heard the click of several guns being cocked. Terrified they were going to be shot by rebels, they told me later they put their hands up to show they were unarmed. A patrol of Indian soldiers emerged from the reeds. Although we hadn't been told there was one, the boys were soundly reprimanded for breaking the curfew. This area was, they were reminded, full of insurgents. Poor Theo.

The next day we arrived at Udhampur. Theo had developed a cough in addition to his stomach problems. I was worried and told Hendrikus he was expecting too much of his friend, but he wanted to ride on the second highest road in the world, from Kargil to Lehn.

By the time we got to Baltal, sixty miles away, Theo was struggling to stay on the back of the bike. I insisted we seek medical help. He looked dehydrated and was clearly most unwell. As luck would have it, we chanced upon a huge Hindu festival attended by vast numbers of devotees to Shiva. Pilgrims from all over India had

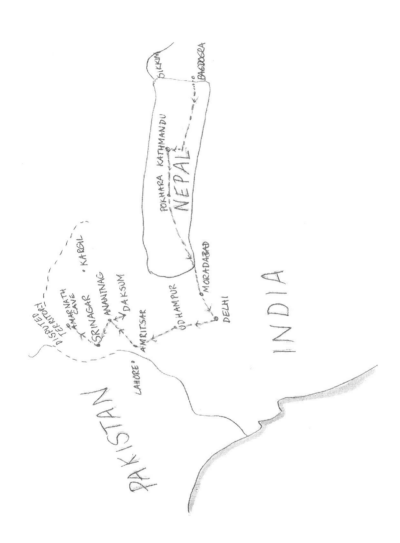

come to show their respect at Amarnath cave where, in the winter, ice forms a lingam, a highly religious symbol. At 12,729 feet, the cave is accessible only at this time when the seven-and-a-half mile walk is free of snow. The festival was supported by the Indian Army, as Muslim and Hindu were not at peace.

The enthusiastic medics fell upon Theo at the camp; within the hour, he had a drip in each arm, antibiotics injected into his bottom, oral sedatives, pills for pain and pills to stop sickness. He was put on a stretcher and taken by ambulance to Ward 7, a brown tent bearing a big red cross. I went with him and held his drip, feeling very much as if I were in an episode of *M.A.S.H.*

Once we knew Theo was being cared for, Hendrikus and I went to explore this stunningly beautiful place. All the poems and words of praise written about Kashmir are true, and we felt sad that so much blood was being spilt over it. It was dusk, so we were turned back from hiking up to the shrine for our own safety. Pilgrims were greeting and congratulating each other with cries of "Bom Bom Bolay." It was a great atmosphere. We were made very welcome and ate curry and rice at one of the stalls set up for the occasion, before sleeping alongside Theo on canvas beds in his hospital tent.

The next day as he was recovering, some army engineers dealt successfully with my leaking clutch case by padding out the rubber gasket with hairy garden string. I was short of petrol too, and they found some in an old jerry-can. It had rust and blue paint in it and had to be strained through some mesh, but Enfields will run on anything.

Theo was discharged but advised to return to Srinagar. We found a beautifully appointed houseboat on the lake where he could rest. We even found a takeaway pizza. It should have been a lovely meal as we dined on our palatial houseboat, but Hendrikus, who blamed Theo and his refusal to eat or drink for our failure to reach Leh, was struggling to keep his temper. Theo was trying to force down some pizza, and I was trying to keep the uncomfortable peace by being over-cheery to compensate for Hendrikus's lack of empathy for his friend's situation.

Theo's "interesting" holiday was not over yet. To make up for missing Leh, Hendrikus planned a "pretty" route back to Udhampur on tracks through forested mountains. We got quite a long way and stayed in a beautiful wooden Kashmiri house near

Daksum as guests of a very well-to-do family. As a female, I could meet the women who were friendly and curious, whilst Hendrikus and Theo could only stay with the men. We were eventually turned back by the Indian Army, who said they had intercepted a message between militants who had seen us. Grateful but disappointed, we re-crossed all the rivers we had just crossed and stayed in Anantnag. We were ready to leave, but the hotel manager told us there was a strict three-day curfew.

On the 15th July, shortly after we had left the festival, militants had indiscriminately opened fire on "our" pilgrims, killing twenty-seven and injuring another thirty-six. We were shocked, devastated. Theo had just about had enough by now and was glad his return flight was imminent.

We decided Hendrikus would go to Pakistan, because his Indian visa was running out, and I'd have to wait in Amritsar for my bike's Carnet de Passage to arrive from Holland. I'd need one to join him in Pakistan but had no success in arranging it through the British AA. The Netherlands one had been simple to organise. The curfew was lifted, and we were free to leave.

Theo flew home, Hendrikus crossed into Pakistan, and I returned to the Golden Temple to await the Carnet. Doubtful that DHL would deliver to the address "Golden Temple, Amritsar, India" the owners of a local glass and plywood business kindly agreed to accept delivery of my Carnet. I felt really sorry for Theo. He'd had a traumatic month travelling with us.

I enjoyed living at the temple. A box of bright, sparkly headscarves was provided for non-Sikhs, and each evening I chose one to wear for my peaceful walk around the lake. The Golden Temple became my home. I arose from my mattress on the floor each morning and walked along a busy street, where I developed a "good morning" acquaintance with a man who ironed clothes with an iron containing hot embers. He worked all day as he stood at his rickety ironing board on the pavement.

Sikh women in shalwar-kameez chose fresh produce from stalls as children in uniform hurried to school. Rickshaws darted about noisily. Businessmen in turbans looked fresh and smart. Most days I breakfasted on banana and the best freshly-made yoghurt I've ever tasted.

One morning, I walked round nearby Jallianwala Bagh Park, reading the information notices. Friendly local people asked where I was from, and I felt ashamed to tell them I was British. It was here in this public park, in April 1919, that an unarmed gathering of men, women, and children were fired on by the British Indian Army at the command of Brigadier-General Dyer. It happened at a time when anti-British feeling was running high throughout India but especially here in the Punjab.

Public gatherings had been banned, but families had travelled to Amritsar to celebrate the Sikh New Year from all over India as they had done for two-hundred years. As they assembled, Dyer imagined trouble and gave the order to fire into the crowd. Between 379 and 1,000 people were shot, depending on whether you believe British or Indian estimates. An elderly Indian man sat down next to me, and I told him how I felt. As he held his hand out for a donation, he said, "Never mind. It is all forgiven now." I gave him a generous amount to appease my private national guilt.

There has been appalling bloodshed in Amritsar. The Golden Temple was the scene of Operation Blue Star, the storming by Indhira Ghandi's military forces in 1984 to quash increasing Sikh power-seeking. In 2014, a remembrance ceremony to honour those killed in that event itself resulted in a sword-wielding fight. In both places, bullet-holes can still be seen in the walls.

Unspeakable violence took place in Amritsar during the partition of India in 1947 when Pakistan was formed. Muslims, Hindus, and Sikhs, who had lived alongside each other for centuries, slaughtered each other because of newly-perceived intolerable religious differences. It didn't make sense, and I began to question religion and who had the right to set neighbour against neighbour.

As a Girl Guide I had promised to "do my duty to God and the Queen." My mother was a Methodist. I attended a Church of England school. I'd got married in a church. I thought about patriotism, too. With everyone else, I'd stood up whenever the National Anthem was played, even in cinemas, when I was a child. Although my parents brought me up to not be bigoted in any field, I absorbed the societal notion that "British is best." What arrogance.

After my visit to the park, in defiance of religious intolerance, I took Oobie, a young Israeli, on the Enfield to the train station to help him out. In the dormitory I made a point of talking with a fervently religious man from Switzerland. He wore a white robe and a large wooden crucifix and carried his Bible. When not riding his "lie-down" bicycle, he looked like Jesus and was inevitably recorded in my diary as Swiss Christian Chris.

My next pillion was Mike from England. We rode the 17 miles to the famous daily border closing ceremony between India and Pakistan at Wagah to see the ludicrous display of posturing. Instead of parading about in immaculate uniforms with a military band and guns, they might just as well poke their tongues out at each other across the barriers.

Ten days later, on the 15th August 2000, my Carnet arrived. I could then go anywhere with my bike. For the moment, the thirty-one mile journey across the border to Lahore in Pakistan would be enough. A straightforward and efficient session at Customs and Immigration on each side of the border and I was through and on my way to Lahore to meet Hendrikus.

3
PAKISTAN

"So free we seem, so fettered fast we are."
Robert Browning

I noticed the differences between India and Pakistan as soon as I crossed the border at Wagha. Apart from a plethora of mosques, it was more what wasn't there than what was there. I couldn't find a cup of coffee anywhere. No cows roamed. After the colour and vibrancy of India, it was less bright; women were not in saris working in the fields or mending roads. In fact, women were scarcely seen at all until I reached Lahore, a university town with some plucky female students.

Men wore grey shalwar-kameez suits, not garish shirts or turbans and white tunics. Traffic was still busy and noisy, but not a gaudily painted temple was to be seen, although huge hoardings advertised films with their startling colours portraying promise of drama and romance in the dark.

Hendrikus and I had a joyful reunion on the campsite in Lahore and discussed the similarities and differences. His thought was that India was the noisy child and Pakistan the sensible older brother.

When we checked our emails later, I heard him gasp. There was a message from Theo. He had returned back safely to Amsterdam, which given his recent experiences, was a relief. But we could hardly believe the next bit. He thanked us both for the best holiday he'd ever had. He'd thoroughly enjoyed himself and planned to return the following year, bringing a friend to share the experience. Looking at each other but unable to speak, we shook our heads in amazement.

After two days' riding north, we spent a few days on the foreigners' campsite in Islamabad, deciding we would continue up the epic Karakoram Highway (KKH) to the border with China at Khunjerab Pass. I was excited. A motorcycle traveller I'd met previously in Bangkok had told me about it. His description of riding a motorbike amongst mountains was tantalising; now I was going to do it.

Almost eaten alive by bed-bugs in one overnight truck-stop, which resulted in my losing two sleepy days swallowing antihistamines for respite from the itching, we favoured the tent. Following a tip given by Swiss Christian Chris, we went to the smartest hotels we could find and asked if we could camp overnight in their garden. Most managers agreed, and at Murree, a hill resort twenty-eight miles north of Islamabad, we had a spectacular view of the mountains from our tent on one of the terraces of the Cecil Hotel.

Our next stop up the KKH was Abbottabad, in the news eleven years later for being the site of the hideout and death of Osama Bin Laden. Not far from his future compound, in August 2000 we camped next to the Pakistani military academy, the equivalent of Sandhurst, so near we could hear the soldiers marching and the RSM barking at them.

We had a vague plan to ride our bikes all the way up the KKH and try to get into China, even though we knew we would be highly unlikely to get permission. But a trip to the Chinese border would be exciting anyway. As usual, we did anything we could to ride on dirt rather than tarmac.

Hendrikus suggested riding up the Khagan Valley to Chilas. According to the map, the ninety-three mile route would shave sixty-two miles off the road route and would, he said, be fun. We would be passing some of the most spectacular scenery in the world.

Fun? It was as hard as I could do. We left the KKH and the last signs of civilisation at Naran and proceeded up the lonely valley on a road more suitable for goats. I fell off countless times and once almost dropped over the edge into the gorge below. Sharp, jagged rocks littered the track which, when it wasn't crusty and rutted, was waterlogged.

I lost items from my luggage (including my lipstick) as the bike was bounced and bashed on boulders. Every inch was hard-won, loosening luggage, nuts, and bolts. I was scared and tired and insisted we camp as cold came with the dusk and I could no longer see the track. I was not having fun.

There was frost on the tent in the morning. An hour later it had risen to forty-eight degrees in the sun as I washed in a stream. On we went, up the treeless valley. We came across a bridge with so few planks (due to people taking them for firewood) they had to be shuffled from behind us to in front by the bridge custodian as we walked the bikes across. The track got harder. I had to tell myself repeatedly, "I CAN do it. I WILL do it!" because I knew there was no going back and there was just a chance it would get easier as we went on.

We met a caravan of nomadic people returning to the lower slopes with their donkeys, cattle, and goats for the winter. Unlike in other parts of Pakistan, the women's heads were uncovered; the mountain people seemed to have their own rules about that. We reached a height of 14,324 feet, from where we could see Nanga Parbat, the ninth highest mountain in the world. Then began the final ascent to lawless Chilas on the KKH. Some shortcut.

Bright daylight faded and became dusk. We were already done in when Hendrikus's front wheel fell off, due to a lug snapping. String and cable ties to the rescue. Then his engine wouldn't start, and countless times I helped him push his bike uphill before running back to get mine. I was happy to redress the balance, as he had picked me up countless times. He was flagging, whilst I found energy and optimism from somewhere, but things became almost unbearable when some children threw gravel at us.

Another, kinder, boy further up gladdened us with a bunch of fresh grapes picked from the garden and the news that we were nearly at Chilas. Oh, the joy! Exhausted, we fell into a good hotel, regardless of the cost. That time I would have refused the usual round town "Let's find the cheapest hotel" rigmarole that Hendrikus always insisted on. Never before had I been so grateful for comfort and rest. What a challenge it had been. I had surpassed my levels of endurance and physical strength. Now we were here, the journey suddenly became an adventure, not the ordeal it had been a few hours before.

In this area, ancient tenacious blood feuds persisted, based on religious differences between Sunni, Ismaili, and Shia Muslims. Next morning, as I checked on the bikes, I gave some paracetamol to a bandaged man who had five gunshot wounds. Lying in the back of an open pickup truck, which served as his ambulance, he was being taken to Gilgit hospital, eighty-one miles away, because the rivals who had shot him threatened to kill him at the local hospital. We waved to each other as the truck drove away.

Once more mulling over religion and the trouble it causes, I went to see the famous petroglyphs between the Indus River and the KKH. The petroglyphs date from between 5000 and 1000 BC. I climbed the cliffs to see where travellers and pilgrims on the Silk Route to and from China had left their stone-chiselled depictions of ibex, people, and references to Buddhism during more peaceful times.

One of my "O" level passes had been in Religious Education. At that time, the syllabus covered only Christianity, as if there were no others, but since wandering around Asia, my education had grown to include Buddhism and the Hindu, Jain, Sikh, and Islamic religions. However, I was none the wiser. Why was violence involved, when all claim to uphold tolerance and love?

Weary from six months on the road, some of it really hard, we were looking forward to a break from travelling. But fate had one last hurdle for us after the long day's travel from Chilas to Gilgit. It was dark as we approached the town, and a warm wind hit us from the front. Suddenly we were blasted in the face by a sand-storm, and the last few miles were painful and difficult. We treated ourselves to a room when we arrived at the North Inn in Gilgit, caked with sand and looking as if we'd just crossed a desert.

Heavy roads and heavy loads had taken their toll on the Enfields. They needed maintenance and repair. With no available spare parts, we had to have things made locally or make them ourselves. Finding plenty of workshops in Gilgit, we were welcomed by the owner of one who allowed us to use his premises and tools every day.

There were no "girly" calendars in this workshop. No hydraulic workbenches, electric tools, or inspection pits either. Just a concrete building in what Hendrikus and I called "Mechanic Street" because the long road was lined with engineering workshops. In one of the most beautiful parts of the world it appeared ugly, but beauty abounded in the human effort everyone made to overcome language and cultural differences.

Hendrikus's bike was having problems. The battery was not charging. On opening the clutch case, we saw that two stator windings in the alternator had burnt out. We bought reels of copper wire, measuring it by laying it out on the North Inn lawn where we were now camping.

Later, in our favourite chai shop, we wound what seemed to be miles of wire round bits of plastic we had fashioned from a bucket lid. The bodge worked. It was then comparatively simple to find a workshop where I could have a new front brake link-rod made with opposite threads on each end and, after those numerous drops and falls in the Khagan Valley, to straighten the skewed crash bar.

The North Inn filled up with people arriving for the Silk Route Festival, a celebration of thousands of years of trading between East and West. Bobby, a performer in a puppeteer company, booked in and befriended us. He was amused at our both sleeping in a tent made for one, calling it our "mobile palace." "Promise you will come for tea if you come to Islamabad," he ordered. We said we would, but a return to Islamabad was not planned. If we couldn't get into China, we'd go to north-west Pakistan. We'd have to be quick too; autumn was creeping up on us. Soon snow would close the roads for months.

The Silk Route Festival was lively and full of things I wished I could buy. For one afternoon, the week's food and crafts festival was set aside for women only. I talked with some of them. They couldn't understand why I would want to leave my home and family to go travelling in strange countries on a motorbike. For Pakistani women to travel without male relatives would be frightening and shameful. I wouldn't have swapped my life with theirs either. We joked about it, but they could not see how I could possibly be happy without Allah in my life.

Posters outside the Wall of Death motorcycle show enticed us in. Excitedly, we climbed to the viewing platform, waiting for the spectacle, the fanfare, the sense of occasion. Instead, a bored-looking bloke strolled in with a cigarette in his mouth wearing, not the anticipated flashy leathers, but a grey shirt and baggy trousers.

With not a vestige of showmanship, he got on a 125cc motorbike, distractedly started it up, and began the ascent up the vertical wall of the wooden drum-shaped structure. Two-stroke fumes filled the air, and the noise was deafening in the enclosed space. Hendrikus shouted something to me, but I couldn't hear what he was saying. Genuinely impressed when the rider became horizontal, lifting his arms over his head, we two clapped enthusiastically. The rest of the audience filed out silently after the two-minute show.

Piling on more layers of clothing, thanks to second-hand market stalls full of European cast-offs, we packed the renovated Enfields and started our reconnoitre towards China. We'd been working on the bikes for four weeks, and for most of that I'd had giardiasis, a persistent and obtrusive intestinal infection that had ruined my appetite and caused weight-loss.

My taste buds were stimulated when we arrived in the bountiful Hunza valley and were given juicy, flavoursome apricots, apples, and walnuts by an elderly couple who invited us into their garden at Karimabad. Hendrikus bought yak meat, which was leather-tough, even after a camping stove-full of fuel had been used to cook it.

Grey shale foothills and autumnal greenish-yellow leaves contrasted with blue river and sky and white mountain peaks. The KKH runs through the Karakoram mountains, and we could see Rakaposhi if we looked one way, Nanga Parbat if we looked the other. When we were in Nepal, the highest mountains had been in the distance, but here, thanks to the KKH, we were riding between them. I had never been anywhere so beautiful.

Hendrikus, so much happier since his Enfield was mended, decided a complete break from motorbikes was due. We would hire a donkey and walk with it up Chaprot Valley. Some schoolboys (not a schoolgirl in sight) had chatted to us as we walked along a country lane, and one of them said he would let us borrow his donkey for a couple of days for a small price. We loaded the donkey with bedding and food essentials for us all and set off up the valley.

The donkey emitted clouds of dust when we patted him, so we called him "Dusty Miller." He was excruciatingly slow and nowhere near as keen to get to the top of the Chaprot Pass as we were. It is 18,500 feet high, and we could have done it if he'd been more enthusiastic. In fact, we could have done it if we hadn't had him with us at all; but we were quite satisfied with our two nights out under the stars, realising that he set the pace and we could do nothing to chivvy him along. We'd become used to Enfield speeds so settled for Miller-speed, too.

Rakaposhi looked like a ridiculously oversized cardboard cut-out, silhouetted magnificently in front of the moon as we warmed ourselves and toasted some leftover breakfast chapattis on our campfire outside a shepherds' hut, the stars clear and numerous, with nothing but mountains to blank them from our vision. It was cold. Had Miller slept lying down we would have snuggled up to him, but he stood all night chomping his hay and burping.

After our two nights in the valley, we made our way down, finding it hard to keep up with Miller, who suddenly found the energy to race home. We returned him to his owner, whose parents invited us to share a meal with them in their lovely home.

The KKH is not the three-lane motorway its name suggests and was often no more than a track along much of its 500 mile length within Pakistan. It continues for another 250 miles in China.

We were surprised when on the final Khunjerab Pass stretch we met a non-local motorcyclist coming the other way. "Turn back!" he shouted desperately through his full-face helmet (we wore none), waving a hand in a heated glove back the way we'd come. Apparently, there was ice and snow further up, and despite riding a proper off-road bike with a support vehicle and film crew, he hadn't made it to the border

After they'd gone, we looked at each other, grinned, and carried on. Together, we'd ridden on deep sand, rutted tracks, gravel, thick mud, over rocks, through rivers, and along potholed roads dodging unpredictable vehicles, people, and animals. A bit of snow wasn't going to stop us.

We rode on the snow, even on road tyres. The border guards didn't let us cross into China but gave us tea and bread as we admired the stunning mountain views. The road levelled out, and we took the opportunity for some fun. My boots had no tread, and I could ski with Hendrikus towing me behind his bike.

To save petrol we freewheeled back down the way we had come. Rare Himalayan ibex, looking exactly like the ones I'd seen depicted as petroglyphs and probably their descendants, hardly stopped grazing to look at us as we went silently past.

Returning to a colder Gilgit, before going west, we sought a cheap room, rather than the tent. Our hotel was also the choice of some families of beggars. We saw them begging in town dressed in rags, looking miserably gaunt. Back at the hotel in the evenings, they would, as would anyone, change out of their work-clothes, have a meal, and relax.

Children who'd seemed barely able to lift a hand towards their mouths in a gesture of hunger were now noisily playing chase around the hotel garden. They were very friendly, and we shared food with each other. From the hot south of Pakistan, they came here every year for the rich pickings of the Silk Route Festival before returning to their warmer winter climate.

It was time for us to think about money and climate, too. Hendrikus was on a tight budget and needed to return to Europe to earn more travel money. If we didn't beat the snow to the Shandur Pass and beyond to Chitral, we would be stranded. Iran and westwards was the plan. Farewells were made to our friends from the chai-shop, charity volunteers we'd met, the hotel chef who'd allowed us use of his kitchen, and of course, our mechanic friends.

We managed only 19 miles that day. Our first night was spent at Singul, on the road to Chitral. A local policeman wouldn't hear of us staying in the local dormitory, insisting we sleep at the police station. We breakfasted on rice and dhal with another officer and the criminal to whom he was handcuffed. Afterwards, they lit each other's cigarettes.

The Hindu Kush Mountains loomed ahead as we followed the mica-blue Gilgit River westwards. The bikes were running well, we were happy, and every day was exciting. I loved my "What's happening next?" life.

What happened next was that I broke my leg.

I was leading on the narrow winding track when suddenly from a left-hand bend, a cherry-red four-wheel-drive truck hurtled towards me. With the river a steep drop to the right and sheer mountainside to my left, I had nowhere to go and nothing to do but wait for the inevitable crash. I looked down and saw shin-bone sticking through a gash in my jeans and my foot facing backwards. My fuss-free upbringing and career in nursing meant that I did not scream or panic.

As a student nurse, I'd held the hands of people who were dying and had to tell a woman in the casualty waiting room that her husband had died after a motorcycle accident. I'd been handed organs and limbs to dispose of in operating theatres. I was trained to assess an emergency and deal with it with a cool head. So I disengaged my foot from the peg where it was impaled, turning it to face the front. It was obvious that my right leg was broken.

"Don't worry. Your leg is not broken." said the driver.

Hendrikus caught up with the scene and, taking command, gave me painkillers, immobilised my leg, and lifted me into the back of the truck that had run into me, just like the man who'd been shot in Chilas. I wondered if I'd see him at the hospital and hoped his would-be killers wouldn't be roaming the wards with guns looking for him. Kind villagers assured us they would look after the motorbikes. We set off back the way we had come, Hendrikus holding me to absorb the bumps.

"Your leg is broken," said the doctor at the Aga Khan hospital back in Singul as he administered more robust pain-relief and applied a plaster cast. A few hours later, hitchhiking locals joined us in the ambulance to Gilgit hospital, until I could be flown to Islamabad. Hendrikus informed my insurance company of the accident and was reassured that costs would be covered.

Among my visitors during the three days we had to wait for a flight was a cat that spent the nights catching cockroaches in my room. I had not been allowed in the main women's ward. More charming was the lad from the chai shop, someone from the British Council who brought a secret and most welcome bottle of whisky, and one of the mechanics who came in with some fresh milk from his cow.

"Oh look—there's where we hired the donkey." Flying over the beautiful mountains to Islamabad in an hour (which had taken three Enfield-weeks) was almost worth breaking my leg. At the hospital, the orthopaedic surgeon explained that he would fit a stainless steel external support frame, to be made at a local workshop. Antibiotics and nutritional supplements were prescribed to build me up following the unintentional giardiasis weight-loss programme.

After the operation, Hendrikus alarmed patients, visitors, and medical staff by racing me in my wheelchair round the spacious hospital and grounds. I loved it, squealing all the way. He was an excellent support to me, making me laugh and snarling at the physiotherapist, who made me walk until I fainted from the pain.

With this frame, or as we called it, my "cage," I was able to hobble about on crutches and there was no reason to remain in hospital. I had decided to stay in Pakistan rather than go back to the UK, but there was the question of where to go. Hendrikus contacted Bobby, the puppeteer we'd met in Gilgit, and he, his brother, sister-in-law, and niece immediately turned up with flowers and a demand that we stay with them. Surely this was stretching the previous invitation to call in for tea a bit far?

Not only did this hospitable family give us the best bedroom in their home, but they changed their squat toilet for a European one just for me. Satisfied I was in safe hands, Hendrikus set off on the eighteen-hour bus journey back up the KKH to fetch his bike and to arrange compensation for the accident from the owner of the four-wheel-drive. True to their word, the villagers had garaged the motorbikes after the accident.

Hendrikus straightened out the worst damage and rode my bike to Gilgit. Vehicle insurance was useless in Pakistan; such matters were settled honourably over tea. Hendrikus returned with his Enfield and enough money to cover the excess on my UK travel insurance.

Living with a Pakistani family would be interesting at any level, but living with this family was hilarious. Bobby's brother was a comedy actor and full of fun. His brother's wife and their little girl soon lost their reserve. They turned night into day! In the mornings while everyone (including Hendrikus) slept, I breakfasted on bananas and biscuits. Then I washed in the tin bath and sat in the garden, waving the flies away and letting the sunshine heal the sites where the metal pins holding the bones in place pierced my leg. As it improved, I was able to hop on my good leg to the kitchen and make tea.

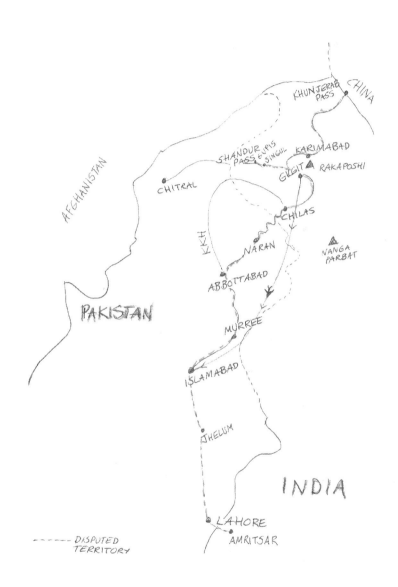

It was now the month of Ramadan, when Muslims fast during daylight hours. Food stalls assembled just before dusk. Men shuffled uneasily, awaiting the signal from the mosques that they could eat, drink, and smoke until dawn the next day. This suited our nocturnal hosts, who slept all day anyway.

There are exceptions to fasting requirements, and my being a non-Muslim, injured, and a traveller absolved me, but it didn't seem fair to eat openly in daylight. As my leg became less painful, and I was able to leave the house with Hendrikus, the search for sustenance and somewhere to eat it became our daily task.

For a Christmas treat, I requested that we fetch my motorbike. It was getting very cold, so I had special trousers made, with the right leg wide enough to go round the frame. Underneath the trousers, I safety-pinned slit leggings together round the pins going into my bones. Every bump painful, I bore the overnight bus journey back to Gilgit.

For the return journey, I rode pillion on my Enfield, clutching my crutches as we descended the KKH. Not only was it Ramadan, but also winter by then. At one hotel, we wrapped ourselves up in a plastic sheet to avoid the bed-bugs and slept with the light on, which kept them at bay a little. Sleeping with the metal frame was uncomfortable, and it was a miserable night.

Wearing all our warmest clothes, we made good progress down the KKH, until about a third of the way, a landslide totally blocked the road, and we had to stay in Dasu whilst it was cleared. Lorries tailed back, and drivers' communities developed with fires to keep them warm, quite a sight after dark. Several controlled explosions sent the bulk of the landslide tumbling into the valley below, and after three days, sympathetic workmen seeing me on crutches took pity.

First the Enfield and then me were carried over the remaining rubble. It was the first vehicle across. Drivers the other side cheered, knowing the road would soon be clear. Our onward road lane was deserted. Hendrikus got off the bike and sat behind me. "You drive," he said. With my feet raised on the crash-bar, he did the foot controls, as I steered and pulled in the clutch. I was so happy I wept.

Christmas and Ramadan coincided that year, and on Christmas morning, all we could find as a festive treat was John West mackerel fillets in mustard sauce and bread from the Afghani bakery. We went to a park, sitting behind a bush secretly eating our food. It was the strangest Christmas meal I've ever had.

Pavements were not flat or hazard-free. When I tripped over my crutches on a lumpy, cracked, uneven pavement one day I went crashing to the ground and was covered in dirt, wincing from the pain as the blow from the pins hitting the ground reverberated into the bones. But I was improving and getting around well on my elbow crutches. In a country where, outside of cities, women are rarely seen uncovered, I was used to being stared at. As a western woman on crutches, I was even more conspicuous.

Hendrikus found jobs building websites, and I was bored. Had it not been for the Coolabah Club at the Australian Embassy and the wonderful British Council library I would have gone mad. There were dozens of language schools all over Islamabad. Surely someone would appreciate practicing their English conversation?

I chanced on The English Language Institute, run by Wendy from Yorkshire. She exclaimed that I must have been sent from heaven, as she was a teacher short. No amount of my telling her I was a nurse, not a teacher, would stem her enthusiasm. "You're English, aren't you? Can you start tomorrow?"

The next morning at eight o'clock I was teaching two diplomat couples from Azerbaijan. I also ran the women's group and had students from Turkey, Italy, Rwanda (a princess), Nepal, Russia, Iran, Lithuania, and Chile. Suddenly, instead of Enfield manuals, bedtime reading consisted of English language books, and I was teaching pronouns, adverbs, and tenses.

My leg did not stop us exploring on my bike at weekends, and we ventured south to Khewra, the salt-mining area. We visited a mine, which was proud to have the world's only underground mosque made from bricks cut from the solid pink salt. Flat, quiet roads were ideal for me to steer my bike.

We stayed at a petrol station one night, the guest of the owner, who was thrilled to have foreign guests. He tucked us up in bed after getting his mother to make us a pea curry. We didn't see her to thank her, but in exchange for his kindness in the morning, we gave him a cup of coffee, the first he had ever tasted. He was not impressed.

Ramadan was coming to an end. I'd been sharing buses with goats for weeks. I watched as a cow had its throat cut in its owner's garden. As a school-child, our class had been taken to a horrifying abattoir.

This cow just seemed to get tired and lay down. It seemed a much less stressful experience for the animal whose life peacefully ebbed away after some prayers.

A communication breakdown occurred between the hospital and my insurance company, who refused to pay for essential out-patient treatment. Needing physiotherapy and X-rays to monitor bone-growth, I decided to go home. I had earned enough for the flight and would sort out the insurance later. A kind Pakistani friend let us secure our Enfields in his garage, and Hendrikus and I flew to the UK together.

Hendrikus went to London to earn more travel money, and I stayed with my mother in Bristol. My new orthopaedic consultant observed that, although the bone was healing, it was not straight and would one day need to be surgically rebroken and rotated. I would have to go through all this again. Regardless of any future operation, this time it would need another few months before the frame could come off.

I happily reacquainted myself with my daughters and set to working as hard as I could at Martin's backpacker hostel as manager and being as much of a help as my "cage" would allow. My ninety-three year-old mother and I lived happily together for eleven months, getting on better than we had ever done before: "Tell me again about when you slept outside in the mountains with the donkey, dear . . . "

Up at 6AM to help my early-rising mother, I'd spend all day and evening working at the hostel. The frame was removed after eight months, replaced briefly by a plaster. Once that came off I was free. It may not have been straight, but I could walk, run, and swim and most importantly, I could ride my Suzuki 500 to the seaside, where I thrashed about in the surf.

Between us, my brother and I arranged a live-in companion for my mother, who she accepted and grew fond of. Social services coordinated visits, and Meals on Wheels were arranged. With the feeling that I was now in the way, eleven months after returning to the UK, I made plans to leave.

Hendrikus and I had almost lost touch, but I emailed to tell him I was making my way back to Pakistan to get my Enfield. Alone and with my bank account looking healthier, I looked with incredulity at my return ticket and grinned.

4
SYRIA

ROMANS AND ROMANCE

"I'll look forward to more of your little holiday stories, dear," squeaked my mother as I left for Syria in February 2002. It was our third "final" goodbye since my long-term departure to go backpacking in 1998, and again when I set off to buy my Enfield in India and travel with Hendrikus in 2000, but I felt she'd still be there whenever I came back. She wasn't bored with my stories of life in other countries.

Apart from a coach trip to see the tulip fields in Holland with my aunt and a trip to Majorca with me in 1970, she'd never been abroad. "Hitler stopped me going to Paris in 1939," she said, as if that was his worst crime.

I'd grown up with my father's accounts of life as a young maritime customs officer in Shanghai, China, in the 1920s. The British discouraged use of domestic opium, and it was his job to search for it. He lived there for ten years and had many anecdotes, but my mother was bored with stories she'd heard so many times. I regretted not asking him to tell me more before he died at the age of eighty-nine. He inspired me to travel, but I too am wary of voicing a recollection with "When I was in . . ." as I see people's eyes glaze over.

The first thing I'd done when my frame was removed was have a celebratory seaside swim at Weston-super-Mare before booking my return flight to Pakistan. But wait . . . it says here on the ticket that as part of the deal I can spend a month in Syria on the way: I was going to have a holiday. All I knew about Syria was that it was where the "Dawn of Civilisation" took place, it was ruled by Bashar al-Assad, America had it on its terrorism blacklist, and that as I hadn't been before, I should definitely go there.

The Enfields had overstayed their allotted time in Pakistan, and I would have some explaining to do to various officials on my return to Islamabad. Showing them my scarred and wonky leg would not be appropriate proof, so I packed my X-rays and letters from the hospital as evidence. My medical insurance company didn't pay up until a complaint to the insurance ombudsman persuaded them to cover my flight.

I had no plans beyond the obstacle of retrieving my motorbike. Hendrikus and I were unlikely to continue travelling together. I'd felt bereft when he'd gone his own way whilst my leg was healing. He hadn't enjoyed visits to me and my mother, and after dumping all his surplus stuff with a "goodbye" note, he left to offer his skills in the IT boom in Ireland. It seemed impossible that two people who had been inseparable for a year and experienced so much together had just slipped apart, but I knew he was a free spirit, I'd had a truly wonderful time with him, and it seemed right for it to end now. I doubted my ability to travel on my own with the seemingly high-maintenance Enfield.

A month in Syria would allow me time to have a rest from domestic duties carried out on crutches and to enjoy myself with cash from working at the hostel. The inevitable struggle with bureaucracy and decision-making could wait.

Good fortune was shining upon me. My Syrian Airways ticket was upgraded to business class as compensation for the late flight, delayed for hours due to pilgrims returning from Mecca. Having a lift from a kind fellow passenger to my pre-booked hotel in

Damascus late at night was another bonus. It was in the centre of the old city, inexpensive but comfortable.

In the morning, wrapped up against the early chill, I started sightseeing. I left the hotel and felt I'd walked into one of the pictures from my childhood Bible. There were men wearing flowing Arab robes and headwear with the "bungie" strap round to keep them on. Some women wore the burka. I was wonderstruck. For me, Damascus was a city on the "Palestine in the time of Christ" page in the map section of my Bible. Other familiar names, such as Antioch and Caesarea Philippi, had captured my imagination since I was able to read.

I felt overwhelmed with the history of this, one of the oldest cities in the world. Bringing it right up-to-date to remind people just who was in charge here now were very large banners of the Assad father and sons, including Bashar, the present leader. Rather than flowing robes, they wore threatening military attire and sunglasses, looking like film stars in a war film.

Now, dismayed for the plight of people killed or still suffering in Syria, I feel privileged that I was able to go when I did. Many of the World Heritage sites have been shelled, looted, and deliberately damaged. Things I saw and people I met may not be there now, due to the brutal civil war between President Bashar-al Assad's government and rebel forces, started in March 2011.

Umayyad Mosque was the place to start my month's holiday. I covered my long hair with a headscarf and went into the vast area under the huge dome. I expected a reverential cathedral hush but found it wasn't like that at all. Emotions running high, men were weeping openly by the tomb of Husayn, a young relative of the Prophet Mohammed, who had been beheaded by his enemies in A.D. 680.

Simultaneously, cheery family snaps were being taken a short distance away, next to the plinth where his head had once been exhibited. Another head, purportedly buried under an ornate pillar in this magnificent building, is that of John the Baptist, recognised as a prophet by Christians and Muslims alike. The Pope had visited only a few weeks before. Despite the tears, it was a beautiful, joyful place with children running around the vast carpeted space; I felt like doing cartwheels across it myself.

The whole of Damascus is a World Heritage site, and the heart, the ground this mosque occupies, has been sacred to Arameans,

Romans, Christians, and Muslims during its long history since the eleventh century B.C. I felt overwhelmed to be in the same place as those people who had settled in Damascus about 5,000 years ago. Alexander the Great might have walked where people from all over the world walked now. I left the mosque and stepped out into brilliant sunshine.

"Come and see my carpets. I give you tea. Best price for you . . . " I wandered around the ancient Souq al-Hamadiyyeh, resisting gorgeous rugs, and saw things for sale that I didn't recognise. Dried up stumps that could be animal, vegetable, or mineral might be edible, to rub on sores, or be ground up for medicine or perfume. Gold was being weighed, and pieces snipped off coins in exchange for cash by men with scales.

Also for a snip were copies of designer clothes and handbags. Someone grasped my hand and very biblically anointed my wrist with perfumed oil. Attar of roses on my skin mingled with piles of oriental spices. It was almost too much. The oil was only fifty Syrian pounds for a vial, less than £1, but I was not in the market for scent.

I spent the rest of the afternoon wandering around Straight Street, the route taken by blinded Saint Paul who, on his way to Damascus to persecute early Christians, had a vision of Christ. Instantly converted, he spent the rest of his life telling everyone how great Jesus was. The Pope had walked here on his visit too, and I wondered if, like me, he'd stopped for some freshly-squeezed orange juice, pistachio nuts, and olives. If he did, I bet he didn't find the little off-licence I did and buy a bottle of beer.

I hardly ever use taxis but couldn't find the station a few days later, so shared one with a man who climbed in after me. This kind man would not let me pay the fare and ensured I caught the right train to Homs, my next destination. It took three hours to get there across desert scenes.

The city of Homs seemed well-off, but I wasn't. I'd brought only enough US dollars for a week or so. I'd found that in countries with no ATMs, banks were always happy to take the commission involved in a transaction with a passport and credit card. Not so in Syria. I calculated that my cash would stretch to six dollars a day for the month. I was used to being frugal, and Syria was not an expensive backpacking country, but I had money in the bank and wanted to spend it.

I admonished myself for not researching. Why hadn't I gone straight to Pakistan? Then I remembered that going with the flow, seizing the day, saying yes instead of no, believing life's too short, and daring to take chances was now so engrained I couldn't have resisted the offer on my return ticket to spend a month in Syria. I may never get the chance again.

In Homs I saw Um el-Zennar church, one of the most ancient churches in the world, dating from A. D. 59. It was built underground to protect it from the Romans and houses the holy relic of a belt supposedly worn by Mary, the mother of Jesus. Relics drew pilgrims (and their money) to places of worship. I remember seeing the head of Saint Catherine in Siena and, rather irreverently, the undergarments of Mohammed in Badshahi mosque in Lahore. I read later that this church was torched by rebel forces in May 2014.

People looked well-dressed, and I saw no beggars. Women and girls were walking about freely, some in tight jeans and tops. Rickshaws, but very few motorbikes, buzzed about, while lots of old VW Beetles and campervans cruised around.

There were times when I felt I was walking along the back streets of Paris; it felt very French, with louvre windows and baguettes in the bakeries. Syria had been allotted to France at the end of WWI, only gaining its independence in 1946. Older people spoke to me in French, rather than English.

The manager of my Homs hotel was Sad; that was his name. He was, indeed, a melancholic but sweet Palestinian who came here after being evicted, together with most Palestinians, from Kuwait in 1991.

Something had to be done about my finances. I had some information and options. There was a cash machine at the Cham Palace Hotel in Damascus, but not wanting streams of tourists traipsing through the exclusive lobby, they adopted a strict "residents only" policy. I could try changing the Pakistani rupees I'd brought with me into Syrian pounds at a bank. I could keep trying to find a bank that would give me money with my credit card. I could change my flight and go to Pakistan earlier. Or I could nip across the border to Lebanon, where there were cash machines.

After a fruitless day asking in banks, none of which would give me any money or change my rupees, I took the most interesting option and planned a dash into Lebanon.

In the meantime, to save cash, I was living mostly on fruit and vegetable juice. I looked at menus as I sipped and was amused to find items such as chick bears (with or without meat); Hand Miss was a possible choice or there was Marina and Ferry. Cook Spray came with rice. In one restaurant "Grenade" was on the menu, and on the list of ice-creams, there was a Charles and Diana made from strawberry, cream, honey and nuts. The weather was warm during the day, so there was a brisk trade.

I passed a cinema and, having enjoyed such experiences in other countries, bought an inexpensive ticket. A Liam Neeson film was showing. Inside, there was no order; the audience mostly consisting of young lads who bellowed to each other as they roamed around. Ushers added to the mayhem by shouting to draw attention to the refreshments they were selling.

The poor quality, scratchy film started, and I was getting into the story but was surprised and shocked when it was interspersed with occasional, brief porn clips: nipple-sucking, lesbian kissing, and trouser-fumbling; it was quite funny how these clips would suddenly appear in a crucial bit of the plot. The audience reacted with cheers and whistles.

Set in Brighton in 1959, the film was about a detective-photographer who set up a business falsifying evidence at seedy hotels for would-be divorcees to prove adultery, one of the requirements at that time. A rich man was murdered who'd had associations with a woman who could have done the murder. It was difficult to follow with all the cheering and porn, but I think the detective did it. Or was it the nipple-sucking lesbians?

For a day-trip, I caught a minibus to the majestic and very French-sounding Krak des Chevaliers, a Crusader castle originally built by Kurds twenty-eight miles out in the desert. In my imagination, I saw knights in armour and heard their horses' hooves clattering on the cobbled internal roadways as I walked the well-preserved ramparts to see the view of the surrounding desert.

T. E. Lawrence, later Lawrence of Arabia, came here many decades before me. Before the current civil war it looked much as it had eight-hundred years previously, when 4,000 soldiers had been billeted here. Although a World Heritage Site, it has recently been severely damaged by airstrikes and fighting, having withstood previous attacks for a thousand years.

Although I'd have liked a bit of a seaside holiday, my trip to Syria was turning out to be a cultural one. Hama was next on my itinerary. I wouldn't find sea and sand there either. A holiday romance perhaps? It took me a couple of nights in Hama to realise that, although it said "Hotel" outside, I was staying in a brothel. I did wonder why the room I was staying in was furnished with pink and red fluffy cushions on a soft double bed with perfume bottles decorating the dressing table.

I wondered, too, why all the other guests were slinky females, who didn't look a bit like they would carry a rucksack. Then there was the owner; a big, pale, moist man who was always there in his Arab robe looking benevolent but shifty. "Call me Papa," he said suggestively. A couple of times he stroked my hair, making me feel uncomfortable. It suddenly clicked when I noticed men sitting around waiting in the foyer and Papa was receiving sheaves of notes from the women. I paid up and left, but not before Papa kissed me. Ugh!

A helpful man at the tourist office took me to where the microbus left for Lebanon, bought kebabs and salad for me, and left before I could pay him back. I bought a visa at the border, and then I was in Lebanon. This wasn't in the plan . . . hurrah!

I withdrew loads of cash, and it was dark by the time I booked into a little hotel in Tripoli on the coast. In the morning, I opened the louvre windows and gasped when I saw the view. I sat on a rickety little chair on the balcony; in front of me was the Mediterranean Sea, sun, and sand; a perfect holiday location.

People were jogging on the esplanade. Women were driving cars. Young men were tearing up and down the sea front, posing in BMWs as the boys did in Minis and scooters on Weston-super-Mare sea-front when I was sixteen. I was thinking I could have my sea, sun, and sand holiday here and looked at the Lebanon stamp in my passport to see how long I could stay.

Next to it was the Syrian one. As I looked, a feeling of horror spread from my heart to my throat, followed by further self-admonishment for lack of research.

Extract from my diary, 7th March 2002:
"Oh NO! What have I done now? Here I am in Lebanon, surrounded by ATMs and can have as much money as I

*have in my bank BUT . . . I see that my Syrian visa is single
entry only, meaning I can't go back."*

Here was the seaside holiday in the sun I craved, but I dared not
stay. I was too worried about getting back into Syria and had time
only for a beer, the best tabbouleh I've ever had, and the worst ice-
cream, so bad it was chewy.

Of course, there was no problem getting back into Syria; I had
only to buy a new visa. I chatted on the bus to a Palestinian, who
told me he had no nationality or home because "Someone else is
living there, and I can't go there." It made me question my feelings
about my own country. Now used to feeling at home anywhere,
and not considering myself to be particularly patriotic, I wondered
inconclusively how I'd feel if I didn't have that anchor.

I arrived back in Hama, and I found a backpackers' favourite,
The Riad Hotel, much more suitable than the brothel I'd stayed
at before. As I was checking in, so was a man called Finn. Not
only did I feel at home at the guesthouse, but Finn and I hit it off
immediately and were inseparable for the remainder of his stay.

He had a guide book, and during the ten days we had together,
we were proper tourists. We visited one of the beehive homes
outside the city and were given tea by a jolly woman who lived
there with her farming family. These conical dwellings are so
efficient at temperature control during harsh summers and winters
in the desert that a computer is unable to design anything better.

Another trip was to the remarkable ruined city, Palmyra,
an oasis in the desert at the crossroads of the Silk Route from
China to the Mediterranean, Greece, and Rome. Celebrated
worldwide for its architecture and art, it was ruled by Queen
Zenobia, who conquered Egypt, Asia Minor, and all the land
and sea-ways to the Far East. She was highly educated and a
renowned military leader. She was, therefore, a thorn in the
flesh to the Romans, so they formed a special army, and despite
this warrior queen giving them a run for their money, she was
defeated at Homs in A. D. 273.

Finn, thenceforth, called me Zenobia. We were two of very few
tourists. Walking beneath magnificent archways, I imagined her
planning her battles whilst swishing in oriental silks and wielding

a sword. Palmyra has since been badly damaged by gunfire, and the archway has been blown up by terrorists.

Back at Hama, I went to the hammam baths, where I enjoyed an afternoon having my hair washed and being scrubbed in oodles of piping hot water inside tiled washrooms by the other women bathers, like me, just in their knickers. They sang a song to me which ended with a high-pitched "Whoop!" It was a lovely, intimately female experience.

Afterwards, Finn and I watched as skilled artisans restored one of the seventeen norias, ancient wooden water-wheels powered by the Orentes River. Pottery jugs attached to the wheel emptied river water into an overhead aqueduct to irrigate local fields. There are reports that they have since been ruined and burnt by soldiers.

We wandered about the streets and were captivated by a cheerful chap in a white traditional costume with a red fez and pointy red slip-on shoes who was selling a tasteless red drink from a huge silver container strapped on his back. He looked spectacular. The apparatus was an arrangement of tubes that siphoned the juice through a cooling chamber into a tall glass. Another tap allowed him to wash the glass, ready for the next customer.

We travelled north-west in search of more seaside. Kesab was the perfect place in this warm climate. The high season still a month away, they hadn't yet turned the hot water on. We were the only guests in the vast hotel and considered playing hide and seek but worried we might never meet each other again.

The next day was as lovely as I remember any being. The temperature was ideal for walking in the countryside between the hills and down the steep valley that eventually led to the clear, blue sea. At the side of the narrow road were wild cyclamen, irises, and daisies. Fig trees were beginning to sprout, encouraged by the sunshine.

We stripped off on the deserted rocky beach but could see the occasional glint of binoculars. Someone was spying on us from a cliff-top lookout. We found him after our swim. Over a cup of sweet black tea, he explained that he was "border control," observing the dividing line between Turkey at one end of Samra beach and Syria at the other. During a lunch-stop at the only café half-way back to the hotel, the owner shouted for her husband to help with our order. "Batkiss!" she yelled repeatedly. Henceforth, that was my name for Finn.

Zenobia and Batkiss went on to Aleppo and were greeted at the bus terminus by Murhaf, a pleasant young man who guided us to his family's hotel. The Spring Flower was every bit as good as he said it was, so we stayed there in a room with thick walls painted a soft orange. Arabic lanterns and woven rugs set the Syrian scene.

My abiding memory of Aleppo is the souk, some of which goes back to the thirteenth century, a labyrinth extending over several hectares. Declining honeyed lizards at one stall, I bought a small "silver" pendant with the world's first alphabet stamped on it. The alphabet, developed in this part of the world, has thirty letters and was used from 1400 B. C. Murhaf spent the day with us telling us things we might otherwise have missed. He pointed out hooks from the ceilings of souk stalls from which ropes were attached to enable the stall-holder to swing from the back to the front to avoid clambering over his elaborate display of goods. He even took us to his parents' home, where we drank thick, sludgy coffee with his mother and sister, who wore burkas, bright red lipstick, and nail polish. They did not speak English, unfortunately, but when we left, I asked Murhaf about women's place in the Syrian family. He told me that men choose to marry girls of fourteen or fifteen " . . . so they can be moulded to suit their husbands, before they develop their own personality." Words like *suppressed* and *repressed* came into my mind, not *moulded*.

Murhaf took us to a shop where we were allowed to look down into an underground labyrinth. These tunnels run underneath the whole city, or used to before the police filled in many of them to stop escaping criminals from getting away. Hidden treasure is often found when people are restoring houses. Thinking of Aladdin's cave, I could well imagine a hoard of jewels down there. We went to a lovely restaurant stuffed with antiquities. Poor Finn puffed himself dizzy with a narghela (hubble-bubble pipe) and, reviewing his former decision to buy one to take home, preferred instead to amuse his friends with a copy of Boss aftershave where the "B" had been replaced with a "T."

Back in Damascus, the night before Finn left, we went for a last meal together to a good-quality restaurant. Between courses, a whirling dervish show was so dizzyingly frenzied I gripped my chair to steady myself. The restaurant was full of people dressed in all sorts of clothing from western-style glamour to full burka. Some women were eating, drinking, and smoking cigarettes and narghelas. But there was a woman near our table who, revealing nothing in black clothing including gloves, was fasting. Everyone else on her table was tucking in, though. What variety.

The next morning as Finn left, I felt very emotional, but I held it in, as I didn't want to spoil his image of my being a really "got it together" woman. Zenobia would have held her head up high, and so did I, until he'd gone.

I went my lonely way, fity-four miles south, to see the Roman remains at Shahba near the border with Jordan. I'd expected hotels nearby, but a taxi driver said, "No hotel . . . " and took me to his home. I spent the evening talking to his seventeen-year old niece, fetched because she spoke English. Far from being moulded for a future husband, she was at college and wanted to be a doctor. We ate bread and cheese and baby aubergines stuffed with pimentos in olive oil. I slept on their sofa, and next morning this kind man took me to the third century villa, amphitheatre, and museum I had come to see at what was once the city of Philippopolis. Unbelievably, I was the only tourist there so had the director's attention all morning.

We walked up Roman streets admiring Corinthian pillars. He showed me parts of the six-mile long aqueduct that had brought water for the three baths. When I told him it was my birthday, he fetched two glasses and some of his home-made wine to drink in the sunny amphitheatre, built not for just two but for two thousand people. The villa's mosaics were well-preserved and absolutely gorgeous. One depicted the story of Orpheus who, missing his dead wife, went despairingly to the desert. He was frightened of the wild animals and played music to appease them. The mosaic shows him playing a lyre whilst animals, including lions, tigers, and snakes, listen to the music rather than attacking him. It was utterly delightful and gave me a lump in my throat. There was even a little mouse sitting on the lyre. I found the place enchanting.

Later that day, I was asking about buses to nearby Swieda, when I was scooped up by a shopkeeper, who took me in his pick-up truck and showed me round Qanawat, another Roman city dedicated to a local god, Rabbos. I noticed people were dressed differently there, wearing black robes with a white headscarf for women and a white turban for men. I learnt that they were Druze, followers of an offshoot of Shia Islam. My guide showed me a Roman prison with diamond-shaped cut-out "windows" in the stone, so that prisoners could talk to their visitors. The tour concluded with a drive to Swieda, past the modern homes of rich people who had returned from working abroad. He delivered me to a Christian church hotel, but I didn't want to stay there and so, thanking him very much, waited for him to go before finding a cheapy in town. The manager there offered to take me out to dinner and away to the seaside at the weekend, but I declined both. He told me he was looking for a wife: "Women here," he explained, "are interested only in money, not love."

The hotel was basic. Everything in my room was hard; a marble-chip floor, a tin wardrobe, and a metal-framed bed with a solid kapok mattress. The bedding consisted of a heavy eiderdown and stiff blankets like carpet underfelt. The sheets might well have been unchanged for several guests' stays, and I was glad of my cotton sleep-sheet. The pillows were so hard I used my folded coat wrapped in my sarong. But the hotel was central, and where else would the manager serenade me with soulful songs on his guitar?

The next morning, I awoke to the sound of a woman's haunting voice so got up to see where it was coming from. I had to have what I'd heard and dashed down to the music shop below to buy cassette tapes of the Arabic singer Firoz.

My next destination on my round Syria tour was Bosra, an important trading town between Damascus and the Red Sea and capital of the Roman Arabian Empire. I stayed in a cold, cheerless room at the citadel, feeling sure the Romans would have had some efficient system of heating, sadly long gone. When the Romans left, locals moved in or utilised the stone from the walls for their homes, and still do. Roman dwellings with a satellite dish on top looked bizarre.

The museum was stuffed with antiquities illustrating their rich and organised lifestyle. The second century amphitheatre demonstrated its perfect acoustics when a group of schoolchildren came round as I sat quietly on one of the numbered seats at the top. Even though they were on the stage area at the bottom, I could hear every syllable. As I sat there I imagined there would have been a ticket booth and perhaps people walking round with trays of snacks and wondered what show might have been performed. It is now severely damaged from mortar shelling.

I returned to Swieda after my short stay at Bosra and wasn't surprised to find the room I had vacated a few days before still had the same, unwashed sheets on the bed.

Back in Damascus I stayed in a hotel dormitory with Amber, an artist from New Zealand, and a heavily pregnant young Australian woman who had become a head-covered, praying-five-times-a-day Muslim. Her Sudanese husband had left her in this guesthouse, and her baby was due in a week or so. Unsure of his whereabouts, she hoped his friends would help when the baby came. As a health visitor, I found her situation alarming, but she didn't seem concerned and kept on praying.

I spent ages at the museum, marvelling that cow-shaped milk-jugs I'd seen in a museum in the potteries of Stoke-on-Trent were the same design as one made here many centuries before. I saw the original world's first alphabet carved on a finger-sized section of stone. There was also a good modern art section in the museum, making a change from viewing antiquities.

Amber and I got a bus to Maaloula, an ancient village where the residents are some of the last in the world to speak in Aramaic, the language used in the time of Christ. We had something to eat at a little restaurant.

The young woman who served us asked to be our tour guide and took us to what she told us was the oldest church in the world. It was built on the site of an old Roman temple for the god Apollo. Our guide insisted on my drinking some holy water at Saint Taqla's Well. She told me it would always keep me safe and well, and it's worked so far. Amber, unwilling to risk the water, had none but is also still alive and well.

Back in Damascus that evening, the night before my flight to Karachi in Pakistan, I reviewed my month's holiday in Syria. I had a tan, a few little souvenirs, and some photos. I had seen so much, had met people from many different places, and even had a holiday romance.

I visited Syria at peace and couldn't have asked for more. I found an Internet café and checked my emails. Hendrikus was going to join me in Islamabad. I had no idea what would be the outcome of my reunion with either him or my Enfield and, as usual, waited to see what would happen.

5
Backpacking in Burma

Reunited and Restored

I was high. I was flying. I felt GOOD. I had my bike back. I knew the Islamabad streets, the traffic. I judged I could get to that turning before that rickshaw would dash out. I knew where I was going. I felt I owned the place. I was queen of the road. I was Zenobia.

I hadn't seen the Enfield for a year or ridden it for seventeen months and was apprehensive. Would I remember the back-to-front gear-changing? Would my wonky leg be up to kick-starting it? Would it start at all? As the up-and-over door of our Islamabad friends' garage revealed the travellers' bikes, I held my breath. There they were . . . Hendrikus's with its sheepskin on the saddle, mine black and beautiful, both displaying their Indian Tamil Nadu number-plates. I wanted to cuddle them.

After charging the battery and one lunge on the kick-start pedal, it started. Nostalgia mixed with euphoria sparked my heart when I heard the engine ticking over. The smoke from the exhaust enveloped me in a mist of scenes from the past and a certainty that, no matter what, I was not leaving without my bike.

Joyously, I rode the familiar wide, modern streets and prepared for the next obstacle, the trail around government offices to enable leaving Pakistan with my bike. I had to grapple with the idea that it may be impounded.

I was staying in Rawalpindi, about half an hour's journey away and had completed this route so many times by bus when we were staying with our actor friends. Each morning on my way to the language institute, I'd hauled myself and my crutches up the steps to the front seats where the women sat, men in the seats behind, all ready for a day's work.

It was spring now, and so warm I slept in my sleeping bag on the roof of my friends' house near Commercial Market, a place that came alive at night with loud, jingly music from the latest Indian films blaring from the shops selling "dodgy" cassettes and CDs. At the same time, the nearby mosques broadcast the call to prayer. People browsed the brightly-lit shops and stalls.

Manikins in snooty poses I'd never witnessed for real in Pakistan were displaying the latest style of shalwar-kameez; always shown as always worn, with a dupatta headscarf. There were plenty of women in the streets with their families, a contrast to some places in rural Pakistan where I'd seen no women; staying inside, I was told, for their own safety, as the outside world is run by and safe only for men.

One brightly-lit stall sold only glass bangles, the jewellery worn by almost every woman, the cheapest ones costing a few rupees. Spotlights made them sparkle. Of every colour, they were displayed on horizontal poles from floor to ceiling. Whenever the arm of a woman moves, the bangles jingle and tinkle together. I recalled the keep-fit class I had run for Pakistani women when I was a health visitor in Stoke-on-Trent. As the women stretched their arms, the old Victorian school hall jingled with the sound of glass bangles and Pakistani music. How lovely, I thought, for a baby to be able to hear its mother's reassuring approach.

I bought some for myself, but my motorcycling gear and boots did not do justice to the feminine bangles. I felt a fraud and then later, on moving the bike, heard a crack and saw my bangles in pieces by my front tyre. Motorcycling and glass bangles did not go together.

I was apprehensive but curious about how Hendrikus and I would be if and when he turned up. In the meantime, I would do what I could to get both Enfields released from the sheaves of official documentation that bound them. I didn't know where to start but thought the Pakistani AA might help. Their head office was in Lahore. On the way there to stay with friends from my previous visit a few years before, I was stopped five times by police officers. I hadn't been stopped like this when riding with Hendrikus.

Mostly, they wanted to chat, but one younger policeman asked to see all my documents, even the International Driving Permit that I'd had for years and nobody had ever asked to see. I kept it "current" by disguising its expiry date. Unable to find fault, he told me I would have to pay a fine for not wearing a helmet, until I pointed out at least a dozen motorcyclists riding past bare-headed as we stood there.

I rode on to Lahore, feeling rather less like Zenobia by the time I arrived after dark, filthy from the heavy traffic grime sticking to my sweat and clothes. I found the gated and comfortable home of my friends. They had a cook, a housemaid, and a gardener. I showered and changed in my en-suite room and was treated to home-cooked food and the company of Imtiaz, Gazella, and their twin daughters.

The next morning, Imtiaz drove me to the AA. The friendly man there said I would need a new Carnet de Passage before appealing to the Central Board of Revenue in Islamabad, but before he could issue me with one I would need a "No Objections" certificate, available from another office in Lahore.

An official there told me to return to Pakistan Customs to get it, but when I phoned them, they didn't know what I was talking about. I got the impression that nobody in Lahore really knew what to do with me and that I was being passed around the different departments. I conceded defeat.

My host took me, instead, to see where the enormous billboards advertising forthcoming films are painted—much more enjoyable than the frustrating paper-chase to free the Enfields. Measuring twenty by thirty feet, the impressive art-work is lost as each new film theme is painted over the last.

After a luxurious stay with the family, I started the return journey to Islamabad, taking back roads to avoid any more police interest. I'd bought a map of the Punjab, but it had so few roads marked on it that I did what I like doing best and asked the way. The countryside was lovely and quiet, and I was tootling alone for miles alongside rivers and a wide canal. Then the bike stalled and wouldn't restart.

The carburettor was leaking. I was just about to tighten the drainage nut underneath and clean the spark plug when help arrived in the shape of a comedy rickshaw. It was one of the new types I had seen; yellow and gaudy and called Quinki. Kinky it certainly was, and I felt part of a circus act when the driver hitched the bike to the back and towed me the half-mile into town.

A mechanic sorted the problem by tightening the drainage nut under the carburettor and cleaning the plug. Neither the Quinki driver nor the mechanic would accept any money. I thought about the times I'd been stuck at the side of the road in Britain and people had just driven by.

It was getting dark, and I looked around for somewhere to stay. I asked at a rice-mill with an upper platform and settled in, happy to be sleeping outside again. But the owner heard about it and came and took me to his home, where I shared a room with his teenage daughters and was fed and cared for by his wife, a no-nonsense ex-army midwife.

Another motorcyclist attached himself to me when I left the next day and took me to see Rohtas Fort, built in the sixteenth century to quell rebellious Punjabi tribes. Impressive as it was, the crossing of five little rivers to get to it was the best bit and reminded me of doing this sort of thing with Hendrikus. I began to think that perhaps it might just be possible that we could be doing it together again. Maybe.

The following day, I set off to the Central Board of Revenue in Islamabad, armed with my X-rays and hospital letters. I filled in and signed various forms and left them with a stressed, but pleasant, man who told me to return the next day. Three weeks after my return to Pakistan, the necessary permission for both bikes arrived and so did Hendrikus.

It was no Hollywood reunion. We were shy with each other, neither of us feeling able at this stage to be any more than politely friendly. He sorted out his Enfield and gear whilst staying on the foreigners' campsite in Islamabad. How long would it be before either of us broached the subject of what to do next? I felt I had gained the confidence to go on alone, if necessary. He said he was a more mature traveller now. We both avoided the subject of travelling together.

Before I could go anywhere, with or without him, I was waiting for the new Carnet for my Enfield. He had renewed his on a visit to Holland. We both needed to replenish our spare parts and do repairs, so it was agreed that we would travel to India together and then decide. We warmed.

He bought me a new petrol cap to replace my leaking one. I bought him his favourite Edam cheese from the supermarket in Islamabad's diplomatic area, where even Stilton was available if you had enough money. It wasn't long before we were as close as before and having fun again.

We went to see the Pakistan Day military procession through the streets. All vehicles, including our bikes, were searched for explosives underneath with mirrors on sticks. I found this amusing, recognising that we were riding Enfield Bullets. The display of military hardware was chilling, and I hoped the two nuclear warheads on parade were copies and not the real things.

My new carnet arrived; we said grateful farewells to our friends and set off the cross-country way to the border. Any new-found, grown-up attributes Hendrikus thought he may have gained over the last year were not evident as we immediately reverted to our childish ways. We vowed anew never to say "be careful" to each other. We'd followed random tracks all over India, Nepal, and Pakistan, kissing tarmac when we'd exhausted ourselves on arduous dirt paths and then, becoming bored with it, dived off-road again, letting tracks lead us to situations and encounters I couldn't have imagined in my previous life.

With unlimited time and no satellite navigation we were free to follow our adventurous noses. One day we navigated using the sun. Amritsar our destination, we abandoned the busy Grand Trunk road and travelled as if we'd never been apart.

That day we rode up and around hills through a coal-mining area. Stopping to talk to some miners, who were dressed only in traditional shalwar-kameez, we were invited down their mine. My guide held my hand as we doubled up and squeezed through the mud tunnel. Down, down, down to the coal face.

They considered themselves well-paid and were proud of their status. A generator piped fresh air to them as they chipped with chisels at the seam. They hauled the coal up to the surface in sacks on their backs and then loaded them onto donkeys, which carried them to waiting trucks. They were a cheerful bunch and so proud to have shown us their mine.

We spent a hot, tentless night on an arid hill, sleeping amongst the scrub and red earth, watching camels grazing in the dawn light. I cried with frustration and a feeling of failure the next day due to repeatedly dropping the bike and needing Hendrikus to manoeuvre it for me as we descended the hill-track made up of boulders and fit only for livestock and four-wheel-drive vehicles.

It was the first time I had ever been unable to ride my own bike due to the awkwardness of the terrain. Finally, I broke my clutch-lever. We were hot, very thirsty, and had no water left. Not usually a worrier, I was concerned about dehydration.

As usual, rescue came into view. We saw a farm. The gentleman farmer welcomed us and gave us tangerine juice from fruit grown on his opulent land whilst one of the farm-workers fitted my spare clutch lever. Hendrikus was cross with me for not doing it myself, but I didn't care.

Afterwards, we found a metalled road and should have stayed on it, but we decided to take a shortcut across a desert. I dropped the bike over and over again. "Full throttle and keep the handlebar straight," shouted Hendrikus. I did, and the bike shot out from under me at full pelt. I clung on but left the saddle completely with my feet off the pegs for a while until I couldn't keep straight and ploughed into the sand.

Only as we collapsed into a cheap room at Jhelum after a hugely difficult day battling with the thick sand did we look at the map to see that since leaving Islamabad, we'd ridden 150 miles to avoid twenty-five miles of the Grand Trunk road. That's how we travelled together. "Why," we wondered, "would anyone go the easy way?"

Perplexed officials at the Pakistan/India border were unsure what to do with a carnet but eventually stamped the bikes officially out of Pakistan. On the Indian side, we stopped for a beer, which strangely, I hadn't missed whilst in Pakistan. When I knew I couldn't have alcohol, I stopped wanting it, but it was lovely to slake my thirst with cold beer.

We stayed again in the foreigners' dormitory at the glorious Golden Temple in Amritsar and started getting the bikes maintained at the workshop of a local mechanic, who renewed the footrests, brake shoes, battery, front forks (I could fill a book with everything I learned about hydraulic front forks), and all the cables. Finally, both bikes were finished.

We had breakfast at a restaurant overlooking a busy street. Hendrikus wanted toast and butter but was told that wasn't possible. When he asked for toast, butter, and jam, it was brought. Hello again, India.

And so the time for someone to make a decision was nigh. I loved him and his ways. He made me laugh. He was childish and never boring. We had resumed the adventurous life we'd had before. We travelled well together. He liked to make all the decisions, and I was happy not to, although when travelling alone, I was equally as happy and managed perfectly well with the Enfield. We were both unhampered by restrictions, neither wanting to spoil that freedom for the other. Which was it to be?

I went to pay for our breakfast and asked the waiters to toss a two-rupee coin. Heads to stay with Hendrikus and go east, tails to go it alone and go west and back to Europe. It came up heads, and I was happy. Apparently, he liked being with me too, because he looked pleased and gave me a hug when I told him of my "decision."

We enjoyed meandering through the back farm roads of Punjab and Haryana on our way to Delhi. From there, we'd ride towards South East Asia but had no specific plan. The word *plan* was banned from the vocabulary.

My bike stalled on a country road at the end of the first day. We decided to sleep nearby under a big tree out of sight. Or so we thought. Before long, we were surrounded by dozens of curious villagers, so there was no chance of stripping off and immersing ourselves in the cool water tank by the tree, as we had hoped. Instead, we saw people arriving with chairs and even a charpoi bed. Ice and bottles of cola were brought.

Things got a bit heated as some of the people saw we wanted to be left alone and tried to push the others away. But they would have none of it, and voices and fists were raised. I went into the fray and separated two men who were getting out of control. Things calmed down, and they all left. We had our bathe at last and slept in peace with the astounding stars. In the morning, we departed after sharing chai brought by some villagers at dawn.

My bike continued stalling. Sherlock Hendrikus to the rescue. Petrol wasn't getting into the carburettor, but each time I peered in the tank, it improved for a while. He deduced that the new petrol cap he'd given me was airtight, causing a vacuum and stopping the flow of petrol. Discarding the cap and securing a pierced plastic bag with an elastic band worked until a proper Enfield cap was bought.

After the more sober Pakistan, India offered us crazy occurrences daily. We stayed one night in a Sikh temple dedicated to Baba Deep Singh, a fierce fighter and leader (the one who carried on fighting with his head under his arm).

The following day, we were overtaken by a motorcyclist whose throttle cable had stuck. He lay on his back on the saddle, arms folded behind his head whilst steering with his feet. Enthralled and delighted, we did our riding side-saddle trick and other acrobatics I had mastered. We all stopped and shook hands before riding on! We arrived in Delhi and saw more bizarre road behaviour, such as large panes of glass being carried on Enfields by pillions facing backwards.

We stayed in an ashram guest house in the Karol Bagh district, well-known as the motorcycle centre of Delhi, but the owner seemed permanently stoned and offered no spiritual guidance at all.

We would have liked to have ridden through Burma into Thailand but found this an impossible ambition. Strict army rule forbad foreigners in remote places, and there were few inroads, even for Enfields. However, it was on the way, and it seemed opportune to visit it whilst the bikes made their way to Bangkok by sea. We found a shipping agent in Karol Bagh and rode there one very hot morning.

No trees offered shade in the back streets of Old Delhi, where winches noisily lifted heavy things on and off trucks, but a piece of corrugated iron dangling from the roof of the freight warehouse served as a parasol. Amid the smell of hot oil and machinery, I waited with the bikes whilst Hendrikus went to fetch Mr. Chowla, the manager, to oversee the crating of the Enfields.

I settled down on an oil drum to catch up with my diary. The ink in the ballpoint was watery from the heat and blobbed annoyingly onto the page at the start of every word. Memory deep in the previous days, I looked up from the page for inspiration and, for a moment forgetting my surroundings, wondered why I was at a Bollywood film gala.

A short distance away was a beautiful Indian woman, incongruous on this set, with its backdrop of engineering workshops and soundtrack of metal being beaten and bent. What brought this glamorous lady dressed in a pink and sparkling silver sari here, complete with dangling jewellery from nose and ears? In her strappy sandals she looked as if she should be walking on a red carpet, not on this backstreet carpet of dirt and old sump oil. I gazed at her, feeling unfeminine in my sturdy boots, faded black jeans, and T-shirt, shabby from motorcycle travel amongst the diesel and dust of India's roads.

As if bowing at the end of a performance, the woman bent elegantly and started scratching about in the dirt, looking for something. She cooed tenderly at her daughter, who had just come into view. No sand pit for her to play in, dry dirt was her playground. The little girl, also in a sparkly dress, was grubby, her black hair dull brown from the dust. Occasionally, the woman found something and put it in a cloth bag. She and the child went past, noticing neither me nor the 104-degree heat that I was drooping from.

As they disappeared round a parked truck, Mr. Chowla emerged from the warehouse and told me that she was gathering discarded washers, nuts, and bolts. She could exchange a kilo of scraps for fifty-five rupees (about eighty cents). It would buy enough food for her family for a day. People would be outraged if this form of making a living were common where I came from.

Not for the first or last time, I realised that as a traveller, I could only glimpse cultures very different from my own. Someone once said to me that he didn't need to travel, he could "look it up on the Internet," but as Einstein said, "The only source of knowledge is experience, everything else is just information"—I mused that even then you are often left with more questions than answers.

"The platform for your motorcycles is there, Madam." Mr. Chowla pointed to a couple of four-by-twos nailed together. Dismayed, images of wheeling our bikes into a large crate dissipated, and we spent the rest of the morning reducing the space each Enfield occupied.

Front wheels, mudguards, handlebars, luggage racks, and crash bars were removed and stacked around the bikes which, resting on their forks, looked as if they were on their knees. Tanks and batteries were drained. Spare parts and tools, camping stove and tent were stowed behind the forks, and finally they were wrapped, boxed in, and nailed up.

We'd be using public transport for two weeks. What would that be like after two years of travelling by Enfield? A label was affixed announcing their destination. "See you in Bangkok," I murmured as I patted the crate and swung my backpack over my shoulder and headed back to the ashram.

India has a way of imposing conflicting emotions on you. The evening before we left we had a rickshaw ride through Old Delhi. The combination of treadless tyres and a wet road led to a graceful rotating slide like the giant tea-cup ride at Alton Towers. Miraculously, although the road was stuffed with the usual amount of vehicles, people, and animals, we didn't collide with a single thing.

We changed rickshaws, and as we were driven along the crowded streets, I was transported by the serenity and beauty of the magnificent Jama Masjid mosque with the rising moon behind it. It was magical. Seeing legless beggars returned me to reality. Moments later, Hendrikus and I found ourselves violently ejected onto the road by the sudden braking of the driver, before we hit the rickshaw in front. We sat in the road laughing as we peered at each other through the spokes of the rickshaw wheels. Magic, tragedy, and hilarity in so few seconds. We were given a lift to our accommodation by two men on a motorbike, making four adults on one bike.

It was May 2002. Airport security was tight after 9/11, and a fellow passenger had to hand over the needles from her sewing kit before the flight. Free to travel unhindered for so long, I just wasn't used to it. It seemed ridiculous. Goodbye, India!

The airport at Yangon is the most splendid I've seen anywhere, with its ornate, golden pagoda-style edifice over the entrance. It was exciting to be in South East Asia. We bought Myanmar Kyat in "'foreigners' money": £1 bought us 600 Kyat; the equivalent for a national would buy 1,000.

Within the hour, after help from friendly local people on three different buses into the city, I was spending a little of it on coffee and a cockroach in the market. Fried and sold by the kilo, there were buckets of them, complete with wings, heads, and legs, that I was picking out of my teeth for some time afterwards. It wasn't too bad, as long as I told myself it was no different from eating a prawn, but still managed only the one.

For lunch I had a more piquant mustard-leaf soup made from carrots, leafy greens, cauliflower, onions, tomato, lemon grass, chilli, and ginger, quite unlike the Indian food we'd been enjoying for many months beforehand.

Also unlike India, there were no beggars and very few motorcycles in the quieter, greener streets. Bargaining was a more serious enterprise too. As a tourist, you know you are a target, and either you pay up, bargain light-heartedly, or make your stay miserable for yourself. Aware of the history of three Anglo-Burmese wars leading to Burma becoming a British colony before independence in 1948, I felt it quite in order to pay more for things than local people as retribution and had been grateful to be allowed into the country at all. Anyway, with beer at 35 cents a pint, it wasn't worth getting upset about.

At a market stall, we watched a fit young man butchering meat. Stripped to the waist, the two meat cleavers he was wielding flowed artistically in his hands. Exotic fruits were displayed colourfully; green mangos and red rambutans, with their fearsome-looking, prickly exteriors disguising soft and delicately flavoured flesh inside.

The only people who approached the few visiting foreigners said they were tour guides. My questions about life under a military regime went unanswered as they looked guardedly over their shoulders. I'd had reservations about coming to Burma, people saying my tourist money would only support the repressive regime. I wanted to know more but couldn't. There were no email facilities either, and international calls were restricted, so it was also impossible to get information about how my elderly mother was.

People were dressed in comfortable clothes, men in smart round-necked shirts and cotton longhi wrapped round their waists like sarongs. The women wore colourful long skirts and short-sleeved blouses. Although fifty degrees cooler than Delhi, it seemed even hotter here, as frequent monsoon showers increased humidity.

After three days in a seven dollars-a-night hotel and despite entertaining daylong karaoke performances in the bars, a boat trip to the coast lured us away from the city. There was ample space on the rear upper deck of the old wooden ferry to allow us to lie alongside our backpacks for the overnight crossing to Patein, but as the boat filled up with people and sacks of produce "our" space decreased, and our backpacks had to double as pillows.

People shuffled to make room, welcoming those who approached. Our neighbours were a young couple and their baby. Hendrikus was concerned at a potentially noisy journey, but I told him I'd seen even small South East Asian children sit for hours on wooden benches on packed buses without a grizzle, squashed by all manner of luggage, sacks of vegetables, chickens, people, and pigs. I decided patience and endurance must be both genetic and nurtured by Buddhism and warmed to these gentle parents and their babe.

Night came like a switched-off light, there being just enough yellow twilight to see a colony of bats flying overhead as the engine started and we left the quay. I was too excited to sleep, journeys of any kind a delight. All through the night, the parents took it in turns to sleep or fan the baby to stop mosquitoes from settling and biting. It was such a touching act of tenderness and compassion, like a nativity scene. I felt I was part of something beautiful, absolutely human, and not a guidebook "must see."

At dawn the sky lightened, showing boats already ferrying people about or fishing. Roads were flooded during this, the rainy season, and the Enfields would have been useless. Palm trees loomed out of the daybreak, and birdsong replaced the sound of the engine as we slid alongside a jetty to allow some passengers off and others on. Food vendors squeezed in between people to sell food they'd cooked.

Breakfast was a hard-boiled egg and some still-warm fried flatbreads sprinkled with sugar.

Hendrikus didn't enjoy backpacking and later made an embarrassing fuss on a bus journey from Patein to the coast, delaying tolerant Burmese passengers, because he resented paying a "foreigners" fare. Not only would he rather be on his bike, but I felt he didn't want me around. However, Chaung Tha Beach was the perfect antidote to the stress and weeks of hard riding, planning the shipping, packing the Enfields, and arranging our flight. Not that it offered a typical holiday brochure setting. Monsoon skies and a windy balcony overlooking the excited sea meant the place was deserted but still very warm. Fish was cheap at the beach restaurant, and when we weren't dining on red snapper, we were eating clams in sweet and sour sauce with rice.

A tropical storm hit one night, and we awoke to the sound of the fly-screen slamming against the window as if it was trying to break it. The tin roof struggled to hang on to the bungalow whilst being hammered by deafening rain. The sea was wild in the morning, and I enjoyed being buffeted about by the waves like a lone shirt in a washing machine.

Hendrikus had a huge kite, and we let the power of the wind drive us across the waves and through the surf. Unfortunately, I wasn't good at steering, and it dragged me across the sand, giving my bottom a thorough scouring, which took many painful weeks to heal.

When Hendrikus said he was tired and wanted to spend more time on his own, I left him reading on our veranda one afternoon and wandered around the village to find the local hospital, the nurse in me never far away. Patients included one quite lovely newborn baby, a man walking about with his head bandaged, and three cases of malaria. A chart on the wall showed that malaria is on the increase and is the biggest killer, followed by respiratory infections, dysentery, and TB. The little hospital looked clean compared with the one I'd once seen in Laos a couple of years before, where chickens scratched about on the earth floor. The beds here had no mattresses or pillows, either. I thanked the nurse who showed me round, even though we couldn't talk to each other. I had learned to say only "hello," "thank you," and to count to ten: "tit," "ni," "thong," "lay," "naar," "chow," "cannit," "shit" (loved that one),"co," "tasay."

The return journey to Yangon allowed us a day or two at Patein, Myanmar's fourth largest city, where people were taxied about by cycle-rickshaw. It had seven cinemas, most showing Indian films, but we chose to go and see a Burmese one at a cinema near our guesthouse. Every seat was taken in the large cinema for the screening of a comedy. The story was about a man and his three sons and how they fared searching for marriage and jobs. Luckily, it was quite visual, and we laughed with everyone else at a woman wearing bottle-end glasses, whose vision was so poor she threw away half the rice when she was picking out the little stones. Another character was shy. His friends matched him up with a shy girl, and their efforts to get together were hilarious but charming.

There was a power-cut halfway through the film. The audience waited patiently unlike in India, where jeering and foot-stamping would ensue until the generator was started. I compared this cinema visit with my recent experience in Syria. Here, there were no gangs of youths roaming and whistling and no porn clips either. This was for families, and everyone laughed together. How interesting to see the contrasts.

Our train journey to Yangon showed us another aspect of Burma as we passed remote villages with bamboo and rush homes, some of them two-storey and with mini spirit houses on a pole outside for good fortune. Oxen pulled ancient wooden ploughs amid miles of rice, rice, and more rice. What I didn't notice was any evidence of anything military or anyone maintaining law and order, but then I was politically naïve and blithely went around with rose-tinted glasses. Back in Yangon, we visited the exquisite, peaceful temple of Shwedagon Paya before leaving for Thailand.

Three days after our arrival, which we'd spent visiting Bangkok's tourist attractions including a snake farm and a Thai Boxing match, our crate arrived. A flurry of paper-shuffling from one place to another caused delay, but finally we unpacked and reassembled the Enfields. As time was getting short and the depot about to close for the weekend, a kind man refilled the batteries for us. We just made it before the bikes were locked in, the gates clanging shut as we rode away. Later, we discovered that the kind helper had not used distilled water, and the ruined batteries, unable to hold a charge, had to be replaced.

The twelve days using public transport in Burma had been enjoyable for me but a revelation to Hendrikus, who had never backpacked before. When riding your own bike, you are in charge and responsible for how things go, and there's pleasure in that. On public transport you are more open to the vagaries of other people's timings and decisions, but you can communicate with fellow passengers and observe the scenery. It's a different way of travelling. Both are a thrill and privilege. I'd experienced both. Having my own motorbike, even with the hassle of piles of importation documents

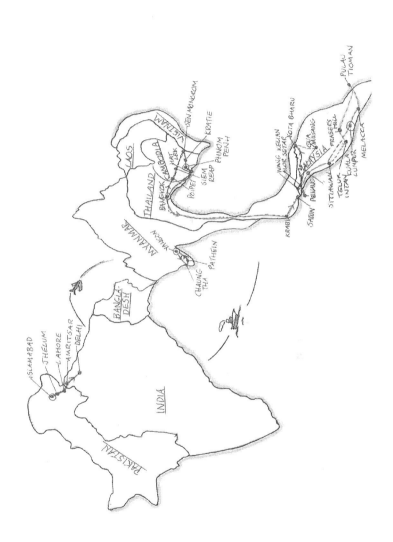

and mechanical problems, is less bother than constantly finding out from where and at what time the bus/train/ferry/rickshaw going to your destination leaves, ensuring a space, and carrying your essentials on your back. The only luggage restriction with the Enfield is what can't be tied on. Rough tracks can be explored on a whim. Unscheduled stops can be made to look at interesting things or to eat at roadside stalls. I enjoy travelling, whatever the mode of transport or destination, but as I rode away from the depot, reunited with my beloved Enfield, I had a huge grin all over my face.

6

Laughter in Thailand, Cambodia, and Thailand Again

If only I'd had a smart business brain it could have been me rather than some quick-witted entrepreneur to bring skin-devouring fish salons to the world.

I trailed my hand in a fish tank at the immense weekend market in Bangkok. The tiny garrarufa fish attending to my palms and fingers felt nice and made me giggle, and I wondered what it would be like to be immersed in the tank with them. But it fell to someone else to start the short-lived craze of "fish pedicures." Anyway, now on the road for two years, I was enjoying travelling too much to think about making or losing a fortune from skin-scouring fish.

Hendrikus and I had ridden from our pleasant guesthouse by the Chao Phraya River through the heavy Bangkok traffic to the market to buy padlocks and chains for the bikes. Many hours later, we emerged goggle-eyed and overwhelmed by the vast array of goods, clothing, antiques, animals, and food; riding back with nothing but our pair of clean motorcycles, which we had washed on the way. Although there was no livestock to contend with, the traffic in the city was on a par with the city streets of Delhi or Chennai. Traffic-smog deluged the city like a polluted sigh in what is known as the Venice of the East.

As I wove around buses and tuk-tuks, I had another one of those moments when I wondered what on earth I thought I was doing riding this funny motorbike in Asia when surely I should be doing something useful and sensible. As an antidote to doing anything sensible, we rode round and round the statue of Rama Vth outside the parliament buildings, for which disrespect we might well have been arrested.

We had a vague idea that we would keep travelling eastwards until we arrived at New Zealand, where Hendrikus hoped to find work in IT. With no goal or sense of purpose, I didn't care where we went. It had become less of a trip and more a glorious way of life. We were travelling because we both relished being accountable to no one but ourselves. For him, it was a backlash to authority and for me, a welcome change to routine and responsibility.

I enjoyed the spontaneity and the lack of planning, clockwatching, and "shoulds" and "musts"; drifting along like tumbleweed in a wonderland of tastes, smells, sights, and experiences. Until I started travelling, I had never before had the opportunity to allow for such aimlessness. I was learning not to get in a stew at having to wait. I was reading books on Buddhism. There were many opportunities to practice patience and non-judgemental observations. Living in the present, according to the books I'd read and monks I spoke to, is all there is.

Dwelling on the past or worrying about the future prevents us from enjoying "now." So all I worried about was the Enfield, my relationship with my family, and increasingly, my relationship with Hendrikus, which I had to admit, was no longer the idyllic one it had been. He was irritable and spent hours on his own in front of his computer. Perhaps things were ailing due to his financial worries and would improve once he found work.

Back at the guest house, he was absorbed in something called a chat-line. I preferred talking with other travellers staying there, most of whom were foreigners like us. It was a great opportunity to discover things about other countries apart from our own and the one we were in.

A couple visiting from Israel lived on a kibbutz. Miriam told me how she'd been vetted for two years to check that she was suitable to marry Joel and live there. She didn't mind having her salary shared out with the others, explaining that whilst she would never be rich, neither would she ever be poor. They'd been allocated a small flat but would have a bigger home if they had children, child-care being shared too.

It all seemed so jolly sensible until I thought about the disadvantages. What if the other people were bossy or had annoying habits? What if they didn't like you? Could you opt to look after your own child instead of going to work? Could you leave if you had a sudden yen to travel when people were relying on your income? This couple had applied for their holiday years before permission was granted. Communal living wasn't for me.

A lone American woman who was "doing" Asia was another guest. She was fully made-up and wore smart, fashionable clothes. She used taxis to take her everywhere, uneasy at the prospect of getting on a bus or a river-ferry. The Royal Orchid Sheraton perhaps more her style, she felt she was roughing it, staying in "this place."

Slightly removed from Khao San Road (the well-loved international backpacker street, now a tourist attraction in itself) Hendrikus and I considered we'd gone steeply up-market being in this new, clean guesthouse. It was all so very entertaining; everything and everybody fascinated me. I strolled to a small local market and ate delicious pad Thai served on a banana leaf whilst sitting on a mini plastic chair at a mini plastic table. At the river, water-traffic was as frantic as on the roads. Little ferries, dodging large boats low in the water with cargo, called at landing stages on both sides of the river collecting and depositing passengers.

The waterways were the best way of getting around the city. By the river I met a saintly woman from Swindon who came every day to spray the poor, flea-ridden, and mangy dogs to alleviate their distress as they scratched themselves raw.

I loved the small portions of appetising food; satisfying for a few hours before the temptation of another dish. Thai bananas, small and sweet, noodle and rice dishes cooked to order in a wok, the combination of salty dried fish marinated in honey was delicious, however odd it might seem. Fresh fruit juice and Singha Beer were good for keeping hydrated in the heat of Bangkok, but however good the fare and the guesthouse were, we were anxious to get away from the city on our motorbikes after three weeks in Burma without them.

Now they were here, we couldn't wait to move on. Hendrikus wanted to see Cambodia; I was curious to find out what I'd see by motorbike that I hadn't seen by bus as a backpacker. I'd had a marvellous time there, but it was bound to be a different experience with my own transport and a boyfriend. We would do a circular route and return to Bangkok before going south to Malaysia.

It didn't start well. Hendrikus was almost arrested by a Bangkok traffic policeman in a close-fitting brown uniform. I waited further on, wondering why the irate officer had blown his whistle. We'd bought helmets as required in Bangkok. Mine was a ridiculous second-hand, silvery plastic one in the shape of a coal-scuttle, whilst Hendrikus had splashed out on a proper modern one, so I knew something else had annoyed the policeman, who was jumping up and down with rage. It was too hot, his uniform too tight, and the traffic too frantic for such discourse. Finally, Hendrikus was allowed to go. He'd ridden in a bus lane . . .

Our first night out of the city was spent by the side of a pond, by a huge ants' nest with squadrons of mosquitoes hell-bent on making us anaemic by the morning. Hot and sticky from the humid climate, I had a refreshing dip in the pond, draped my mosquito net over the bike from an overhead branch, and safe from ants and mosquitoes, watched fireflies and listened to crickets and frogs before sleeping well on the bike with my feet on the handlebars and my head on my backpack on the rear luggage rack.

Frogs are soothing when you are sleepy at dusk after a day's motorcycling if you don't want a conversation without shouting over the croaking. I was living my childhood dream and having *Famous Five* adventures. I wasn't scoffing big farmhouse high teas with lashings of ginger beer as they did, but I adored the sleeping out bit in these hot countries we were travelling in.

Awoken at dawn by a sleepless Hendrikus, who was really too big to sleep on his bike, I offered to navigate that day, as he complained he was doing everything. I drew a straight line on the map from our current position to the border with Cambodia, finding little roads as close to the line as possible. I was in a happy travel bubble, almost a meditation. I was growing into the bike, my thoughts centred on how it sounded and whether I could manage the terrain. My route took us through quiet Thai farmland, the earth tracks as red as paprika.

Bangkok was used to western tourists. Rural Thailand was not. At a farmhouse, we stopped to check we were going the right way, and all concerned got a shock. The men and women were wearing sarongs up to the waist but were bare-breasted. At the sight of us, an old, toothless woman became helpless with laughter, her breasts wobbling about with her shaking shoulders as she pointed out Hendrikus to the other people who gathered to see the spectacle. His ginger hair was about two inches long all over and stuck up like a brush.

I must have looked a sight too; the choc-ice I'd bought and eaten whilst riding along had melted rapidly in the heat, and my face was smothered in chocolate. It was an amusing situation, but Hendrikus didn't like being laughed at, so we rode away leaving them in a heap of mirth.

The road I chose next disappeared into what was now a lake. An optimistic man who had set out wearing white ankle-wellies was whistling merrily as he waded along up to his thighs. Hendrikus cheered up when we had a swim over the flooded road, turning what could have been a negative situation into a positive one. When we found an alternative route, an out-of-control driver almost wiped us off the road; my day in charge was turning out to be rather odd.

Next, a man in a car flagged us down and indicated he wanted us to come with him. Thinking he needed help, we followed. He approached a young woman sitting with her child on the balcony of a house. The interaction between them led us to realise that she didn't know who he was either. We left, bemused at our strange day. Thenceforth Hendrikus resumed navigation as usual.

Crossing into Cambodia at Poipet was straightforward; nobody seemed too concerned about scrutinising or stamping any paperwork. I had travelled in the back of a pick-up truck on this road before and had hoped that in the intervening years, the road to Siem Reap would have improved, but the ninety-three mile journey was even worse on two wheels than it had been on four. Not only was it potholed, but it was constructed with sharp rocks designed to be hard-wearing but also resulting in a punishing ride.

Our poor Enfields were almost shaken to bits during the journey. Each bump had made Hendrikus wince, and by the time we'd booked in at a cheap guest house at Siem Reap, he'd decided he didn't like Cambodia. Over the next few days, spent tightening loosened nuts and bolts on both bikes and searching for the cause of an electrical fault, he decided he no longer liked Enfields either.

He even wished he had a BMW, something he'd sneered at when meeting some Germans at the foreigners' campsite in Islamabad, stranded whilst they awaited sealed units from Germany. We'd done a bit of spannering on our bikes and ridden off feeling smug. I compared how things were then with how they seemed now.

"We are getting more and more distant," I noted, sadly, in my diary.

Siem Reap is famous for Angkor Wat and thousands of other ancient Khmer temples, some of which I had previously explored. Hendrikus didn't want to go where everyone else went, so once we'd found and repaired the loose connection on his bike, we rode forty-seven miles to a lesser-known temple on muddy, barely passable, potholed tracks with makeshift bridges.

After eight and a half centuries, the unrestored Beng Mealea Temple was losing the battle with roots and tendrils of rubbery trees that appeared to be devouring the roofs and terraces. We clambered around the columns and galleries, admiring the stone-carved mix of Buddhist symbolism and the Hindu gods Vishnu and Shiva. Stylised temple girls depicted all over the temples were smiling welcomingly, not at all stony-faced. The mythical snake Naga formed a balustrade.

I felt as if I were in a scene from *The Jungle Book* and half expected Mowgli and Baloo to swing by on creepers. Not Mowgli, but other children joined us to show us the temple, their future as tour-guides mapped out for them, as they already spoke English. They were delightful, and one little chap stuck to Hendrikus like glue.

The once vast Khmer empire was raided and claimed as theirs by Thais from the western border and Vietnamese from the east. Colonised by Japan and then France, Cambodia gained independence in 1953 before getting involved in the Vietnam War.

As if that wasn't enough, with the Vietnamese War came the Khmer Rouge and Pol Pot. Snatching total control, he decided to return Cambodia to an agrarian society, murdering millions of his own citizens and sending those who were left to work on the land until the Vietnamese, now victorious over the Americans, liberated them.

Despite this miserable and violent history, Cambodians show a surprisingly happy disposition but still live with an unimaginable number of landmines. They are surely entitled to the foreign charity organisations who come to do good works in their beautiful country.

Our efforts to communicate in Khmer were met with sniggers or guffaws. Hendrikus tried bargaining with the same result, so he'd storm off from the stall or shop and ask at the next one. Sometimes it would take all day to get what he wanted at a price he thought fair. I got fed up and, whilst wanting to be supportive, felt embarrassed. He was making himself more and more angry over a few pennies.

Half-way between Siem Reap and Kampong Cham we looked for a suitable coffee stop. "That looks a nice place," I said as we approached a pretty wooden hut accessed by a little bridge over a stream. We parked the bikes and ambled across the bridge in our muddy gear to be greeted by sweetly perfumed women wearing heavy make-up and high-heels, as opposed to the usual satin pyjama suits and hats women wore in the streets and shops. I'd chosen a brothel again. They didn't serve coffee so we left with red faces.

That night, choosing the cheapest place in Kampong Thom, we realised that it was yet another brothel as well as a guesthouse. Some friendly Indian men, travelling round Cambodia selling mosquito nets and delighted to see our Enfields, were staying there too. They cooked curry over a small stove in the corridor and shared it with us.

We were grateful for this, not tempted earlier with dried monkeys for sale on a food stall on the way. I tried to ignore the men trooping sheepishly by as we ate.

"No more brothels," I instructed Hendrikus as we left the next morning for Kampong Cham, a good day's ride in those muddy road conditions.

In contrast, we stopped at a peaceful monastery, where flamboyant yellow and blue butterflies the size of birds fluttered amongst the orange-flowering shrubs, as if they knew nobody there would hurt them. Between 1975 and 1979, the Khmer Rouge killed almost all monks, because the Theravada is a scholarly sect of Buddhists, and intelligent people were hunted down.

The violence had left no discernible atmosphere here. It was so peaceful, I felt uplifted and ready for anything, which was just as well later when we headed east away from Kampong Cham on muddy provincial roads. We were riding further from the capital on our way ninety-three miles east to Sen Monoram to see what life was like in a more remote area.

The road conditions were dreadful. I had no tread on my boots and could touch the ground only on tip-toe whilst seated on my bike. If it had been deep mud I'd have managed, I was used to that, but this was a thin layer of wet mud on top of smooth, dried mud. The tyres couldn't sink in and get a grip, as it wasn't deep enough. The top surface was like ice, and the tyres couldn't grip that either. Logging lorries were slithering and sliding, doing graceful pirouettes all round us. I was worried I'd be in the way and get swiped by one like a curling stone.

People who lived in houses overlooking the road were having a great free show from their balconies. Hendrikus could easily touch the ground with his army boots, but even he was sliding about, engine racing as the back wheel spun. He skilfully manoeuvred a patch of dry track between two enormous puddles. I knew what was going to happen as I tried to navigate the same track. Splosh! Followed by gales of laughter from the onlookers. Hendrikus couldn't immediately come to my rescue.

The bike and I lay in the puddle. Bubbles were emerging as my gear absorbed the chocolate brown muddy water. The audience was gleeful at the spectacle, and I wish I could have laughed too. But my pride was hurt, and to make it worse, Hendrikus, who had managed to secure his bike, took a picture of me. I was most ungracious about it and sulked for some time after.

We booked in to stay somewhere, and I hung everything outside on a line. Our food supplies were bagged and tied to a washing line that we'd rigged up in our room to avoid raids from rodents. I awoke to rustling in the night and turned my torch onto an acrobatic rat which was tightrope walking along it to get to our stash of noodles.

Next morning, someone light-fingered had taken my fingerless gloves, and I rode with unprotected hands on the road to Sen Monoram. Luckily, the soft mud didn't hurt during the many times I fell that day. Loud birdsong and the buzz of thousands of insects serenaded me as I had a swim in a beautifully clear jungle pool wearing my clothes to rinse off the mud, which was beginning to harden and restrict my movements.

Red mud tracks with rickety bridges led through the rainforest which, although thick with trees, was clearly being logged, and we saw many huge lorries loaded with massive tree-trunks. It wasn't only my clothes that were restricted by the mud. It had got under the mudguards and was acting as a brake. So I had to free the wheels with my screwdriver before the stuff dried like cement. No wonder the Angkor temples had survived for so long; the earth dried like iron.

An hour or so later, it was starting to get dark, dusk lasting only minutes in Asia. We were still some way from Sen Monoram when I fell badly. Hendrikus had to come and pick me up. We started to panic. We were close to Vietnam. There were landmines there and possibly bandits too. Or even leopards or snakes, or stampeding elephants. I cried, and an exhausted Hendrikus almost did too. It had been an incredibly hard day; the bikes heavy with the extra weight of thick, sticky mud. The uphill and now totally dark road was getting worse and worse. What could we do but keep going? We couldn't risk going off-road to camp amongst landmines.

On the unlit road ahead we reached a drier, flat bit and then saw lights further up the track. We rode up to the guesthouse with unbounded relief. If they'd had no room for us, I would have slept outside in my clothes. As it was, they not only had a room but served food and the best beer I've ever had anywhere; as it always is after a day like that.

We'd gone as far east as we wanted to go, but before we made our way to Phnom Penh, we had a rest day, lazing and swimming in a clear freshwater lagoon fed by a waterfall from a river. I dreaded riding on that same road again, but there had been no further rain, and we travelled easily in daylight down what was now a remarkably easy track, not at all the arduous journey we'd had on the way.

A frisky cow making a bid for freedom is softer than a vehicle, and the blow to my left shin was not severe enough to break it this time. The crash bar that had swivelled and smashed into my right leg in Pakistan during the collision with a four-wheel-drive now swung the other way and bashed my left leg when I hit the cow, which then ran off with its owner in pursuit. I rode painfully and hastily away to avoid a kerfuffle.

Hendrikus was a long way ahead. He'd missed the incident but had troubles of his own. When I caught up with him, he was taking his front wheel out, ready to repair a puncture. I took it on my bike to a nearby village for repair. During the wait, I watched a woman performing a healing procedure by the repair shop. She was scratching another woman's skin with a coin to bring the blood to the surface before putting hot cups over the marks. They didn't mind me watching until the puncture was repaired. The healer was kindly. I wanted her to soothe my painful leg, but the tyre was ready.

We stayed at Kratie to the west, a good day's ride from Sen Monoram. The next day a boatman took us in a small boat with an outboard engine for a river trip to see the rare Irrawaddy dolphins. They are critically endangered in this area due to fishing nets and habitat degradation. The Mekong River is a milk chocolate brown, so as well as thinking it unlikely we would be able to see any dolphins, I wondered how they saw each other.

At a calm bit of the river our guide clung onto the branches of a submerged tree and cut the engine. We held our breath. Fortunately, the dolphins didn't hold theirs, and we heard them taking in air before we saw them looping in front of us. Although we could see nothing below the surface, we saw their rounded heads and long silvery bodies as they emerged from the water. The photos we took in our excitement just show a few wavelets in unimpressive muddy water.

We asked some locals about river transport to Phnom Penh from Kratie, but either we couldn't make ourselves understood or they didn't want to take us and our Enfields, so we rode on, quite literally sticking to the roads.

A puncture on the way necessitated a stop at a roadside repair stall. The T-shirt of the repair man proclaimed him to be Jesus, but there was no miracle repair. Not only did he rip a huge gash in the inner tube by not removing the nail from the tyre first, he pinched the now much-patched tube when putting it back in.

We got about a mile down the road and had to do it all over again at another repair shop, this time using a new inner tube.

It must have been the Buddhist equivalent of graduation day; riding through a village on the way to Phnom Penh, cymbals and bells were tinkling everywhere as we passed dozens of young monks walking about. I could still hear tinkling even after we'd passed the yellow and orange procession. It was a familiar sound that was getting a little louder every day; the tappets needed adjusting.

Tappets are the rods that open and close the valves when the engine is running. Gradually they wear and have to be lengthened when you can hear them. Now this is a job requiring three hands. It is a frustrating game of trial and error to get them just right.

I took comfort from something I'd read in *The Grapes of Wrath* and thought that if the theory was good enough for John Steinbeck, it was good enough for me. The poor family he writes about is uprooting from Oklahoma to California to pick fruit, as the bank has seized their unproductive farm. They buy an ailing truck from a shifty salesman, who advises them to listen to the motor and ignore the tappets which, he adds, could rattle until the second coming of Jesus, because the noise did not indicate a problem.

Hendrikus would have none of it. The tappets had to be done. It's not a filthy job. It's not a heavy job, and there's even a little window into the engine for ease of access, but getting the tappets set just right, not too loose nor too tight, is a tedious, fiddly, nerve-wracking, infuriating chore, and you have to tweak patiently with three little spanners until the nuts will just turn but not spin. Just as you think you have it right, you tighten the lock nut to complete the job, thus altering the whole thing, and you have to start again. It would test even a Buddhist's patience. I managed to do it without hurling the spanners out of sight, and we rode on. I'd proved I had patience.

Now my riding skills were tested. Even if we were going to Phnom Penh by road, instead of by river as we'd hoped, the journey still required crossing rivers caused by rainy-season floods. This meant balancing the heavily loaded bike whilst riding slowly along unstable planks onto small, wobbling, shallow-sided wooden boats that were too narrow for more than one bike at a time. Even locals found it difficult on their nippy Hondas.

The boatmen, used to a few passengers or small motorbikes, were surprised by the amount of water displaced. With my heart in my mouth and adrenaline pumping, it took real effort to overcome my fear, let out the clutch in first gear and set off along a plank from the water's edge. I got a huge sense of achievement when I did it.

I told myself I wasn't doing too badly for someone who was told she'd never achieve anything. Who cared if I failed an interview for a holiday job in a high street store? With a stop-clock ticking, I couldn't add £2 eleven shillings and sixpence and £5 nine shillings and tuppence ha'penny and then calculate a refund of £1 four shillings and a halfpenny in the allotted time. Stuff that! I could ride an Enfield along planks onto wobbly boats.

Hendrikus told me I was the best motorcyclist he knew (after himself), which further boosted my confidence.

A ferry took us across the wide Mekong River to Stung Trong, where we broke our rule not to ride in the dark. Leaving in the late afternoon to ride twenty miles to a pleasant guest house we'd stayed at in Kampong Cham on our way east, all we had to do was follow the river and not bother with roads. It was one of those days when I'd got on the bike and felt as if we were one machine. With a goal, pure concentration, and a race against the failing light, I felt invincible.

It was a challenging but enjoyable ride. Passing through riverside villages, I flew round puddles and trees in the gathering dark. In one area I thought we were back in Pakistan, as people called out, "Assalam Alaykum!" as we passed a small mosque (I later found out they were Cham Muslims).

The sunset was a blaze of different colours, and as dusk fell, a cloud of large flying insects rose and buzzed audibly over the engine noise, wing-cases doing a drum-roll against the Enfield and on my face. The moon turned the Mekong from brown to silver and lit our riverside path as we entered Kampong Cham.

The kindly landlady recognised us from the previous week and greeted us, giving Hendrikus a special gift of a fried spider, a local delicacy. As I'd eaten a cockroach in Burma, I didn't feel the need to prove my gastronomic prowess and declined.

Following a day doing little else than sitting on the guesthouse balcony watching the river, we rode to Phnom Penh along Highway 1, in sections like riding through brown butter churned by heavy lorries.

Once settled into a hostel there, we did a few bits of necessary maintenance, including straightening my "cow-catcher" crash bar and fitting a new clutch cable. I went for a test-run around the capital's streets.

A policeman blew his whistle to stop me, pointing to a traffic sign I'd missed amidst the myriad other signs at a junction. Because I'd turned left down a "no left turn" street he started to write my registration number in a large notebook. I revved the engine to leave the scene but was not quick enough. The policeman gave me a hefty whack on the head with the book. Fortunately, he was on traffic duty and didn't follow me, but I hid the bike in the alleyway behind the hostel for the rest of the day.

Not a keen sight-seer, Hendrikus did not want to see much of the capital, so I was glad I had seen the market, palace, and museums when I'd been there before.

There was occasional but very heavy rain as we headed away from Phnom Penh through serene national parks to the Hat Lek border with Thailand. Neither of us cared to repeat the Poipet Road experience we'd endured on entering Cambodia, so we took a different route out and stayed at Sre Ambel overnight, drying our soggy clothes and boots by tying them onto the whirling ceiling-fan.

The journey there was the loveliest ride on pleasant and quiet roads through mist-shrouded, hilly forest and the most enjoyable part of our three-week trip. It was testing enough to be interesting but not so difficult as to be well-nigh impossible, except for when we came to rivers.

Three times we were left with no choice but to ride onto little boats to take us across, some so small I feared they would capsize. All my skills were called upon when riding onto these unstable craft. Once on the boat, stopping also required some expertise as it shifted wildly from one side to the other, but I was getting better at it with each new encounter.

Now across the border and into Thailand again after our circular route, we thought we should see Pattaya on our way to Bangkok.

Pattaya is best-known as an attraction for older European men wanting the company of pretty young Thai women.

We stayed in a guesthouse with our bikes in the room with us. I had washed mine first, concerned that the red Cambodian mud would set solid. Hendrikus didn't have his washed, and it did; despite many subsequent washes, the red mud always stuck to all the little creases and nooks on his bike.

As we had a beer in a café that evening, we got talking to some women travellers, one of whom verbally attacked me for saying how much I liked India where she considered women to be exploited. I was puzzled. Here we were in one of the biggest sex attractions in the world, and she condemned *ME* for enthusing about India. I shut up and sipped my beer as I watched gorgeous young women on the arms of seedy, unattractive blokes wearing terrible T-shirts and shorts. I started thinking about choice and free will and whether either of them really exists.

Back in Bangkok, it was out with the atlas and the maintenance manuals. I needed new indicators, as mine had stopped working due to frequent bike-drops. I needed a Thai massage too. Then we said a final goodbye to Bangkok and rode south towards Malaysia.

So far, there had been much amusement and laughter in South East Asia, either from us or at us, and sometimes at my expense. One way or another, it had been a funny experience.

I didn't expect to find much to make me smile in Kanchanaburi at the Burmese Railway, built under the harshest of conditions and disease during the Second World War. The ruling Japanese occupiers wanted a railway to connect Thailand and Burma to defeat the British in India.

At the museum, I discovered that it was the humour and optimistic attitude of some of the prisoners that made life bearable. They put themselves at enormous risk by writing forbidden camp newspapers on smuggled scraps of paper and putting on group sing-alongs and comedy skits for each other to keep morale high. Even in the most brutally punishing circumstances people still have a sense of fun.

Whilst we were in Kanchanaburi, tempted by an entry in the guide book, we popped in to see the Floating Nun at Wat Tham Mangkhon, a Buddhist monastery. As the audience sat round the small pool, she appeared, enrobed in white. Not a skinny woman by any means, she lay on her back and slowly circled round the little pool in various yoga poses. I wasn't impressed, but as retribution for my scepticism, one of the temple elephants knocked me over.

The elephant had ambled over and gripped my hand quite tightly with its trunk. It scared the wits out of me. I tried to move away and fell over backwards. The next day, we visited an elephant sanctuary, and a baby elephant, aged ten months, playfully gave me a nudge and I was unbalanced again.

The days passed uneventfully until, as we rode closer to Malaysia, I saw quite an unusual sight. More often depicted cross-legged, seven large concrete standing Buddhas were in a line on a hillside.

We rode up the steep incline to a monastery where we were made most welcome and shown around. The wat was dedicated to the monk who had founded it, and he was displayed in a glass case like Snow White's, wearing a saffron robe and, strangely, his glasses. He had been dead for seven years.

A living monk blessed our motorbikes, and entranced myself, I fell at the bottom of the slope as we left.

It wasn't my last encounter with the dead. Entering a town at lunchtime, I suggested we stop and eat at a restaurant where lots of people were seated. I thought it must be good food there, as it was so popular. I parked the bike and walked up to it and then noticed the cream-coloured coffin decorated with gold Chinese characters, fairy-lights, and flowers. What I'd thought was a Chinese restaurant was a wake.

Noppharat Thara beach, near Krabi, is just as beautiful as it looks on the postcards. We enjoyed some diving and snorkelling, my mask and snorkel always packed in my luggage and perfect for scanning this turquoise sea paradise with black, yellow, and white angel fish, soldier fish, and cup-shaped coral. Soft green coral draped itself over the rocks like a blanket, and another type, like blue string, swirled through it. A sea-snail as big as my fist was moving along quite perkily in the surf.

Just as I'd laughed with joy when we rejoined the bikes in Bangkok, so I laughed as we left Thailand. Before we crossed the border to Malaysia, I bought a bottle of whisky to use up my Thai

Baht. After going skinny-dipping on our last night, we sat and drank it on the beach. I looked upwards and laughed with the stars. My lucky, lucky stars.

7

Malaise in Malaysia

"Don't cry because it's over, smile because it happened." Dr. Seuss

Asia was doing its "magic" thing again. We left Thailand on Enfields but, mysteriously, entered Malaysia on Harley-Davidsons.

At the quiet border post, the solitary Customs officer didn't have "Royal Enfield" on his list and considered "Harley-Davidson" the nearest alternative. So frustrated was he at the lack of ticked boxes that, after two hours, he waved us through without stamping our carnets and even accepted my expired British insurance documents.

Hendrikus had no such papers, but the pleasant and hitherto patient officer let us both pass on my paperwork alone. Without a stamp in the carnet, the bikes were not officially in the country and could be left there. This was more than just a possibility.

Things didn't seem to be suiting Hendrikus. He would withdraw but wouldn't say why. The enchantment of India hadn't hitched a ride with us. Uneasy silences reminded me of times when things were strained between my parents or I had been naughty. Familiar with the crippling effect of the "silent treatment," I drew deeply upon my inner resources and said nothing, because the good times were better than the bad times were bad; travelling together was fun most of the time. I loved him and wanted to stay with him.

We had left Satun in southern Thailand and ridden through the gorgeous Thale National Park to the border at Wang Prachan. Although it was part of the same huge park on the Malaysian side, it became Perlis State Park at the border. The same heat, eerie mist, and heavy tropical rain welcomed us at Wang Kelian, our entry point on the north Malaysian side. It was so lush I smiled for all twenty-five miles to Kangar, through the forest, and onwards to Alor Setar.

Hendrikus seemed enlivened by being in a new country. I realised that my reliance on him must be a burden but still had no foreboding regarding the manner in which I would eventually leave Malaysia.

Alor Setar was a small town, so when we got separated I knew we would soon be reunited. With no mobile phones, we usually kept within sight of each other in built-up areas, but heavy traffic sometimes divided us. Outside towns, if one of us felt like racing off they would wait at a visible point until the other caught up.

A cheap Chinese-run hotel provided us with a large room containing two enormous double beds, an outdoor toilet, a balcony overlooking the street, and some rodents and cockroaches that scuttled about after dark. I rigged up my mosquito net, the one provided being full of holes offering mosquitoes the chance to search and attack.

In contrast to Thailand, a strong Islamic influence was evident here in the north-east of Malaysia. Muslim women wore shape-hiding but brightly coloured clothes and headscarves, secured under the chin. Hardly a hair showed. In Pakistan, women's headscarves often needed rearranging and hair was exposed. In Syria, some women were completely enrobed in black.

Here, women worked in shops and offices and walked unaccompanied in the streets, whereas I hadn't encountered this in Pakistan. There were different rules about Muslim women's dress and lifestyle wherever I went. Here, non-Muslim women wore western clothes. Malaysia has a perfect climate, making it unnecessary to assess the temperature before dressing for the day. There is very little wind too.

Since leaving Islamabad, we'd been slowly moving south to more humid climes, and my minimalist travelling wardrobe was further reduced to a T-shirt, sandals, and dress in addition to my riding clothes of jeans and long-sleeved T-shirt. A black plastic sheet tied over my luggage kept the torrential rain off when we couldn't find shelter for the ten-minute daily downpours. Even if we did get a refreshing natural shower, we dried soon after the rain stopped.

Main roads were good. Roadside stalls offered noodle and rice dishes, fruit, and other delights and were always worth investigating. Impromptu refreshment stops were a good opportunity to pause and discuss things seen along the way and to look at the map.

We were heading south to Penang to treat the bikes to new chains. In India it was common to remove the links to tighten them, but we wanted good quality, less elastic ones.

As I crammed my mouth with fried bananas at a country roadside stall, a grinning Malay motorcyclist on a Norton stopped to greet us. Easily side-tracked, we abandoned our Penang plan and accepted the invitation to stay at his nearby home.

The next day he took us to his mechanic, where we bought and fitted new chains. He and his friends in the Sungai Petani Classic Bike Club urged us to join them in a weekend Independence Day rally to Khota Bharu on the north-east coast. A breakdown truck would accompany us.

Off we went with fifteen keen Malaysians on BSAs, Triumphs, AJSs, Nortons, Ariels, one English Enfield, and a few bright and cheekily-coloured Honda Dreams, largely responsible in their day for putting an end to the British motorcycle industry and now "classics" themselves. Nobody could have been anything but joyful at being in the company of these smiling enthusiasts. It was exhilarating, as was the speed which, at fifty miles per hour was racy for us. It was hot and sunny, but I thought it was snowing when, in front of me, a rider's tyre repair aerosol exploded and clumps of white foam erupted from his pannier.

Hendrikus made use of the breakdown truck when he got a puncture, blaming cheap, Cambodian tubes, heat, and excessive speed. No sooner was his replaced, than mine went too; the valve had blown off.

We paraded in convoy through the crowded streets of Khota Bharu. The traffic was being controlled by the king and queen's own guards, and I felt like a queen myself as people cheered when we all rode past. We even received a special mention at the evening's awards ceremony, a local affair attended by other motorcycle clubs.

Whilst staying in Khota Bharu, I had my motorbike seat re-covered. The cheap plasticised fabric had given up under the strain of the rigours inflicted on it. In Asia, you can have anything repaired. I'd even seen a man in India having his worn flip-flops mended at a cobbler's pavement stall.

The party was over, and everyone went home. We travelled south-west through rural hills and, finding no villages by dusk, chose a forest clearing for our bedroom. The shooting stars were astounding, and I made a wish for everyone I knew. We slept out again the following night too, having done our ablutions in a lake on the way near Gua Musang, where I explored some large caves on a hillside. I'd had to squeeze through a small gap and follow a long passage before it opened out into a beautiful space as big as a church. There was a reachable ledge, like a balcony. I climbed up and looked out over the town below.

I could see the KFC, where Hendrikus sat with his computer. He delved into it at every opportunity. He didn't enjoy the things he used to, like exploring and trying local food, and I felt sad that he seemed bored, not just with me, but with travelling too.

Later, as we rode along, I composed a poem in my head:

> *I may not have a keyboard*
> *But my lips are full and red*
> *Could you use your fingers*
> *On MY software instead?*

> *Your fingers pass so swiftly*
> *On each and every key*
> *You used to be MY hotmale*
> *Why not logon to me?*

> *You used to be so loving*
> *Before you got a Dell*
> *You prefer computers*
> *Am I losing you as well?*

The next day we went south-west to a hill resort in the Cameron Highlands district, where we stayed at a basic backpackers' hostel, inappropriately named the Cameronian Holiday Inn. Hendrikus was working on something important on the Internet so I went for a long walk. I thought I'd be able to find my way back easily but had wandered far further than I'd intended. By the time there was that "end of the day" feeling in the air I was lost in the jungle. Although I was desperate to see a tiger, I hoped it wouldn't be then.

The New Straits Times newspaper reported rubber plantation workers being eaten by tigers in the area. Would it be safer to hide up a tree or in the undergrowth? I spent hours wandering round in circles and, at one point when I reached a road, hitched a lift some of the way in a car. Later, in the dark with my mini-torch, I recognised a path that led to a safe return without my hearing even a meow. Hendrikus, unconcerned, seemed not to have moved all day.

Eventually, we made it to Penang, a large island on the west coast reachable by one of Asia's longest bridges at over eight miles long. Hendrikus's clutch cable broke at the handlebar end as we approached Georgetown. He cleverly clamped a mole-grip tool to it and pulled on that in order to change gear in heavy traffic as we rode to the Wan Hai Hotel in Love Lane, where I'd stayed before. I didn't know what was going to happen in the following weeks, but I sensed Hendrikus was making plans for himself. He was distant and vague.

In this old street there was a large shop calling itself an emporium that sold mysterious bits of engines and tools. Foreseeing a time when I might no longer be sharing the one in Hendrikus's tool bag, I bought myself a comfortingly robust old German square-type adjustable spanner to add to my own tool kit, just in case. It opened up wide enough for the nut on the front wheel hub, yet closed small enough for the nut that tightened the wing mirrors (newly bought to comply with Malaysian law). Due to the bumpy roads we usually travelled on, they swivelled round like radar dishes searching for UFOs.

I also had a new nut made for my front wheel, the thread on the old one worn due to being taken off and put on so many times to repair punctures. As I waited for the new one to be cut, I wandered to an Indian temple, drawn to the musical beating of drums and more unfamiliar sounds.

The source of the cacophony was a trio of musicians: one drummed, another squeezed some kind of bagpipe-type instrument, the third blew like Louis Armstrong into a nadaswaram; so loud and frenzied it must have been a version of the trumpets which brought down the walls of Jericho.

In Penang there was a mixture of the three different cultures: Malay, Chinese, and Indian, providing food choices beyond our dreams; coconut drinks and curry, roti (a version of fried flat-bread stuffed with savoury or sweet fillings) and refreshing watermelon juice. Nasi goreng, noodles and dumplings, took the place of western food, which I little hankered for after two years of Asian cuisine but there were always banana pancakes, the staple backpacker food.

I found myself increasingly alone and spent the time exploring. One stifling day, I went to read and sunbathe on the beach, even though the sea was too warm to be refreshing and I yearned for cold British coastal waters.

I pondered again the requirement of the Qur'an that men and women should "dress discreetly." Fathers and sons in swimming trunks were cooling off in the sea, whilst mothers and daughters sat and watched, fully covered from head to toe and wrist, surrounded by non-Muslim Chinese women in bikinis. I watched the Muslim women. Did they envy the women in the sea? I wondered if anyone else was puzzled, and imagined trying to explain the scene to an uninformed visitor from space.

"A Muslim Response to the Attack on September 11th" was the title of a talk advertised by posters. It was now September 2002, a year after the US Twin Towers attack.

Prior to the talk, there was an exhibition on display called "The Deceit of Darwinian Evolutionism." Anatomical diagrams of the eye were shown to demonstrate that surely only a supernatural power could have designed such a structure. There were also detailed explanations of how bombardier beetles mix two deadly chemicals internally to use as a missile but aren't themselves harmed. The exhibitor claimed that it is so complex that only the hand of God could have created it. Honey bees make too much honey for their own use, so the assumption (rather arrogantly, I thought) was that it must be provided for humans.

The talk about "9/11" was disturbing. The speaker, a Sheik from the USA, expounded the theory that Israel had organised the attacks for its own ends.

My head was in a spin. Recent news highlighted the case of an unmarried Muslim Nigerian woman due to be stoned to death for having a child after she'd been raped. Nothing seemed to reflect a kind and loving God. I'd sung *All Things Bright and Beautiful* since my toddler days. How did that tie in with Darwinism?

I had previously wafted around Asia as a backpacker in an air of "it's not for me to judge how people live. I'm just observing. There's no right, no wrong, just different." Now I was doing rather more thinking and was questioning what I saw. Religion seemed to be about oppressing people and fighting.

I told our Chinese hotel manager, called "Girlie," about the talk. In response, she invited me to accompany her to her Baptist church. Off we went on the bus to a church in a tower block. It was the antithesis of the previous grim Islamic talk. Many storeys up, people were singing, clapping, and smiling to happy young people with tambourines and guitars, led by a preacher in an ordinary suit. I thought of a hymn my mother used to sing, *Closer my God, to Thee*, as we were that bit nearer to heaven up there.

Hendrikus and I were invited, by someone he had kept in touch with from the rally to Khota Bharu, to attend a motorcycle get-together on the mainland near Sitiawan, 111 miles to the south, and it was there that we met Wilf, a large and likeable ex-pat Australian who had lived there for years.

His village home was a sprawling complex of bungalows on a jetty overlooking a large river, where he ran a water-sports venture. We stayed a week or so, helping him repair the jetty and meeting yachtsmen repairing their boats at the local marina. We watched monkeys in the trees and sea-otters eating fish on the rocks as we canoed on the river.

Later we'd get squiffy on Anchor lager at Wilf's local bar. He enjoyed the company and issued an open invitation to return. I sampled a coconut drink called "toddy," made with sap from a slashed coconut flower at the top of the tree. It is fermented for a day and then POW!—one refreshing and very toxic drink.

We rode on to see more of Malaysia and settled on Teluk Intan, only thirty-seven miles south. It had few tourist attractions, other than a leaning water tower. Hendrikus wanted to see what an ordinary town was like. I didn't mind where we went, happy to be led and not make decisions. I had all the choice I wanted, always finding something of interest.

But Teluk Intan was far from ordinary. At the festival of the Nine Emperor Gods the emperors' spirits are invited to come from heaven to earth. Devotees wore white clothing, or if plain white couldn't be found, white Carlsberg T-shirts sufficed. Temple priests and followers went to the river to collect the spirits in ornate gold sedan chairs, becoming entranced on the return trip with rhythmic drumming, chanting, and bell-ringing.

The procession ended at the dark, hundred-year-old, incense-smoked temple. Entranced devotees then sat on nail-spiked thrones and whipped themselves whilst emitting blood-curdling cries. Gongs, drums, and cymbals were struck. Blood-soaked paper money was burnt as offerings as some of those in a trance (brace yourself) sliced their tongues with razor-sharp knives. They held the knife horizontally and drew it from side to side across their tongues and then beat their backs with machetes accompanied by more chanting, bell-ringing, and drumming. It was like a scene from Hell.

Milling about amongst this spectacle, the children of the congregation were as wide-eyed with alarm as I was. Up until this point I had found Malaysia mild and agreeable. As I watched, I compared the ceremony with some church services where men also perform rituals, dress up in highly embroidered silk cloaks, and carry golden ornaments whilst other people swing incense about; similar offerings and chanting but no tongue-slashing, as far as I know.

It seemed that Teluk Intan would be our home for a week or two whilst Hendrikus was looking for work or building websites, so I took the opportunity to have some more dental work done. An Indian dentist removed a false tooth (wobbly for thirty-four years), made a new one, and created a bridge for me, all for a reasonable price and of enduring quality.

When, after ten days, Hendrikus was ready to move on we went south a further hundred miles towards Fraser's Hill, a cooling-off resort for summer retreats. We were following no particular route as we zigzagged our way through Malaysia. Plantations of trees for rubber, coconuts, and controversial palm oil were everywhere, apart from the National Parks. We stayed a night in a plantation workers' tin hut amongst miles of palm oil trees. Eerily gloomy and with no wildlife, the usually ubiquitous cicadas were noticeable by their absence.

Hendrikus had another puncture on the long, winding road up to Fraser's Hill. At this cooler altitude, it was less effort to repair than at many other roadside "workshops." He was worried that a crack in his rear tyre was causing the punctures.

We were lucky to find free accommodation in a workers' unused dormitory and met a teacher from Glasgow who had been just about everywhere whilst travelling on his bicycle. He'd taught geography in Taiwan, Tasmania, and Timbuktu. He recommended a seven-mile walk to Pine Tree Hill, so up at 6AM with porridge inside us and sandwiches made for lunch, we set off. Hungry by 7AM, as the cooler climate stimulated an appetite, we sat on a log a little off the forest path quietly munching when we heard "thumpety-thump" on the dry, hollow-sounding path and stopped eating, wondering what on earth was coming.

Two otter-like animals with bright yellow chests came bounding round a bend. They didn't notice us at first but stopped dead five metres away. I grabbed Hendrikus's arm. The weasely creature that had seen us first almost did the same to its companion. They froze. We froze. They looked at us. We looked at them. They warbled to each other and scampered back a few yards. Then, much to our delight, rather than running away, they came back for a second look. It was a charming experience, and we talked about little else for the rest of the day. They had faces like cute Disney animals.

Even things like shining black giant centipedes, gibbons, macaques, butterflies, and rivers of ants we encountered during the hike couldn't compete with the creatures we later found out were yellow-throated martens. We never did see the pine tree at Pine Tree Hill.

We continued our haphazard tour of Malaysia by going east 155 miles to Mersing and, leaving our bikes at the hotel we were staying at, continued by ferry to Tioman Island off the east coast.

I had a morning ritual to protect myself against sunburn and mosquitoes. After a wash, I would apply sun-screen, to which I added a squirt of 100% Deet. Hendrikus did not bother, believing his fair skin should get used to burning to toughen it up. It had lots of opportunity to when we went snorkelling. Protected by a long-sleeved T-shirt, I watched large, beautiful brown and purple-spotted rays as they "flew" gracefully beneath me. Hendrikus was soaking up the other sorts of rays from the sun. After an hour, his back was an angry red. His skin just wouldn't learn.

Tioman was not only a swimming and snorkelling paradise, it was ideal for jungle exploration. We walked for hours amidst tropical rainforest with drooping, loopy vines trying to garrotte us. When exploring the Andaman Islands, Hendrikus had bought a machete, and he hacked through what, we liked to think, was jungle never before walked upon by humans, but there was probably a path.

We reached Monkey Bay, a deserted, perfect beach on another part of the island and played chess on a board drawn in the sand. Shells made excellent pieces, but my black king suddenly came to life, and the occupant, a hermit crab, unwilling to accept the responsibilities of monarchy, wandered off the board.

We went for a snorkel and saw, horror of horrors, "crown of thorns" starfish, the ones responsible for destroying coral on Australia's Great Barrier Reef. Knowing that these sinister-looking carnivores suck the life out of coral, we decided to "do our bit" and, avoiding the fearsome spines, lifted the things as large as heaped dinner plates out onto the rocks. They looked alarming with red and purple stripes in the water but collapsed in a grotesque heap when out of their environment like creatures from outer space.

We thought we were helping. Later, I mused in my diary that if we'd been told they were rare and endangered, I might have viewed them differently and done my best to ensure their safety rather than hacking a couple to pieces. I realised how suggestible we humans are and that we should question everything we are told, especially when it comes to attitudes to all living things. I don't kill anything now, with the exception of mosquitoes.

Our random journey took us 150 miles over to the west coast again. Even for us, we had no sense of purpose and seemed to be bouncing off the sides of Malaysia like pinballs. Melacca was a place I had enjoyed in 1998, and we stayed a while to sort out luggage and the bikes.

I'd heard from home that someone asked, "What does Jacqui DO all day?" A fair question, and to anyone who has not experienced long-term travel, it might appear to involve endless days of riding, stopping to admire the scenery, eating, sleeping, and riding on again. But it isn't like that most of the time. Especially with Enfields.

There are endless things that have to be done. Apart from bike maintenance, there are facts to be found out, photographic film to have developed, documents to be obtained and photocopied, mosquito nets and clothes to be mended, washing, shopping (for tea, coffee, and dried, easy-to-pack food), sending things home like gifts, diaries, postcards, photographs, and letters and greetings cards. Once written, the post-office had to be found and the item weighed. Writing a letter could take all day. Constant repacking and jettisoning surplus things is necessary. I needed batteries for my Walkman. I had listened to my cassettes of Joe Cocker's *With a Little Help from My Friends* and Bette Midler's *In My Life* over and over when I felt lonely.

My bike was using quite a bit of oil. The engine needed to be delved into. So did Hendrikus's. We found a Chinese mechanic who very generously allowed us to work on the bikes on his premises. Mine needed new piston rings, which we found locally. I was gradually changing from hating maintenance and repairs to getting satisfaction from it as we performed "operations" on the bikes.

There was such a difference in doing emergency repairs in the midday sun at the roadside, and working in a well-ordered workshop made all the more inviting by the proximity of nearby enticing food stalls. Hendrikus's exhaust valve needed readjustment, and I was given the task of making a more snug fit, using grinding paste. It took many days to rid my fingernails of the ingrained carbon from scraping it off both piston-heads.

Mr. Koh, the workshop owner, and his family were very kind to us. He arranged for a journalist of a local newspaper to come and interview us, thereby getting some publicity for his business, but the article was in Chinese, so we couldn't read it.

We were staying in a more comfortable guest house than usual. I was delighted when another couple with motorbikes booked in. Kirsten and Chris were from the UK; she riding a Triumph Tiger Cub and he a Tiger. She was four months pregnant.

When she discovered I was a health visitor, she asked my advice about further travel. They had been on the road for many months. Irresponsible health visitor that I was, I told her there was no reason why she couldn't carry on riding until she could no longer lean forward enough to reach the handlebar and, at that stage, to look for somewhere to have the baby.

They were on their way to Tasmania, where they had relatives. It was such a relief to be able to communicate with people from my "neck of the woods" after such a long time. They didn't ask what my religious belief was or how much I earned, quite a normal and unobtrusive question for Asian people to ask.

They could see things were uncomfortable with Hendrikus and me and offered to take me with them as they travelled through Indonesia. I would have had a very different journey had I accepted their offer, I heard from them later. They had made it to Tasmania and named their little boy Lucas, the company name of a former motorcycle electrical components manufacturer. Afterwards, she had a sidecar fitted to her Tiger Cub for him, and they went on to Fiji before continuing to the UK. What a woman!

A week later, our bikes were all fine and dandy again. We went north ninety-three miles to the capital, Kuala Lumpur, to meet Hendrikus's parents, who were coming for a holiday. As we approached from the hills to the south, the dusk cityscape seemed like a film-set with the needle and twin-towers. I didn't dare stop for a photo in case I lost Hendrikus, and so as on many other occasions, I had to take a "memory photograph."

We stayed in The Coliseum Hotel, an old colonial building with the grumpiest manager imaginable, who might well have worked there since it was built. He lurched around turning off the lights behind us so we could hardly see where we were going in the funereal gloom. He wasn't amused when Hendrikus brought in a ridiculous helium balloon, a blue grinning ant with antennae and just four legs. It was a present to welcome his parents, who were arriving the following morning.

I was lying on the bed as he released it in our spacious room. I watched it rise and become involved in the vortex of the ceiling fan. It circled the room slowly in ever decreasing circles, accelerating as it approached the fan, eventually getting entangled in it. The sound of rubber bumping against spinning metal filled the room as the ludicrous face went whizzing round and round and spun free only to be drawn in again. We were helpless with childish laughter. Hendrikus rescued it, but not before it lost its hind legs, and it was this sorry offering that he took to his parents' hotel as a welcome gift. It was a good start. He was in a cheery mood that I hadn't seen for months.

We took his parents to the butterfly house in a park with a small enclosure exhibiting creatures that could make themselves invisible. Stupidly, at first we thought there was nothing in the display-cases. Then gradually we could pick out the frogs and insects that had evolved to look like leaves, twigs, or even orchids to resemble their background.

His parents continued their backpacking tour of Malaysia, and Hendrikus and I went back to Wilf's home in Kampong Baharu near the town of Sitiawan. Because we had spent some time there before, it felt like home. We helped Wilf with some jobs around the complex and made friends with Ben and Marcel, some yachtsmen at the marina. Then Hendrikus went back to Teluk Intan on his own to do some IT work.

The time had come. We both knew it. One morning I rode there to discuss the situation. I wasn't surprised when he said that he didn't want to travel as we had been doing and planned to fly with his Enfield to Australia from Singapore. He'd been my mentor, my partner, and friend for nearly three years. He'd shown me everything I knew about the Enfield and how to travel with it. I'd been exposed to situations and encounters I couldn't have imagined. We'd shared a pretty unusual way of life. We parted amid reminiscences, hugs, and tears. There were no harsh words. It was simply a parting of the ways.

I went back to Wilf's "sanctuary," where I cried all over Christmas and New Year and considered what to do next. I missed Hendrikus and was now on my own with this demanding lump of machinery, this Enfield Bullet motorbike. Then I realised that I had been coping largely on my own for the last couple of months, anyway.

I reviewed my options. I felt I wanted to call this all off and go home but then remembered I didn't have a home to go to. Everywhere and nowhere was my home. I liked Malaysia so stayed there for a while. It is a country with everything: hills, rivers, good diving and snorkelling on "could stay here forever" beaches. Most villages had traditional bamboo houses contrasting with modern cities.

I learned that many ex-pats go to Thailand and re-enter Malaysia with a new six-month visa. I could do that, or as it wasn't officially stamped in, I could even abandon the bike and travel without it. But I was damned if I'd give up. I had to go on.

I had lost track of my former life after so long on the road and just couldn't see myself going back to what was now the unknown. So I continued with the familiar sort of uncertainty. I'd had only had short stints on my own with the bike before, and the prospect of travelling solo with something that I had always had Hendrikus to help with daunted me. It needed constant attention. How would I know what to do? What would happen if it stalled in a jungle or desert or busy city as it had done before? It would be no good waiting for Hendrikus to come and pick up the bike to sort it out.

I taught myself how to pick the bike up. This meant taking off all of the luggage, standing with my back to it, gripping the lady's handle and luggage rack, and using the strength of my legs, rather than my back, slowly ease it up. With enough determination and adrenaline, I COULD do it.

I now had faith in myself to be able to cope with things if they went wrong. I discovered at the age of fifty-two that not only is the world a wonderful and surprising place but that, with this recognition, I had become capable of surprising myself within it and could grow to fit this expanse. I embraced this feeling, which I envisioned as an opening up of something that had been there all along but that I had only just become aware of. With this feeling also came trust that I would cope. I felt rather high, and whilst I would not have been so daft as to try flying from the top of the Petronas Towers, I thought I should at least have a go at travelling on my own.

Encouraged by this new feeling of wobbly invincibility, I knew I must test myself so rode to an Indian festival at Bhatu Caves 136 miles away to the south-east. There I saw Hindu devotees, equally as determined to prove their devotion as the Chinese had been at the Nine Emperor Gods festival. They had hooks in their backs attached to ropes and chains and pulled chariots through the streets to pay tribute to Lord Muruga.

Hotels all full to bursting, I slept on the Enfield under a bridge surrounded by a sea of sleeping Hindus. Luckily, nobody was hurt when due to "dead-arm" I fell off when shifting position during the night. Resembling a dishcloth myself, I marvelled next morning whilst they unpacked fresh clothes, washed discreetly with bottled water, and looked immaculate in suits and saris.

After the festival, I followed a lead to a place in Ipoh that apparently sold Enfield spare parts. I thought I had better stock up so rode north another 125 miles to see what I could find. I had just got there and was looking for the dealer when the spring broke in the gear-change lever, and I was stuck in first gear. "What a fix I'm in," I thought as I stood beside the bike at the side of the road outside a motorcycle showroom. I went in and asked if there was a mechanic who could help. He phoned some friends, and within the hour, I had a whole bunch of members from the Ipoh Classic Bike Club to help me.

Mani and Appu invited me to stay with them whilst I got a new spring made. "Hmm . . . " I wondered again, "Would this happen at home?" I recalled pushing my lifeless Suzuki along a road in Stoke on Trent to the sound of people beeping their horns and jeering as they drove past.

The next day, the broken spring was removed from the gear-change lever and I was taken to a Chinese spring-making factory, where I had a new one made for the equivalent of a couple of quid. The Enfield dealership had burned down some time ago.

I was invited to stay at the vacant bungalow of Mohan, one of the club members. I stayed there for about a week whilst I got used to being alone. Nearby was a cosmetic surgeon, or as it said on his shop front, an "Architect of Beauty." Droopy eyelids are a family trait. My mother's almost covered her poor old blind eyes, and so I went in to make enquiries. Tired of endless bike maintenance, I felt I needed some myself.

My diary entry for 14th January 2003 reads quite nonchalantly: "Today's highlight has to be the plastic surgery on my eyelids. Better than going to the dentist! £90 and I looked like a zombie with eyelids dripping blood down my cheeks later. I'd been told to rest but the chaps from the Ipoh bike club invited me out to a club in the evening and I thought "What the hell . . . ' I danced with Mani, Mr. Lee, Appu, some of the waiters, a doctor and the assistant manager. Felt wonderful."

The operation itself had been performed under local anaesthetic. I lay back after the "architect of beauty" had drawn a couple of lines on each eyelid with a felt-tipped pen. I was told to close my eyes. A few minutes went by, and even though I had my eyes closed, I could see. That was the worst part, as I knew he had sliced through my eyelid. I thought of the Chinese devotee slicing his tongue and decided that was worse so didn't whimper. After ten days, I took my own stitches out and couldn't see much difference to my eyelids.

I said my farewells to my Ipoh friends and went back to Wilf's. My first solo journey had been a success. I'd got to where I wanted to go, seen what I'd wanted to see, found a place to sleep, had a problem with the Enfield, managed to get it repaired with help from friendly local blokes, had cosmetic surgery, and returned. All in about three weeks.

Out came my mini atlas, and I decided to go to Indonesia. Marcel, one of the sailors we'd met at the marina, suggested that I might accompany him on his catamaran to Australia. That meant sailing via Indonesia. "What bliss that would be," I dreamed, imagining sailing between Indonesian islands, lazily adjusting a sail or something, whilst relaxing on deck and mooring at idyllic deserted island beaches. He was a tree-hugging vegetarian, and I thought I'd be safe. My agenda was to pay half the expenses and do half the work; his was similar but had some added extras . . .

8

MEN WHO SCARE ON BOATS UPON THE VASTY DEEP

Sailing with my older brother in a small dinghy in the bay at Weston-super-Mare before we were teenagers was scant preparation for sailing from Malaysia to Australia in a thirty-two foot catamaran when I was fifty-two. Weston lies on the Severn Estuary, which has one of the highest tidal ranges in the world, at fifty feet.

I understood about tides. I'd regularly paddled my red canvas kayak the three miles from one side of the bay to the other on my own and managed to not get sucked into the North Atlantic with the outgoing rush of brown silted sea I'd been larking about in since I was seven. I'd often sailed with my boyfriend in a National 12 and a Fireball. I understood about wind and sails.

But I didn't know about charts, I didn't know about diesel engines, and I didn't know that for the first time in my life I thought

I really might die. I had learned to be respectful rather than afraid of the sea as a swimmer, occasionally going out too far or feeling the undertow. I'd sensed danger several times and swum adrenaline-driven like a cartoon character to the shore. I'd had frequent narrow squeaks whilst racing my bicycle down the steep hills to school, feeling invincible against traffic. I'd had moments of fear when climbing up and down the quarry walls near our home wearing plimsolls on my feet, but I'd never knowingly looked death in the face before.

The skipper, Marcel, would know what he was doing; after all, he'd sailed this catamaran to Malaysia from Australia. I grew hopeful and, in my current state of leaving things to the Universe, trusted that all would be well; we'd have a marvellous time cruising through Indonesia and, several months later, land somewhere near Darwin.

There would be fresh coconuts, fish, tropical fruit, beautiful sunsets, and idyllic islands to wade onto. Twenty-three inches of water was all the catamaran needed to float, so we'd be able to get closer to white-sandy beaches than with a monohull. Wildlife would be unafraid and behave naturally and delightfully in front of us. My rose-tinted spectacles became wide-angled and telescopic.

The aft cockpit was just big enough for the Enfield if I removed the front wheel.

Aware of knowing winks and suggestive comments like "the crew gotta screw" from yachties at the marina, I made it clear to Marcel, also in his early fifties, that this was to be a business arrangement and I was not interested in anything other than a working relationship. I still ached for Hendrikus and didn't find small, humourless Marcel remotely appealing. He had already made several suggestions and advances, at the same time pointedly telling me he made frequent visits to Thailand "where women really know how to please a man." Did he expect me to find this declaration alluring? He had a daughter and a girlfriend somewhere. He agreed that he'd accept me as crew without "favours." I'd have my own cabin. The trip was on.

My father would have been pleased at my embarking on a voyage. He was fifty-two when I was born. A Victorian, born in 1898, he went to sea at the age of fourteen and had been in the Merchant and Royal Navies. In my teens he restored *Fuss*, a twenty-

foot gaff-rigged sloop with a cabin and we became family members
at the local yacht club, where I met my future husband.

I was fourteen and still running around with a sheath-knife,
climbing trees and rowing and paddling on the River Axe on the
south-west side of Weston Bay. Happily immature, I wanted to be
outside, walking in the woods behind our home, identifying trees,
birds, and wild flowers or swimming and messing about with boats.
"Learn all you can," my father encouraged each day as I went to school.
I must have worried my parents dreadfully. So when a sensible
nineteen-year-old, who was studying to be an estate agent, came along
my parents did not discourage him. I married him eight years later.

When my father implored me to "Travel, my dear," I mistakenly
imagined doing that with my husband when we retired. Dad died
aged eighty-nine, ten years before I finally fulfilled his wish. It
would have been nice if he'd known that I was riding a motorcycle
around Asia. He'd had a BSA and an Ariel that I barely remember,
but I still bear the mark of an exhaust-pipe burn on my leg from one
of them. Now I was embarking on seafaring too.

Marcel was replacing two outboard engines with one inboard
one. He had bought an old thirty-three horsepower tractor engine
that, with much jiggery-pokery, would reincarnate into a ship's
engine. Alterations to the gearbox and pump were necessary, and
a propeller had to be fitted. It was Christmas 2002. Our estimated
date of departure was 18th February 2003. There was much to do.

I worked hard. Up to my neck in sea water under the boat,
undeterred by a black and white striped sea snake wriggling near
my ankles, I connected the new propeller shaft. I ran Marcel around
on the Enfield and fetched and carried things. I waterproofed and
painted the wooden dinghy. In addition to the country of origin's
flag, it is a courtesy to fly the flag of the country being sailed
through, so I borrowed a sewing machine and made an Indonesian
flag, happy to be doing some sewing again.

I tidied and sorted tools, nuts, bolts, and screws and replenished
the first aid kit. I varnished the cabin interior and the newly-built
engine-cover, stapling egg boxes to the inside to muffle the noise. I
scraped the barnacles from the hulls. I turned out cupboards and
found a concealed ferocious-looking machete.

Sails, dormant for eighteen months, were unfurled. Ropes
and lanyards were replaced, having unaccountably shortened or

lengthened, behaving like Christmas-tree lights that don't work when plugged in after a year's repose. Menus and shopping lists were drawn up. The catamaran had not been "clothed" for eighteen months, and Marcel had to relearn the rigging, climbing up and down the mast.

I did my share of labour, arriving early in the mornings from Wilf's and staying until dusk. Expenses were halved between us.

We couldn't just sail away as I had imagined. An expensive certificate had to be applied for to give us permission to cruise Indonesian waters. We had a month to finish the boat and have an extended test-run up the coast to Langkawi Island before setting off on the voyage proper.

The Enfield's International Carnet de Passage wouldn't expire until April, giving us the chance to use it to explore islands on our way. But I learned some disturbing news from the AA: I wouldn't be able to renew it. India had stopped the AA issuing carnets for vehicles bought in India by non-residents. Not only that, previously registered vehicles were also illegal.

What on earth was I going to do without a carnet? My Enfield wasn't just in Malaysia illegally, it was stateless everywhere. I had legal ownership and Indian registration documents and hoped Customs officials wouldn't know the new rules.

Australia's Department of Traffic and Road Systems (DOTARS) had an informative website. I was relieved to find that, with a tourist visa, I could import the Enfield for three months and extend after that. I didn't need a carnet. First, I had to get myself a tourist visa for Australia.

I rode to the Australian Consulate in Kuala Lumpur, staying in a hotel in colourful, lively Chinatown. The hotel had the surprising and enjoyable novelty of a bath, most unusual in Asia. Neighbourly police officers offered me free parking in their compound. Luckily, they didn't ask to see my documents.

On the trip back to Sitiawan, I looked at the map and made a "there must be a shortcut" decision, found an unmade road, and was right. The road had a mix of mud, puddles, and sand. Hey—I could do this travelling alone thing.

Now in possession of my Australian visa, I applied for "Permission to Import." It was a lengthy procedure, accompanied by much cursing during frustratingly poor Internet connections. I was overjoyed when I received my permission by post. No mention of an illegal motorcycle. I was all set.

The first time I thought I was going to die was when I started to update my sub-aqua diving documentation, hoping for some diving in Australia. I went for an X-ray, as mine had expired. Unlike our NHS system, referrals and appointments are unnecessary; if you want one, you go and have one at a clinic and pay. I had my reasonably-priced X-ray in Sitiawan and awaited the result in the waiting room. After about half an hour, I was called in to see the doctor.

"Have you got a cough? Have you lost weight?" and "Do you smoke?"

With those questions, the chill of fear began. "No," I croaked. He showed me my X-ray. One lung was splattered in white dots. TB? Widespread cancer? He listened to my chest and requested a repeat X-ray. When it was done, I waited outside, thinking . . . In Pakistan when I saw my leg was broken, my first reaction was annoyance that our travelling would be curtailed. I felt the same now.

I'd spent three months getting the boat ready, and now I'd have to forego the trip in order to get this sorted out. Or die. I wondered how my ninety-five year-old mother would feel if she outlived me, and thinking that my daughters and brother would be sad. Then I remembered that only one lung was affected and decided that I could cope with that. I went through a very interesting half-hour thinking over my life. I wasn't afraid. Pissed off, yes, but not afraid.

The repeat X-ray was clear, and I hugged the doctor and cried with relief. It was a fault on the film. Death was not on the doorstep. Not yet, anyway.

I went to a restaurant for my favourite meal of masala dosa and told a fellow diner what had just occurred. After he heard my story, he reached into his pocket and handed something to me. "I want you to have this . . . " he said solemnly, "It's a lion's claw"; I struggled to accept it, as I didn't really want it but knew it was an item of great value to him. A refusal would have caused him great offence, so I accepted not only the claw but his empathy and concern that I had escaped a grave situation.

Many times in Asia I had tried to pay for kindnesses and by so doing had upset the giver. It was very hard to tell when accommodation or a meal was offered freely or not, but here and now, I knew what to do. I'd learned another great lesson . . . that by accepting, you also are giving.

Back at the catamaran, I was astounded one day to receive a severe reprimand from Marcel starting with the words *Sit down I want to talk to you*, reminding me of childhood ear-bashings. He accused me of not working hard enough. I was incredulous, as I felt I couldn't do more. I was working eight hours a day, seven days a week. I no longer thought of this as a friendship and was on my guard.

We'd agreed to be equals in this endeavour. Had I not already done months of work and paid my share of expenses I would not have stayed. He blamed me for all the delays, mishaps, disasters, and general bad luck that befell the boat (which, although plentiful, hadn't even started yet). The gearbox, pump, and propeller had been problematic. If something could go wrong, break, not fit, or get lost, it did.

He implied I was jinxed but hinted strongly at romance. I still found him unattractive in every way, especially when I saw him wearing his wife's lacy Lycra control panties as swimming trunks.

My Buddhist books advised tolerance and bending like a blade of grass in the wind. I tried, but rather than listening to the universe, I was fighting it, defying the disquieting signals it was sending. I stayed. When Marcel made me sign a disclaimer alleviating him of all responsibility for the safety of me and my motorbike, I started to get worried. However, I carried on, optimistic that things would improve once we started the voyage.

My horoscope in *The New Straits Times* read, "Do not be surprised if dates made two months ago are cancelled . . . "

We'd been due to leave for Australia on Feb 18th, but it took until March to have a trial run to Langkawi Island. The propeller was too small, with a left-handed screw instead of a right-handed screw, so when put in forward gear the boat reversed. The rudder was too big, so more time was spent having that cut down and reshaped. The catamaran had some protrusions at the waterline and picked up and dragged someone else's mooring chain whilst out on a test run to see how the rudder was performing.

Crashes into the wooden jetty at the marina were frequent, and Marcel lost his best glasses overboard when observing the rudder's performance. The autopilot wasn't wired up correctly, so the deranged tiller sent us the opposite direction to the one required. That horoscope was right.

I bought myself a mobile phone (my first) and rang a very understanding Claire at midnight my time, 5AM hers. Then I spoke to Abby, who had bought a Honda CBR600 motorbike. I learnt how to send texts. I was catching up with technology.

We did make it to Langkawi. It was beautiful, and we both enjoyed it. I put his bullying down to stress and let it pass. The wind was just right for some pleasant sailing, and I had the thrill of sailing unaided under what I was told was Asia's second longest bridge to Penang from mainland Malaysia whilst Marcel slept. I had been over it, both by bus and motorbike, now I was sailing underneath it. It was a special "grin" moment.

With no engine racket to mask them, "boat noises" could be discerned, and between the hulls a combination of disturbance between wind and water made a sound like a convivial party. I could hear voices and clinking glasses so clearly I had to peer down to check.

On my birthday, as we moored off a quiet island on the return trip, he cooked a special dinner as I swam in the dark. I squealed with delight, because as I moved, phosphorescence lit up like fireworks in the sea. We could see squids lit up by the phosphorescence too. The day was rounded off by a spectacular thunder and lightning storm, which lit up the crocodile-like monitor lizards on the beach as we sipped our wine. I wished Hendrikus was there. I missed him.

A new propeller was purchased on our return so we didn't have to be in reverse gear all the time, and once fitted, we had a little run around the harbour with the by now customary crash into the jetty. An email from Hendrikus told me he was flying with his bike to Australia from KL. He was missing me, too.

Diary entry 26th March 2003 (I had already been away from my job for four years):

> *"Wrote email to my former manager at Stoke-on-Trent Combined Healthcare to say I probably wouldn't be coming back from my five-year career break!"*

Treasured childhood gifts of *The Observers* books of wildflowers, dogs, birds, and trees had sown the seeds of delight in living things. Being in the same place for so many weeks, I observed Malaysian creatures aplenty. At the marina a lizard caught a frog by the leg and dragged it for consumption under a bush (I'm glad to have missed that bit). When painting the dinghy I clearly heard *Rudolph the Red-Nosed Reindeer* being whistled, only to discover it was a bird singing.

One morning, the tide just right, instead of riding the bike to the marina I borrowed a canoe and paddled there. I saw a huge eagle lazily flap away as I silently rounded a curve in the river. A one-eyed gecko lived on the boat that, predictably, we named Cyclops. It wasn't the only creature to catch flies and mosquitoes. A skilful jumping spider stalked a fly that was relishing leftovers from a plate. It leapt eight inches and caught the fly. These spiders hunt and do not have webs.

Day after day outside the marina toilet block, a yellow bird unceasingly pecked its reflection in a shaving mirror. I felt sorry for it, wasting its life in such futility, and moved the cable it used as a perch, but it didn't give up and hung upside-down from the frame and continued to torment and shout at itself.

Wilf's balcony over the brackish river offered further opportunity for wildlife gazing. At low tide, dozens of small orange fiddler crabs with one massively out of proportion claw to repel rivals and attract females waved their claws as if signalling "Oi— Come over 'ere." Striped archerfish cleverly spat at hovering insects to bring them down into the water by judging the refraction and knowing just where to aim the jet.

The longer I lingered quietly with a beer after a day's work at the marina, the more I noticed. Woodpeckers, herons, hornbills, monkeys, and monitor lizards were all seen whilst either sitting there or languidly drifting in a canoe amongst the mangroves.

Apart from the animals, insects, and birds, there were interesting people to study too. I met long-term sailing families who were doing repairs and restocking their boats. The delightful and gregarious teenage daughter of a French couple who did home tuition had been sailing round the world since she was born, knowing no other way of life. A Canadian couple brought up and educated three children aboard. They'd later graduated from universities and now worked in various parts of the world. With all the choices the world has to offer, why do we stick to "normal" regimes? Some people step away from the treadmill and gain enviable experiences, but what, I asked myself, were the sacrifices?

The Enfield needed a bit of attention before setting off. I did an oil change, feeling pleased until finding a washer in the bottom of the oil tray. The oil chamber didn't leak without it, so I hoped it wouldn't all drain out once aboard. A miracle product . . . "End Rust" that converts rust to a hardened black surface did two jobs in one and made the bike look quite smart for its voyage. I fitted a new plug, then tried kick-starting it for ages, sweating in the hot sun before realising I'd left the plug cap off.

Water tanks were filled ("Of course there will be enough water to wash my hair, Marcel"). Batteries were fully charged and would be topped up by a solar panel and wind generator. Fuel tanks were filled, and extra diesel in twenty-litre jerry cans stashed on deck. The fridge was full of food, and cupboards were stashed with tins and packets. We had enough rice and tinned New Zealand butter to last until we got to Australia. Fresh food was stored in the cool bilges.

The last thing to go on board was the bike. Well used to riding it along narrow planks onto wobbly boats in Cambodia, I rode it down the beach, along a descending line of planks, before revving up the last, very steep and bouncy one onto the catamaran. After I removed the front wheel and tank, Marcel and other yachties lowered the bike into the cockpit. I stuffed an oily rag up the exhaust pipe, massaged it with grease ("Wish you'd do that to me," said Marcel), and covered it with a tarpaulin to protect it from salt spray.

We went to immigration to be stamped out of Malaysia, unable to sign into Indonesia until we got there. It felt liberating to be officially nowhere. Just as we were ready to go, the British Foreign Office advised UK citizens to avoid trips to Indonesia and to consider leaving if already there. Indonesia has the largest Muslim population of any country. It was the 6th April 2003, and we had just invaded Iraq.

Nowhere near the proposed leaving date of 18th February, we finally left the marina on 8th April 2003. With a final bump into the jetty for old times' sake, we waved to the others on shore and went on our way.

Leaving as late in the season as we did, the current was against us, and the prevailing wind was largely unusable, as it came up the Straits of Malacca "on the nose." This meant we soon used up much of the fuel that ran the old tractor engine. The new propeller was too big, and the stressed engine achieved a feeble three knots at best. But we were on our way and were more relaxed.

Sometimes, the wind would be kind and let us use it, and it was so nice when we were sailing instead of motoring, often reaching between five and seven knots. The first night was ideal, and after a good day's sailing, we had dinner in the cockpit off Rumbia, one of the Sembilan Islands. I put all the previous hassles behind me. Things, for a while, were looking up.

The daytime heat from the two land masses of Sumatra and Malaysia caused turbulence in the strait as we sailed between them at night. We were blown all over the place, and the current was taking us backwards and forwards. We saw the coastal town of Malacca three times in two days. This sort of going with the flow wasn't at all what I wanted.

The wind crazily changed force and direction, and I got into a muddle in the dark on my watch one night with the torrential rain obscuring my vision as I frantically tried to don waterproofs, cling on to the mast, and keep control of the catamaran. The sails flapped about noisily, as if the devil himself was trying to shake them from the mast. Amidst this tempest I was frightened and feared I would drown. I thought the boat was going to sink and shivered with fear. Marcel came out, saved the situation, and we headed for calmer waters nearer the coast.

After two days of motoring along between Malaysia and Sumatra with no land in sight, we spied what looked like a waving man in a small boat ahead. As we approached, there was not one man, but five; and no boat. Desperate to be rescued, but wary of letting go of the jerry-cans, slabs of polystyrene, and bits of wood that had been keeping them afloat, they climbed aboard and collapsed exhausted on the deck. I rushed about making tea and gave them rice, noodles, biscuits, and bananas, which they gratefully and greedily devoured.

We ascertained with the help of two dictionaries, sign language, and our limited Malaysian that they had been dumped three days previously by the skipper of a fishing boat, who they had paid to deliver them secretly to what they hoped would be a better life in Malaysia. As skipper, Marcel made the decision to deliver them to the police at Port Klang, a big Malaysian port that would mean a major detour for us. But as we got to know them over the course of the day, he changed his mind.

We exchanged currency with them so they would have some money to start with. They were very relieved and, at dusk, helped choose a quiet area just outside the docks area in waist-deep water. We all shook hands before they waded ashore with their few possessions held over their heads. We had probably saved their lives by rescuing them from the sea; we'd fed and watered them and should have registered their (and our) arrival with the authorities. But we didn't.

Marcel and I moored up for the night and rowed ashore for a meal, marvelling at what had happened. Next morning when it was light, we saw to our horror that where we, illegal ourselves having "checked out" of Malaysia, had deposited our human cargo and put down anchor was amongst six occupied police launches, also moored since the night before. We'd been right under their noses. We left Port Klang as unobtrusively as we could, wondering how our guests were faring. I still do.

Marcel decided we must register our arrival in Indonesia but saw from his paltry collection of charts that we desperately needed more detailed ones. The area was scattered with hundreds of small islands, just waiting to be bumped into at night. He set the autopilot for Batam Island, not too far away in Indonesia.

Going there meant cutting across the very busy shipping lanes between Port Klang and Singapore. The engine was shaking itself loose, and its jumping about caused the propeller shaft to bend. Progress was so slow that even sailing miles out of our way and zig-zagging was quicker.

I enjoyed the sailing. It was as good as I'd hoped. Reaping the benefit of the months of waiting and hard work, I relished my solo night watches. Four hours of serene solitude allowed me to do yoga stretches and listen to the *BBC World Service*, hearing about the proposed London congestion tax and what was happening in Iraq.

I'd learned how to operate the automatic pilot that needed only occasional manual alignment with the GPS. At first, I wondered why the stars occasionally disappeared and then realised one of the massive tankers was blocking them as it slid silently by. Container ships, the size of huge blocks of flats, loomed up on us. It was necessary to keep a watch for ships, fishing boats and their nets, or any large floating objects. Some of the ships had lights ablaze, others had just a stern-light and got so close I felt sure we would be crushed. I felt tiny and vulnerable but found it thrilling. I hoped the small catamaran was visible on their radar, as our lights were feeble even when they were switched on, which to save the batteries, mostly they weren't.

A paraffin lamp in the cockpit was usually the only light we had. We couldn't see the dozens of small, unlit fishing boats either and nearly got caught up in their nets a couple of times. My neck ached from looking at the stars during my night watch and from observing frigate birds during the day. Marcel was a great cook and produced elaborate meals from our stores; whilst we still had food and cooking fuel that is . . .

We were now in Indonesian waters. As there were no detailed charts aboard, we couldn't find the marina and moored off an undesirable part of Batam Island, not far from Singapore. Even with my optimistic eyes it looked shifty, with a shanty-town built on the shore. We rowed the dinghy ashore, as the outboard engine didn't work.

We needed to register with immigration, but it was Easter and all offices were shut for four days. We couldn't find any charts either so went back to the catamaran. Someone very small had squeezed through a porthole Marcel had left open. Gone were his cash, credit cards, passport, tools, ship's radio, binoculars, and radio/cassette player. I'd taken all my documents with me, and only my mosquito net, water-colour painting set, and first aid kit were stolen.

The thieves also took two full twenty-litre jerry cans of fuel and the cooking gas cylinder, so thenceforth we cooked on a tiny meths stove whilst the fresh food went off, the fridge also being gas-fuelled. Whilst he could still produce food of a high standard, my efforts were reduced to pale, tasteless slops of things from the pressure cooker. He said I was being a bad cook on purpose. I wasn't, I really was that bad. The one thing we hadn't run out of was water. It was satisfying to collect it from the sails during storms. A well-placed bucket where the rain ran off my bike cover added to the supply.

To avoid further trouble due to inadequate charts I went in search of some, asking at the makeshift village by the shore. A lovely woman called Angel (she could well have been one) who spoke a little English told me that the navy divers were stationed nearby. I visited them. They were most helpful and took me into town to photocopy their plentiful selection of charts. Very pleased and feeling I must have redeemed myself in the skipper's eyes, I returned to the catamaran holding the treasured sheets of paper. Far from looking pleased, Marcel had a face like thunder.

In my absence, he had been reading my diary. Now I confide in and confess all to my diary. I had written sufficient to infuriate him. I endured another "sit down I want to talk to you" session. He said that what he'd read was little short of treachery and told me to leave. I knew my legal rights and reminded him that he would have to pay my expenses either back from whence we'd come or onward to Australia.

He raised the matter of our relationship again, blaming me for not finding him worthy of desire. I reminded him of our "business only" agreement. A less attractive sight than Marcel in a red fit of rage was hard to imagine. He banged his fist on the table, shouting, "I can get any woman I want!" I tried to look contrite, lowering my eyes as he ranted on. I thought about his swimming attire and struggled to keep a straight face. He could shout and be unpleasant to me, but he couldn't make me like, respect, or admire him.

Three days later when the offices reopened, he nearly had a punch-up with the immigration officer, who unfairly tried to arrest him for being an illegal immigrant. I had my passport so was stamped in and legal. Eventually, he was issued with a temporary permit.

We bought some sturdy bolts and secured the engine to the floor again. The police had told us that the bay we had moored in was aptly called Pantai Stress, in other words . . . "stress beach."

To pass the Easter break we read and played cards. We played "Find the Lady" by candlelight. The unwelcome Queen of Spades appeared in every single game, even though only half the pack was being used after shuffling the whole pack each time. Marcel lost and blamed my bad attitude for bringing out the queen so often. He was beginning to frighten me.

Ashore, I withdrew as much money as I could with my bank card and gave him most of it, as he had no access to his bank. He said I didn't have to leave after all, and a truce was made. We now had to go to Jakarta to pick up his new passport. My dream of island-hopping looked like it was coming true when we called in at Bangka Island and had a very pleasant day there buying a few supplies and talking to the islanders. Muslim women were not hidden away but out on the streets wearing cool dresses. No animosity was shown to me, despite the Foreign Office warning.

It was Marcel's fifty-fourth birthday, and he seemed elated, chatting about everything as we walked round. I bought a new sketchpad and some crayons from a stall. We bought new jerry cans and filled them with forty litres of diesel. A throng of villagers helped us to the dinghy. I had my hand held by a pregnant fourteen-year old girl who asked if I would be her mother. I gave her a hug. They gave us coconuts and waved until we got on the boat.

At some stage we crossed the equator. Panicky flying fish scattered airborne at our bow in contrast to languidly looping dolphins. Sea birds rested on old barnacle-encrusted flip-flops and polystyrene. Crabs clung to bits of wood, and coconuts bobbed about. It was fabulous on deck. Things were improving. I was sketching a birthday card for Claire. Marcel played his guitar and saxophone. We were doing alright until . . . "Get down below quickly and keep out of sight."

I dashed below, wondering what he could have seen to give such an order, and I peeped through a porthole to see what was happening. A large wooden fishing boat had sped alongside from nowhere. Much yelling and waving of brown, weathered arms was going on. Surly-looking men dressed in tattered jeans, T-shirts, and neckerchiefs were leaning over the side of their boat, poised to jump aboard the catamaran. I couldn't hear what was being said for the noise of the engines, but they clearly hadn't called for a friendly chat. They seemed to be barking orders to Marcel, demanding something. I heard him explain that he had no money, or passport, or credit cards, as these had already been stolen. Somehow, he prevented them from boarding, the discourse lasting for ages.

They settled for a large quantity of food, almost all we had, which he handed to them as they stood on the gunwales of their boat reaching across. I was able to see their faces as they snatched bags of rice, cans of meat, butter, and vegetables. Even then, they hovered around as the skipper put the engine into gear. They seemed to be having second thoughts, some pointing back at the catamaran, but eventually they meandered away. I did not dare emerge until they had been out of sight for a long time. Their engine was so much more powerful than ours, and

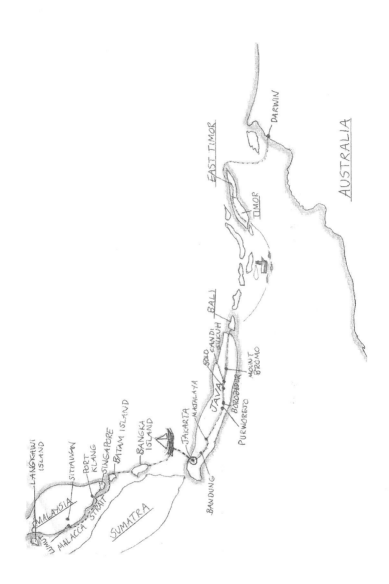

they could still come back to see what else was on the boat. I thanked Marcel for keeping me safe.

We now had little food and could not use the wind, so fuel was getting desperately low. Because the wiring was not connected from the engine, the battery was so exhausted that we couldn't use the auto pilot and had to steer manually day and night, which was tiring. Marcel blamed me for bringing bad karma to the boat. "I could cut you up into little bits and throw you overboard or creep up on you and push you into the sea on your night watch. Nobody would know or ask questions," he said to me one night. "So . . . ," I said to myself, "THAT'S what the machete is for." Henceforth, I slept uneasily with a knife under my pillow and made sure I never had my back to him. I decided I'd had enough of the sea. What with castaways and pirates, little fuel or food, the frightening storms, and deranged skipper, I promised myself that if I lived long enough to land in Jakarta, I would never get on that boat again.

I could see from the chart that there was a nearby off-shore oil field. "Where better to go for fuel?" I said, delighted to accept the chance the Universe had presented, naïvely thinking we could somehow tap into oil straight from the sea-bed. Marcel, too exhausted to point out how ridiculous my idea was, steered towards the area using the last dregs of diesel. "Excuse me!" I shouted up to them as I threw ropes up to a platform to stop us crashing into the metal struts in the huge swell, "We have no fuel or food. Could you spare some diesel so we can get to Jakarta please?" They were concerned and so kind, throwing us loaves of bread, hauling up our empty fuel cans, then lowering them down full. We gratefully received sixty litres of diesel, enough to get us to Jakarta.

On the 10th May, on dry land and a month after we'd started the voyage, I assessed my emotional state. I'd gone from the pain of separation from Hendrikus, triumph at managing without him, hopes of a pleasant voyage, fear of death (from cancer, the elements, pirates, or Marcel), optimism, and enjoyment of the sailing trip to what I felt now . . . relief and determination. I threw myself on the mercy of the Indonesian Customs, dismissing their suggestion that I continue my voyage to Australia. "I am not getting back on that boat."

I told them all about the voyage and that I would rather rot in an Indonesian prison. They not only bent the rules to let the now carnet-less bike in, but in conjunction with the chief of traffic police, made new ones. They gave me a map and a letter demanding that I be given all help and assistance from the police on my way through Indonesia. Despite Marcel's invitation to sail on with him once he had his replacement documents, as I had been "very helpful and generous, really," I refused, choosing to flee that nightmare.

Two burly dock-workers helped me to manhandle the bike off the catamaran once the customs officers had checked it over for their purposes. The reassembled bike ashore, none the worse for its voyage, I said, "Thank you and farewell," to Marcel and set off with a loud whoop of joy to be on solid Java ground. I rode until dark, when I fell off on a potholed road and begged overnight shelter on a police station floor. They were happy to put me up, and I was allowed to sleep on the inspector's desk.

I liked Java already.

Forget the open sea . . . I was genuinely happy to be alive and back on two wheels on the open road. At least if things went wrong I could stop.

"I'll never put us through that again," I said to the bike, which if able to voice its premonitions, would have replied, "Oh yes you will; and next time it will be even worse."

9
INDONESIA

RUSHING THROUGH PARADISE

I'd been warned against going to Indonesia (by people who hadn't been there):

"They're all corrupt. The police demand your documents then keep them, unless you pay them huge amounts of money. Don't talk to anyone. Get through as quickly as you can."

I knew differently, having been treated most sympathetically by the authorities already.

Unfortunately though, I did have to hurry through Indonesia. I was allowed sixty days to see the country. My time had started ticking away when my passport was stamped on 17th April at Batam Island, where the catamaran had been robbed during the voyage. I was so happy to have survived. It had taken four days to arrange the paperwork and land the bike. Twenty-two days had gone already. Indonesia is a big, spread-out country comprising 16,000 islands. I'd have to get a move on and travel east towards Australia as fast as I could.

In the mini-atlas I used for general navigation I could see that Java, 620 miles long, is the largest of the islands that make up Indonesia as they swirl between the Indian Ocean and the South China Sea towards Australia. Island-hopping would be essential, and I wondered about boats. The very thought of getting on one again made me feel sick. Or was the nausea due to another bout of giardia? Either way, I wasn't keen on any more marine experiences.

Before I left Cikalong police station after a good night's sleep on mercifully motionless dry land, I checked the bike over for damage inflicted on it by the dastardly pothole into which we had plunged at 11PM the previous night. It was my first solo fall. I'd had to remove the luggage, use every bit of strength to right the bike, and then re-pack it. The headlight cowl was bent, now resembling a droopy eyelid. I'd ridden about fifty miles from Jakarta, only stopping to refuel with *benzin*, the first Indonesian word I learned apart from *terima kasih* (thank you).

I chose a road heading south-east towards the city of Bandung. After being at sea-level for so long, I planned a route to include mountains whilst travelling to the east of Java, where I hoped there would be a ferry to Bali, the next island. Later on, I looked for my mobile phone. It was not in its usual place. Lost or stolen at the police station? I wasn't sure, but I laughed at my short foray into technology.

The spasmodically tarmacked road gradually climbed towards Bandung. I passed watery terraces of rice being harvested by people in conical straw hats, some of whom straightened at the sound of an unusual engine and waved to me. It was the first time, after much exploring of South East Asia, that I had seen mature rice, Asia's staple food. I'd seen huge rotating barrels removing the husks and polishing the harvested rice. I'd seen it being planted after the paddy fields had been ploughed by benignly disinterested water buffalo plodding along, coerced into moving by kindly men guiding wooden ploughs behind them. Now I was seeing it ready and ripe for picking, each stalk heavy and bursting with grains. Women were carrying sacks tied in a sarong across their shoulders. Despite its dense population, the Java I was seeing didn't feel crowded. It was like tootling along in someone's vast garden.

Even at only 2,526 feet, Bandung felt cool and refreshing after sticky, polluted Jakarta. I bought some cassettes, as I had discovered my Bette Midler and Elgar ones had been stolen from the boat. The only appealing choices at Gromedia, Indonesia's department store chain, were KD Lang and Bach's greatest hits. I found a book, George Eliot's *Mill on the Floss*, and bought that too. An apotik shop supplied, without a prescription, some metronidazole tablets, which had ridded me of giardia in Pakistan. My symptoms suggested I had it again.

A local man and his son riding a Vespa scooter had led me on a country back-road to Garut, saving me miles of main road. But now there was squeaking from the Enfield's front wheel and speedometer. At a mechanic's workshop I saw as I rode along, the Enfield was keenly attended to by a young man who had the wheel off, stripped apart, and brake pads cleaned in no time. He greased the speedo and straightened the cowl before the matter of cost was considered. "Berappa?" I asked. I was charged the equivalent of £1. A little later, the squeaking returned, along with a much more serious sound that couldn't be ignored. There was a grinding, whirring noise coming from the clutch-case. My heart sank. This was like travelling with a sickly relative.

The weather changed from bright and sunny to overcast and cool. I'd find somewhere to eat and consider what to do next. My appetite had deserted me at the same time the giardia returned, so I had to force myself to eat. I recalled my mother making me eat when I was a child. Born in 1908 in a little village near Bath, she remembered horses and young men being taken off the land and sent to the Western Front. Food became scarce, and her pet rabbit was dished up on the dinner table. Later, she managed the severe rationing of the Second World War. She knew about hardship, and I thank her for making me a person without food fads. We ate every conceivable vegetable, pigs' trotters, tripe, chitterlings, home-made brawn from a pig's head she'd boiled for hours, picked all the meat from, put in a basin, and then given to my father to press with heavy things in his shed. Nothing was wasted in our house.

A thatched bar at Majalaya loomed out of the mountain mist. Loud Asian music and wailing burst out as I opened the door. I glanced around. A melancholy monkey was chained up near the bar, too depressed to look up. The bar-tender hardly acknowledged me either. Two men were dancing closely and singing into a microphone. Clearly not there because of its expansive menu, all that was on offer at this karaoke bar was something black in a congealed sauce with cold, lumpy rice. "It has to be better than it looks," I reasoned brightly, remembering many delicious, if visually unappealing, meals I'd had during my travels in Asia. I asked what it was. The bar-tender pointed to his ears and snorted. It was some sort of ear, then. "Oh well—I'll have a plate of that please." It was horrible. Not only was it black and rubbery, I was given a fork and spoon with which to eat it so couldn't cut through the tough ears that might have been from any animal, or even human. Even my imaginative mother had realised there wasn't much to be done with pigs' ears and gave them to the cat.

I felt out of place and left as soon as I could. I was upset about the monkey. As I approached the bike, the rain descended, and being fairly high up in the mountains, it was chilly as I dug out my wet-weather gear. It was dismal and murky like a November Sunday. "I'm cold. I'm miserable. It's raining. The food's horrible. I'm lonely. I feel ill. I'm missing Hendrikus. The bike's not running properly. I can't cope." The bike was lifeless. I thought of Basil Fawlty beating his car with a tree-branch when it wouldn't start. I knew how he felt. I shouted at the bike: "I could chuck you down a volcano!"—there are seventy-six volcanoes in Indonesia and twenty-two of them are in Java, so I'd be spoiled for choice. Then I remembered that I'd been fiddling with the idling speed, and once I'd put that right, the bike started. I felt so ashamed I never admonished the Enfield again. I didn't get very far that day, recognising that I was weakened by the tummy bug, and gave in to that "time to look for somewhere to stop for the night" feeling after only about thirty miles.

No doubt there were more luxurious hotels to choose from, but I was wet from the heavy drizzly rain and grumpy with myself so stopped at the first losmen (guesthouse) I saw on the outskirts of gloom-grey Cipenas. There was a safe place for the bike, and they had a room with a bathroom, instead of the usual WC. I didn't care as long as it had a bed. I found the room, dumped my stuff on the floor, peeled off my wet gear, and fell on the bed.

A bit later, I felt like exploring so opened the bathroom door and was met by billowing steam. "What on earth . . . ?" Gradually I could make out a large sunken bath. I had chanced upon a spa village with natural springs; each room had its own hot bath. I threw off my clothes, grabbed my Walkman, new cassettes, and book and walked down the concrete steps into the soothing water that made me gasp and then smile with pleasure. Life suddenly became sweeter. The restaurant had been fun. The monkey was fed, warm, and dry. The food wasn't that bad really; the bike had got me here and could be put right. I had music and a book to keep me company, and the antibiotics would start to work soon.

From being a miserable thing I suddenly became the luckiest person alive and wallowed in my private hot-pool. I read that, at sixty, George Eliot had married a man twenty years her junior. "Wait for me, Hendrikus!" (His emails hinted about meeting in Australia) but then I read in the next paragraph that she died within the year. Hmm . . . then I remembered Hendrikus's moods and thought I shouldn't chase after him. But, as I wrote in my diary: *"I have a short and selective memory."*

Cipanas gave me just the boost I needed. I left the next morning, the grinding noise no worse, sun shining as usual, and me in a much better frame of mind as I wound my way round the hills, rising and dipping, to cover 150 miles that day before stopping for the night at Cipatuja. A small town, it had three mosques, and my losmen was equidistant to them all. At 5 AM, the call for morning prayers began, each muezzin seemingly competing for volume and earnestness. In addition, it was a special day of loudspeaker preaching until 7 AM.

Sleepless, I left early and was surprised to be greeted at the door by a tour guide I had spoken to briefly about the bike the previous evening. He had kindly taken it upon himself to find me a mechanic and led me to him on his Jawa motorcycle. My speedo was by then not working at all. Indonesian mechanics don't waste time. Off came the clutch case. The bolts holding on the clutch plates were loose and would not tighten due to a stripped thread. Imperial measurement Enfield nuts were not available and metric ones did not fit, so this innovative man made a device to hold the clutch plates firmly in place. Then he set to on the speedo. From a bit of tin, he fashioned a square lining for the hole the square end of the cable fits into. It had become rounded with wear and no longer gripped the cable, so the speedo wasn't registering that the wheel was going round. This time I was charged about £9 on the basis that I was foreign and could afford it. It was worth every rupiah. With no grinding noise and a working speedo, I left for the next town and rode almost immediately into a circumcision party.

The giardia caused a metallic taste in my mouth, and I hadn't managed any breakfast, but some appetising food would be very welcome now. I slowed down when I smelt cooking and was invited, even before I'd stopped, to join in a party. "What sort of party?" I enquired. "My son's circumcision celebrations!" said his proud father. On my caseload as a health visitor, it was customary for baby boys of Pakistani origin to be cut at about eight weeks, so I was expecting to see a baby somewhere, but the star of the show was an eight-year old little chap sitting uncomfortably on a plastic chair looking forlorn and clearly not enjoying himself. He had almost the same expression as the monkey in the karaoke bar. I tucked in to the feast and ate some really lovely dishes, all home-cooked, with not a pig's ear in sight.

I rode on, south-east to the coast. It was heavenly. How could I tear myself away from here? I had a dip in the sea on a beach with rough waves and black sand but left the next morning, although I could have done with a rest day. Midday meals continued to be interesting. A group of Indonesian Christians gave me a free lunch and told me I should be with my husband, as it states in Revelation apparently. I didn't know what to make of all these religious messages. Was it a conspiracy? Why was I supposed to have a man with me just when I was learning to manage without one?

In the late afternoon, I stopped at a motel and waited whilst a room was got ready. Breathy sighs and groans came from within the rooms. Oh no—it was "rent by the hour." I repacked the bike and found a police station. They allowed me to sleep in the mosque, so again, I was awoken at 5AM when someone came in to pray. I stopped to refuel the bike and myself at Purworejo, a noticeably upmarket town, and spoke for a long time to a chubby young man over lunch who'd trained as a chef in London but felt duty-bound to work here in his parents' oil shop. I found people opened up when they knew they'd never see me again, and I was free to listen as he poured out his disappointment at being stuck here when he dreamed of running a restaurant in Jakarta. Meeting people as I grew on my own journey meant I carried a little of them as I went.

Next stop was ninth century Borobadur, the largest Buddhist temple in the world. The tourist blurb told me it measures 2,730 square yards. It was a massive structure built to precision without mortar, looking like a topless pyramid, but was abandoned in the thirteenth century; some say when Java became Islamic. Sir Thomas Stamford Raffles started its restoration in 1814. The most stunning thing about this huge step pyramid on nine levels is that if viewed from above it is a giant tantric Buddhist mandala, a representation of the Buddhist cosmos and the nature of mind. Volcanoes spewed their acidic ash all over it in 2010 and 2014, and since then, Islamic extremists have tried to destroy it with bombs. At the time, it was hard to think that this soft, beautiful place could harbour anyone with malicious intent.

The Cambodian temples of Angkor Wat had been serene, but at this temple loudspeakers blared all day. However, I slept for twelve hours without stirring and, feeling refreshed, decided to tighten the chain to stop it clanking against the chain-guard. I studied the instruction manual and found a quiet space at the losmen to do this procedure that Hendrikus and I usually did together. After a couple of hours I wiped the oil from my hands, satisfied that I had done a good job. The chain was now not floppy, and I had time to read.

The Mill on the Floss is a story about a brother and sister, set in Victorian England. Maggie, wounded by harsh words and neglect, adored her disapproving brother. He was sent to a good school. She was given religious books instead and, rather than developing her own interests, devoted her attentions to duty and good works. Eventually she drowned, trying unsuccessfully to save her brother. I was cross with George Eliot for making her heroine so selfless. She was not showing her readers the "scandalous" life she, herself, was living. She lived with a married man for years. She was a translator, journalist, and storyteller who, knowing that she would never be published as Mary-Ann Evans in those times, published under a man's name. She could have done so much for Victorian women but chose instead to have her heroines overcome with a sense of duty, settle for good marriages, and support their husbands in their endeavours. But, I reasoned, she had to sell her books.

From Borobadur I rode fifty miles in countryside strewn with volcanoes. Merbabu, a dormant volcano, and Merapi, an active one, were either side of the beautiful road to Solo, where I found a quaint losmen. Backpackers were staying there, but I hadn't seen another motorcycle traveller since leaving Malaysia. Rooms there were like oversized dolls-houses within a courtyard. Everything was little and painted pastel colours. The courtyard contained a garden filled with lush plants.

Caged birds sang charmingly, and I fought with my own disapproval of anything caged, as it was lovely to hear them. I found myself thinking, "If that's how they do things here, who am I to interfere?" Then, "If everyone thought like that, we'd still have cock-fighting and bear-baiting. Women would still have their feet bound or throw themselves on their husbands' funeral pyres, if someone hadn't done something about it." Some things, I was beginning to realise on this journey, were definitely not OK with the world I was tripping through. I suggested to the owner that the birds would be happier if free. He laughed. Was I losing some of my acceptance and sense of wonder, finding things less delightful than when I'd started out?

Later, at an outside pavilion at the palace at Puro Mankrunegaran, I thought I was eavesdropping on fairies. Ethereal, mesmerising, tinkling bells, cymbals, and gongs from the huge to the tiny and soft xylophones were confusing to my western ears, which couldn't find a rhythm or catch a tune. Seated on the floor, the musicians looked happy as they sang or blew, strummed or tapped their instruments. Although it sounded haphazard, everyone knew what they were doing. Contentment swept over me, and I felt full of gratitude for all the good things in my life and for the people I loved. This music was like a wellbeing drug, and I slid down the pillar I was leaning on and sat against it on the marble floor for support. I found out the music was called Gamelan. Java was becoming softer the further I moved eastwards towards Bali.

My relationship with the bike became ever deeper. I thought of myself and it as "we." I projected a personality onto it, just as children do their teddy-bears. In the absence of a human travelling companion, the Enfield became my friend with a knowing persona, whilst my diary remained my confidante. It didn't matter that neither spoke back; I had contact with people all day during stops for fuel and food. My daily ritual with the dipstick indicated it was time for an oil change. I bought some at a garage. and as part of the service they did the job for me. which not only included draining the dirty old oil but blowing out the residue with compressed air before refilling with fresh. I was pleased that

I remembered to refit the omitted washer from the previous oil-change.

Unable to tear myself away from Solo, I allowed myself a day-trip to see Java Man, who had lived there half a million years before my visit at his home in Sangiran nine miles away. The museum was delightfully undeveloped. Millions of years before, tectonic plates had been pushed up, forming a dome, which over the millennia, has eroded and exposed the things previously buried under the sea and in swamps. Java Man's *Homo erectus* skull appeared. Sharks' teeth and mammoth bones had been gracing local homes for many a year until it became a World Heritage Site seven years previously. I enjoyed having a sight-seeing trip on the bike, returning to where I'd started from that morning. It felt like being on holiday. I'd forgotten how easy it was to ride without luggage but had to load up and move on.

A tourist leaflet suggested a visit to Candi Sukuh, a Javanese-Hindu temple. It said it was fascinating with fabulous views, but it didn't say that there were stone friezes and statues of penises everywhere. It was like an ancient reproductive system lesson. A statue of a naked man, grasping his oversized erection (a "selfie" by the boastful sculptor, perhaps) had his head knocked off by a disapproving visitor at some stage. Everything else at Candi Sukuh was anatomically correct, even a beautiful stone-carving of a penis and a uterus together. Ganesh, the Hindu elephant god, was depicted, but the temple itself resembles Mayan design. Strange, dwarfish mythical creatures huddled in friezes round monuments as if telling a story.

As Islam was enforced in ancient Java, there was a civil war, and it is thought that Hindus fled to these mountains and built their "fertility temple" to spite the more prudish Muslims. The unusual designs have prompted theories that ancient aliens had something to do with it. How interesting, I thought, that when we don't have the answer to something, things supernatural or visitors from space provide possible explanations. However, bird-people statues are similar to those in ancient Assyria and Mexico, and how those designs reached here is certainly a mystery.

The bike had struggled to get there in the heat, emitting clouds of white exhaust smoke as it chugged up the dramatically steep climb. Gunung Lawu, the mountain where the temple is situated, is

3,280 feet high. Poor Bike. I noticed a new noise coming from the rear wheel and a tinkly noise from the engine that my father called "pinking." Poor quality petrol? Too much strain on the engine? Heat? The bike and I both appreciated the breezy, cooling descent.

Moving on, I wound along lush country roads, passing through little villages. I paused for grilled sweet corn at a stall with a tray of glowing charcoal and looked at the rear wheel for the cause of the grating noise but could see nothing obviously wrong.

I chose Ponorogo as my next stop because it was in the right direction and I liked the name. On the way I passed a village celebration with a "greasy pole competition." Young men were trying to climb a very long and thickly-oiled bamboo pole to reach presents tied on at the top, but they were sliding down. I watched for a half hour amidst the food stalls, but nobody managed it. Such simple fun, enjoyed by everyone.

Ponorogo looked more prosperous than other towns. Its town square had a magnificent statue of a warrior-hero wielding a whip over a pack of panthers. The street-food stalls were festooned with strings of electric light bulbs to show the customers their wares, rather than the usual paraffin storm lanterns. Shops sold quality goods.

Scooters are popular in Java, and I got involved with the Ponorogo Vespa Club. A kind woman rider gave me stickers and a club T-shirt. Her father organised a mechanic to clean out my carburettor and alter the timing, solving the "pinking" problem. The back wheel was examined and spokes tightened in an unsuccessful attempt to resolve the noise I was hearing.

I was introduced to the town dignitary who had a BMW, a Kawasaki, and a Harley-Davidson, all in immaculate condition. He organised a surprise for me that evening. I was led to the equivalent of the town hall where a men-only feast (like the Freemasons, I thought) was served by waiters, who then backed away on their bottoms, bowing as a sign of respect. Then the show started. Acrobatic males danced the local traditional dance accompanied by musicians. The performance culminated in a man wearing a massive tiger head with gnashing teeth. He danced, advancing and withdrawing into the shadows mimicking a hunting tiger until the dance was over. I was completely overwhelmed—this had been arranged just for me. I went to pick up the tiger-head after the display and could just about lift it off the ground. The dancer had leapt about as if it were weightless. I found it hard to leave Ponorogo. My heart was full of Javanese hospitality and culture. It was another "stay forever" place, but it was now the 26th May. I had a long and unknown journey ahead, the only certainty being that, due to my visa restriction, I had to leave this wonderland behind.

Under the watchful eye of a mechanic, before I commenced the next leg of my solo journey, I cleaned out the carburettor yet again and drained the petrol tank, as I felt somehow fuel was being blocked. It was all I knew to do. I wanted to help the bike, which kept going regardless of the conditions and what I did to it. This mechanic had a calming aura, giving me confidence and help when I needed it. I remembered the lion's claw, given to me after my X-ray fright and felt it timely to pass it on. He was genuinely pleased to receive it. Giving and receiving are so binding, somehow. The poor bike struggled up more mountains, stalling whenever it had the chance.

I reasoned that I had to keep the engine cool. It was probably a foolish thing to do, but I took the air-filter off and rode with some oily T-shirt fabric stretched over the entrance to the carburettor, secured with an elastic band, to get unrestricted air to it.

I hate riding on sand but had been told I mustn't miss Mount Bromo in Tengger National Park. I had to cross the two-mile "Sea of Sand" to get there, and I also needed to prove to myself that I could do things like that on my own. It was as if no discomfort or difficulty was enough. Who I needed to prove things to I did not know, but perhaps there I would reach that point where I could say, "Enough." Anyway, I'd never ridden up a volcano before. There are several other peaks within this space-scape but Bromo, a crater within a crater at 7,847 feet, is active, and I wanted to see it.

I remembered going into the desert in India when Hendrikus and I first met. He'd let his tyres down to ride with both of us and our luggage over the thick sand. But he carried a compressor for pumping them up again. I was wary of deflating my tyres, as I didn't know what would be on the other side of this massive bowl in front of me. Unable to find a track, let alone a road, I repeatedly dropped the bike, unloaded, righted, and repacked it and set off again, only to have to do it all again 60 feet later. I was frustrated at my failure. "Keep your arms stiff on the handle bar, let the clutch out, and go as fast as you can," I could hear Hendrikus say, but as soon as I got any speed up, the handlebar was wrenched out of my grip by the force of the deep sand and I fell again. The bike stalled, and petrol leaked out of the tank.

After an hour or so of this, a four-wheel-drive rangers' truck scurried up behind me, and the occupants offered help. Although they wanted to put the bike in the back, I let them carry only my luggage. The bike was easier to control the rest of the way. "Where do you want to go?" they asked. I didn't know, so they took me with them to the rangers' station hut, where I slept on the floor, huddled fully dressed in my sleeping bag to keep warm. I was up early for a walk to see the renowned sunrise at the crater. On the way, I was invited by a man with a couple of horses to join him. Riding a horse at dawn was a pretty nice thing to do. I peeped over Bromo's frightening rim and saw clouds of sulphurous gas escaping and felt my nostrils burning.

I thanked everyone for their kindness and started the descent down the other side of the volcano. I turned the engine off and recorded the mileage. I didn't restart the bike for twenty miles. I refitted the air-filter and continued south-eastwards, accompanied by Mount Semaru in the distance, which puffs out clouds of smoke every fifteen minutes. It was so exciting to be there.

Led by a couple of lads on a motorcycle, I stayed at a homely losmen near Lumajang, where laundry was done communally in the stream. Leaving volcanoes behind me, I headed for the coast to Bandealit, where I swam and slept on the beach between the bike and my camp-fire; my first lone wild-camp.

Next morning, I stopped at a café for breakfast. Someone suggested going to a beach, where after a shortcut through the jungle, I'd be able to see turtles laying eggs that night. "Oh I'd LOVE that." My direction-giver looked at the bike with its panniers and soft bags on each side, the backpack on the back, the extra bag on top of that, and the plastic bags tied on. "It's a rough road," he said. My ears heard only "road," and by the time the words got to my brain, I envisioned a bit of rough tarmac, a few potholes, perhaps. " . . . and there's sand and a river . . . " he added. I imagined sand at the side the roadside; "Huh—I can do rivers, mate . . . " I thought, imagining a pleasantly challenging ride. I'd be there with a beer in my hand ready and waiting for the turtles in no time—"Which way?"

I have two charming little brass bells on my yellow, coiled plastic bike key-chain. At one end I have the keys to the petrol filter, at the other are the ignition and side-box keys. It is an indication of the roughness of the terrain how much the keys and bells jangle. On that run, had they not been attached, they would have been airborne. The twenty-five mile shortcut took all day. I saw only one man, who was cutting bamboo with a machete, as I rode from Mayang along ten miles of jungle tracks with huge ancient trees closing in on me. That was the nice bit. Then I joined a never-ending downhill track where the soil had washed away, leaving protruding sharp stones. It was uneven, sometimes muddy, and so difficult to ride that I couldn't take my eyes off it for an instant—or my hands off the clutch and brake.

I feared the tyres were being cut to ribbons and that every nut and bolt on the bike was shaking loose. Dip . . . Crunch . . . Oil leaked from the front forks and the suspension was squealing like a banshee as I inched down the wooded hillside. The luggage was slipping, but I couldn't stop to readjust it on the steep downward gradient, even though I was going so slowly. It was terrible. My teeth were clenched, my eyes wide with concentration and alarm.

After the stony road that abruptly ended at dusk, there was a river to cross. Half-way across, I fell. Apart from the man with the machete, I hadn't seen anyone all day, a day which had worsened as it went on. Water was flooding my luggage. I knelt by the bike to remove what I could. Suddenly, a couple on a Vespa sleeked up to me and helped me lift the bike up. They said I had chosen the deepest part of the crossing point and showed me the shallow route. They gave me the good news that I didn't have far to go, waving as they scooted off down the river. Were they angels?

A kilometre or two of manageable sand in the dark and I was there. And there, that night, I saw the miracle of a hundred-year-old green turtle about a metre long wheeze her way up the beach, dig a hole with her flippers, lay dozens of eggs, and struggle back to the sea. I was astounded, moved to tears with that reward for my hard journey to get here. She and I had both put in a lot of effort to get to the same spot. It was a serene event, as any birth should be. I was allowed to touch her soft, leathery skin and hard shell before, with a loud sigh, she plunged back into the surf.

I had expected hordes of people to be there, but there were just a handful of us; myself, the ranger who collected the eggs as she laid them, and a Spanish tourist with his driver. He was the only Spanish person I'd met since starting the trip. They had a room, and I bunked down with them for the night, all of us talking about the event. As if the privilege of seeing the turtle wasn't enough, next morning we were allowed the extra treat of releasing baby ones from the nursery above the tide-line where trees and bushes grew. It was an emotional time as they orientated themselves towards the sea and hurried their flippery way as if they were trying to fly, before disappearing into the surf. Nobody spoke. We all felt the same. Would these little creatures live their possible lifespan of 250 years?

The driver offered to take my luggage to the main road, leaving me free to negotiate the obstacles of the day before. Unable to cross the river with his four-wheel-drive, he took a longer route. Now I knew where I was going I could cross. I found the return even more difficult than the night before when fully loaded in the dark. I didn't know how I'd done it. I continued up the horrid stony track until, almost at the top, I fell off in some mud. I turned the petrol off to stop it leaking. I could hear them approaching and, not wishing them to know I'd fallen, righted the bike before they arrived, hoping to get to the top before they did. But the bike wouldn't start. We all stood around thinking it had flooded and it just needed time. Again and again I kicked, hot and sweating. Twenty minutes went by before I realised I hadn't turned the petrol on again. Unseen, I turned it on, kicked again, and the bike leapt into life. I didn't own up and even wondered about admitting it to my diary. "It just needed a rest," I said weakly. We met at the top and said our goodbyes. I refitted my luggage.

A while later, I bought some plain paper and made myself a certificate: "This certificate is awarded to Jacqueline Claire Furneaux. She is now exempt from ever having to prove her worth to anyone including herself ever again. She now knows she can do ANYTHING." I had reached the point I'd been searching for. It was my zenith. I wasn't puffed up, just free for evermore. It didn't mean I wouldn't accept challenges; but I didn't have to.

On the 2nd June, I rode onto the Bali ferry. Then began the work of finding out about getting to Australia. Hendrikus emailed and told me he had left Broome and was heading to Darwin. We might meet up. I was happy on my own and knew I didn't need to be with him. I wanted to be with him; which is entirely different.

I went to Denpasar airport to enquire about flights to Australia and went to the docks to find out about boats to Timor. There was no time left for seeing other islands on the way. If I waited for a boat, it might not take the bike by which time I would have missed the flight to Melbourne, the only destination for planes big enough for such a large item of freight. I had less than a week left on my visa. After a day or two fact-finding and thinking, I risked the boat option, gambling that the captain would agree to shipping the bike. It was a tense, hurried time, and I didn't really enjoy my stay in Bali after the delightfulness of Java.

I made daily enquiries at the docks and eventually learned with relief that the Enfield could go aboard if it was wrapped up. It didn't have to be crated, a big saving for me. Someone found some sacking at the freight shed, and with a huge upholstery needle and string, on the day of departure I sewed it up. That evening it was manhandled onto a truck, taken to the wharf, and lowered into the hold of the ship by crane. I shared a cabin with some happy, guitar-playing Christians, whose hymns and prayers kept me awake. We arrived at Kupang on Timor very early next morning, and the bike was unloaded and unwrapped. After a cup of coffee to enliven me, I rode on.

What a beautiful place: Pastoral scenes, pigs snuffling about on beaches, and warm sunshine as we tootled eastwards along quiet country roads. All was calm. So calm, so calm . . . calm . . . I woke up with a start at the change of engine sound as my hand slipped from the throttle. I had gone to sleep. It was time to stop before I crashed into a buffalo or something.

At a friendly losmen in Soe, an elderly gentleman gave me a small carved bamboo tube used for storing lime powder, mixed with betel nut for chewing. It had a stopper at the top carved in the shape of a head. He had made it himself.

The bike, miraculously, didn't stall, smoke, or make worrying noises. It clearly liked it here too. What a shame we couldn't stay. I still didn't know how I would get myself and the bike to Australia, and there was the problem of having no carnet. It was fine here in Indonesia, and I had permission to enter Australia, but what if it wasn't allowed into East Timor, our next destination? I'd find out the next day.

The customs officers shook their heads, because there was no carnet for them to stamp. I gave them the letters from the Jakarta police and customs not showing the apprehension I felt and trying to appear cool. I smiled, got my book out, and sat down to wait. Eventually, they said I could go. Tidak apa apa! (No problem!) We'd done it with four days to spare.

The officials on the East Timor side stamped my passport and waved me through. One man did mention a carnet, but I said, "No, I haven't got one, thank you," as if it was optional.

Suddenly, I was on the set of a war film: A helicopter descended from the sky, soldiers with guns were patrolling the area while armoured cars trundled around the border post. FRETELIN, The Revolutionary Front for an Independent East Timor, had successfully struggled for independence only the previous year, but there were still problems of instability due to the incumbent president declining another term of office. The violent election build-up necessitated the presence of special UN forces as FELANTIN, the armed rebel force, were still active. A young soldier guardedly let me look at his map so I could see which road to take to ride away from the noise and drama.

Things settled down as I reached the coast road. Paradise was restored; up and down hills with bends, sometimes a huge drop onto the rocks below. Certainly not a road for riding after dark but one of the most pleasurable rides I'd ever had. I parked the bike when I could resist a swim no more. There was no other traffic, and the only sentient being to see me strip off was a charming she-dog, who was happy to sit by my clothes and wait. I shared my picnic with her; she took bread, banana, and peanuts from me in a most ladylike manner. I dried off in the sun and said good bye to my luncheon companion.

Just as the sun disappeared in an orange sort of way, I bought a pineapple at the roadside and enquired about accommodation. I was directed to a police station where a sole twenty-one-year old woman officer was in charge. I shared the pineapple with her. She told me she didn't like men and would never marry. I showed her photos of my brother and implied he was my husband. As I settled down in a spare office for the night, I reached into my daypack for my book and learned that if I'm going to show unconcern at borders, I shouldn't ruin my coolness by leaving my book behind.

I slept well; East Timor is a Catholic country, so there was no morning call to prayer. Next day, I rode on to Dili, the tiny capital of East Timor.

Kevin, the unpleasant, greedy Australian manager of a vehicle-cleaning outfit relieved me of much money and made sure I had the most awful experience when preparing the bike for shipping to Darwin. I hoped all Australians would not be like this. I dismantled the Enfield and degreased and scrubbed every part of it. It was even hoisted airborne so the underneath could be power-washed (I found unmistakable red Cambodian soil behind the front sprocket). It took me twelve hours to do it, helped occasionally by sympathetic men when the boss wasn't looking. Eventually, it was ready for shipping.

I collapsed and was allowed to sleep overnight in an on-site cabin, ready for my flight the next day. I was not allowed to travel with the bike. In Darwin I would wait for the bike to arrive, whereupon it would be inspected by the "we're not letting any foreign muck into Australia" department before I'd be allowed to ride it away.

Suddenly it dawned on me that not only was I leaving East Timor, I was leaving Asia and about to start a whole new continent. Goodbye, Asia. Goodbye bamboo, flip-flop scuffing, heat and humidity, spitting, concrete hotel rooms, rice, NGOs, thatched huts, pigs, chickens, and goats in the streets, people squatting on their heels, bargaining, plastic tables and chairs, coconuts, people with brown faces and brown eyes but black hair, guards with rifles that could be from WWI, T-shirts with wrong spellings and fake brand names, saris, religious differences, religious similarities (but religious influences everywhere), exotic fruits, colourful clothes, street food, lively evenings after dark, cocks crowing, calls to prayer, sarongs, rhythmic sweeping with twig-brooms early in the mornings, train journeys, bus journeys, rickshaws (motorised, bicycle, and sometimes hand-drawn), squat toilets with washing-water instead of toilet paper, livestock on buses, bad roads, monsoons, little geckos that catch flies and mosquitoes in your room and make kissing noises, big geckos that say "gecko," toothpicks, people with stalls who mend everything (shoes, zips, bags . . .), people who sew up white cloth parcels and put a red wax seal on them outside post offices, people who will write letters for the illiterate, "Hello Mister!," "Hello Auntie," "Hello Rickshaw," "Hello taxi."

Good bye, Asia. Good bye. And thank you. Thank you for everything.

10
AUSTRALIA

RUNNING AWAY

For all the concern about removing every microscopic speck of Asian dirt from the bike, no-one scrutinised me as I went through Darwin customs. I realised later that I'd walked off the plane wearing boots with mud-crammed treads. The turn-ups of my jeans shed similar amounts of good old Asia onto pristine, protected Australian soil.

As I was ejected into the Darwin airport arrivals lounge I felt like a reluctant parachutist having to be pushed from relative safety into the void. Everything was different. People were not brown-skinned; they were like me. I was like them too, and unlike everywhere in Asia, I was invisible, just another backpacker in a tourist destination. Asia was comfortably familiar. Here, no-one approached me offering help. I found myself reluctant to leave the airport. It had sliding glass doors the like of which I hadn't seen in Asia, my home for the last three years.

Exposure to extremes is fascinating, but I wasn't ready for this plunge. Riding the bike along a plank onto a wobbly canoe would have been far less daunting. It was the first of many puzzling contrasts I would encounter over the coming months. I looked around, dazed by the clean, quiet smartness of the airport. No longer disconnectedly part of another culture, I was, to all intents and purposes, back in mine. But I was caught between cultures and didn't feel part of this one.

I couldn't stay in the airport all day. I needed to phone the contact number Australian Wilf had given me when I stayed with him in Malaysia. I changed currency, got some coins, and approached the public phone. Just because everything was in English didn't make it easy. I was used to booths where you gave the number to the assistant, who dialled it and handed you the receiver. After the call, you were told how much you owed. Here, I was confronted with a pay-phone familiar to everyone else, but for me it was like trying to break the Enigma Code. Finally, I spoke to Maggie, who gave me her address and advised me to get a taxi. I stepped outside.

Where was everybody? Had a plague decimated the population or a neutron bomb been dropped? No, I had just left the most populated country in the world for one of the least populated countries in the world. The wide streets were empty, a huge contrast to any transport hub in Asia. No rickshaws, nobody offering to carry luggage, sell a postcard, soft drink, or freshly made samosa. No frantic bustle. It was dull.

Staying with Maggie was a godsend. She was kind, informative, and reassuring. When I learned the Enfield had arrived at the docks, I went to fetch it. The quarantine inspector gave it a cursory glance and allowed it into Australia. Paying AU$50 and dissolving the skin off my hands with degreaser and wire wool for twelve hours had been worth it. I had no customs duty to pay. The cleaning charge, wharfage, shipping, and my flight totalled £150. My paperwork was in order, so after washing the salt off the bike (it had been out on deck and must have had waves washing over it, poor thing), I rode off to check my emails. Hendrikus was in Darwin!

I was wandering around the small centre of town and ran across the road when I saw him dismount from his Enfield. We hugged and kissed each other with none of the shyness we had had at our reunion in Pakistan. It was different this time, as we had kept in contact, despite believing our parting in Malaysia six months before to be final. We had more than a three-year, six-country history by this time and had expressed missing each other in emails. For me this was a "getting back together." I loved him, loved being with him, loved our travelling life.

Of all the places to go, he chose a topless bar for our catching-up session. It came as a shock after modest Asia, where people generally covered their bodies. I found no modesty here and mused that some people look down on cultures where such things are valued. It didn't make sense. Early white missionaries made "godless" people cover their bodies, but here in this "advanced" society it was acceptable to employ women so their bodies could be ogled. I felt I had retreated into an out-dated culture, not a modern one.

Hendrikus and I exchanged our news. He was astonished at my disastrous sea-voyage, and I was hungry for information about what Australia was like. He was, in fact, very much taken with Australia and had been riding in daylight and sleeping when the sun went down since leaving Broome on the west coast. It was, he said, perfect for our sort of travelling, so after he'd sorted out the details of a new business venture, we went into the bush for some wild camping and billabong-swimming. He was right. Australia was right up my street.

He had a job building a website for some people with a business near Katherine, 186 miles south of Darwin. Included in the deal was accommodation at their goat farm whilst he designed it. After my alarming trip on the catamaran and subsequent journey through Indonesia coping on my own, I was more than happy to "go with the flow," stay with Hendrikus, and adjust to this totally new environment.

His caravan backed onto the Katherine River. We watched young goats jumping about on tree stumps and heard the dull clattering of their rubbery little hooves on the corrugated iron roof of their hut. Tommy, a pet billy-goat, followed me everywhere round our compound. There was a cat called Mister Chan, who caught some unfortunate creature and presented it proudly to me one day, which didn't please me at all. It was a sugar-glider, a marsupial with skin between its limbs for gliding from the tops of trees. I felt sorry for the little thing but examined its limp body with wonder.

Hendrikus worked all day, so I did lots of wandering about. I didn't have to go far before walking into a nature-lover's wonderland. When I saw my first wallabies I nearly cried, I was so overcome. There was a billabong surrounded by bushes and coolibah trees. When I sat still for a while, the birds, frogs, and insects forgot my presence and continued their cacophony of twitters, hoots, croaks, peeps, screams, trills, whistles, tweets, squeaks, buzzes, toots, whirrs, cuckoos, rasps, rattles, honks, quacks, grunts, wheezes, clucks, coos, and cackles.

Hendrikus bought me a little bird identification book, and I happily ticked them off as I saw them. Then there were the double-barred finches, sulphur-crested cockatoos, galahs, brolgas, black kites, bee-eaters, ibis, spoonbills, butcher birds, and pelicans amongst others that I heard but couldn't see.

Katherine town, nine miles away, was another wonderland. The Woolworth supermarket provided every imaginable item, from kangaroo burgers, pork (unobtainable in most of the countries I'd travelled through), French sticks, hummus, and muesli to bedding and tablecloths. Australians refer to fabric items like these as "Manchester" after the town that supplied them during the early years of colonisation. Huge, blemish-free fruit and vegetables I hadn't seen since I left the UK were arranged in chilled cabinets, not perfectly ripe on sunny market stalls.

The weather was ideal, hot in the daytime but cool at night. It sounds silly to say the sky was big, but with no tall buildings in the way out there, it was huge; light blue on the wide horizon, stretching to deep blue as I raised my eyes heavenwards. The stars also kept my eyes cast upwards at night, with no light or traffic pollution to shroud the vast display. This was well and truly Australia.

Any doubt we were in farming territory was dispelled by the annual Katherine Show, a rodeo and agricultural event with sideshows and stalls. I was most impressed with the way the male and female participants handled their mounts, as if each horse could mind-read and turn at its rider's will. The wild-eyed cattle seemed surprised at their sudden inability to run away when lassoed. Many of the participants and spectators wore large, white, wide-brimmed felt hats to show they were serious cattle-people. The piglet-racing was more light-hearted and down to chance, though no less entertaining!

We watched an outdoor rendering of Shakespeare's *A Midsummer Night's Dream*. It was the most overacted, ridiculously costumed performance I'd ever seen. It was more like a pantomime. I revere Shakespeare and watched in disbelief as his words were mangled and spat out in over-the-top Aussie accents. Was I outraged at this raucous display? No, I loved it.

Everyone knows about Australia's dangerous creatures, many of which I'd heard would rather kill you than not. I had an encounter with a snake when crouching on a path overlooking the river. I'd heard rustling leaves and hissing as it moved. I turned my head and saw it. The finger-width yellowy-green creature with a kindly face stopped when it saw me. After looking each other in the eye momentarily, we both shot off, terrified, in opposite directions. I learned later that it was a harmless tree snake. However, I don't know the identity of a different snake that appeared as I was washing up at the outside kitchen sink one day. I saw some movement from the corner of my eye and, instead of running away, froze. This brown snake was much thicker and longer and didn't have the cute appearance of the tree snake. It looked evil, and I felt very vulnerable. I'd heard of the aggressive "taipan" and "king brown" that chase people. I didn't want it to notice me so held my breath. Its tongue was testing the air as it slithered between my feet and slunk into the lush, damp grass at the sink's soak-away. Only when I could no longer see it did I run away. I'll never know what it was. Australia's Northern Territory has dozens of snakes, many highly venomous. They are mostly brown.

Having been surprised several times in the toilet by dear little bright green frogs and not so dear enormous spiders who frequented there for moisture, I learned to check under the seat and rim before I sat down.

By the river, careful not to dangle my legs in the water, I sat waiting to see what I could see. Terrapins came up for air and sat ponderously on a semi-submerged log. I watched another log floating down and then went cold as I realised it was a crocodile. No it can't be—yes it is. It was over a yard long in the water, but I hadn't accounted for tail or snout, and when it emerged and zig-zagged onto the other bank about fifteen metres away, it was over six feet long. I knew there are two types of Australian crocodile, freshwater ones, which are relatively harmless to humans, and saltwater ones, which definitely are not. I didn't know which type this was, but I stayed stock still. It stayed motionless in the warm sun for exactly an hour, as if it had booked a session on a sun-bed after work, before disappearing back into the water. I could no longer see it and then imagined it underwater coming for me, so ran away again.

In between running away from risky creatures on my part and designing websites on Hendrikus's, we managed some work on the bikes. On examining my rear sprocket, we found all but nine of the teeth had worn away or snapped. The Borobudur chain-tightening session may have given me pride and satisfaction, but I little knew that when I'd adjusted the chain, I'd over tightened it, thus causing the sprocket damage. So that's what the noise was. We ordered some new parts from a dealer in South Australia, and after three weeks, a box arrived with a shiny new sprocket and chain, as well as some parts Hendrikus needed for his bike. At a scrap-yard, we found some Honda motorcycle valve springs, the perfect size and tension to keep my clutch plates in place.

With the website almost finished and both bikes fitted with new Enfield goodies, we left the goats and rode sixty miles south. I loved this country. It was open and free with masses of space, no traffic, and best of all . . . off-road wild camping without having to search for a suitable spot—everywhere was a suitable spot.

At Mataranka, Hendrikus carried on with his work while I found a job at an Internet café near our campsite and learned how to make proper coffee with a machine, but what the Aboriginal owner really wanted me to do was to organise his paperwork. So I sorted bills, put everything in order, and tidied his accounts. He apologised for being unable to pay me but gave me two authentic aboriginal paintings, which I sent back to England in case I ever had a home again.

One day, I visited the local homestead where an early settler, Jeannie Gunn, had lived and written *We of the Never-Never*, a good read describing how hard it was for the first pioneers. There I saw dozens of red flying fox bats clambering over each other for the best hanging spot on the branches.

In the evenings, I went to the natural crystal-clear hot springs and floated peacefully and unobserved between the shrubs, trying not to disturb the Saint Andrew's Cross spiders, which pair their shiny "just painted" legs on their webs forming a saltire. Wallabies hardly noticed me as I wallowed amongst the clouds of steam and vegetation. I watched a baby climb out of the pouch and hop along behind its grazing mother on the bank. Afterwards as dusk fell, I rode past a field of ant-hills looking like giant bottles. I recalled horror films where aliens used such "farms" to breed. Nonsense of course, but by moonlight they looked sinister, as if the throbbing life within was otherworldly and ready to hatch.

With money in the bank from building two websites, Hendrikus was ready to move. We aimed for Cairns. I bought two jerry-cans for water and petrol and, as Hendrikus had done with his, tied them to my crash bar. My bike, now dented and dusty, looked great, and I felt like a real motorcycle traveller. We would be riding for long distances between water and fuel stops. "How perfectly exciting," I thought, " . . . to be back on the road with my man!"

We turned eastwards off the Stuart Highway onto the Roper Highway. Alarming, massive ant towers, some as high as six feet, cast shadows on the dry, sparsely-grassed land. Some looked like huge modern abstract sculptures or gothic tombstones, others like Antoni Gaudí cathedrals or groups of people in frozen conversation. Inside, the ants would be building, breeding, feeding, and surviving the heat of the day by shifting from one side of the construction to the other. Like my Enfield has external fins to cool the engine, they cool their nests by making fins for shade and to make the most of any breeze.

We employed our own temperature control, stopping often for brews under gum trees, petrol from my tank fuelling the cooking stove. This was heaven for me. As a Girl Guide I used to live for the annual camp and, when I had to go home, would sleep on my bedroom floor grieving for the week I'd had sleeping in an old army bell tent in a field in the Quantock Hills with the 10th Weston-super-Mare Guide Company. I'd complete all the camp challenges, such as flora and fauna identification, lighting fires, and with my sheath-knife, make racks from sticks for holding kit bags off the ground for the patrol I led. I had a natural ability for that sort of thing and gained more proficiency badges than anyone else. "If only you'd put as much effort into your school-work," my mother complained. But that was what I excelled at and loved. Here I was, contentedly doing it again forty years later.

We both had soft luggage on our racks, but being next to the bikes meant we didn't have to unpack them, everything in our mobile homes was to hand. We spread out our groundsheet and the blanket Hendrikus had bought in Pakistan and slept beside a campfire. He even made bread in two billy-cans. Eucalyptus trees were everywhere with their orange bark and blue-green leaves. I'd never been anywhere like it.

I could have done without the "corrugations," though. It's a peculiar thing that when tracks are used by heavy lorries, slowly, over time, the tyres all fall into the same slight dips and then cause a ridge as they climb out. They then become deeper and more regular, every half-yard or so. It makes riding on them very uncomfortable, and we found the best way was to keep our speed up. By doing this we could "float" over them.

There were water-crossings with Outback names like Poison Creek and Kangaroo Creek, most of them fairly shallow, but at Robinson River, one was deep and best done without luggage. I went first and managed well, so well that I received a round of applause from some nearby campers, who rewarded us with freshly caught black brim fish and a couple of beers after we'd waded back for our luggage. They said that although it was "saltie" terrain, they hadn't seen any and had been swimming. Being a wild-swimming enthusiast, I couldn't resist it so went in too. It was delicious after a dusty, hot day. Had I read a newspaper report that I saw a few weeks later, I might not have had that swim . . . "KILLER CROC EATS BIKER," screamed the headline. Some motorcyclists had stopped "out bush" near Darwin to wash. One was grabbed by a thirteen-foot long "saltie." The other two had to stay up a tree for twenty-two hours as the croc was waiting for them, having stashed the first one away for later.

The corrugations flattened out for a while enabling more relaxed riding. It was then that I rode over a chasm of a pothole that had been covered with bull-dust. Bang! I found myself flying through the air and landing in front of my fallen bike. The headlight was broken, the cowl twisted, my Enfield looking like it had been in a fight. Bull-dust is dirt as fine as icing sugar that fills holes in the road, making them invisible. The bike had nosedived into one. I could feel pain but at first but wasn't sure where. I was able to get up and move under the shade of a tree. Hendrikus looked at my poor bent bike. "Soon get this straightened out," he reassured. "Oh—you've gone grey. Better lie down." My right shoulder hurt badly. We made a sling from my scarf, and I ate some painkillers.

Almost immediately, when we hadn't seen more than three all day, a car stopped. The driver, amazingly, was a first aid instructor. "Don't worry, nothing's broken," she said, observing my swelling eye, applying an instant ice pack, and immobilising my arm in a proper sling. "That's not very reassuring," we said as she drove away. "That's what the driver in Pakistan said after the accident when my leg got broken."

The leafy Outback roadside was our undisturbed bedroom that night. After some porridge and more painkillers in the morning, I considered riding on. What other choice was there? Hendrikus had straightened out the bent mudguard and number plate. I got on the bike and could just outstretch my arm enough to reach the throttle. I checked my black eye, and we left before the silly flies woke up and bothered us, as they do when the sun warms them.

Later that day, about twenty wild black and brown horses ran through the sparse woodland and set off some others on the other side of the track. For some time they galloped magnificently beside us like an escort, manes and tails streaming, then joined up in front of us before peeling off and galloping out of sight.

As we crossed into Queensland the track got even worse. Every corrugation caused pain, so we stopped at Hell's Gate, where there was a surprisingly high rock formation, the only thing for hundreds of miles to stick up more than a gum tree. We climbed to the top and could see the curvature of the earth over the forested terrain 360 degrees round us. We slept there and breakfasted at the roadhouse.

Next morning, Hendrikus's bike wouldn't start when we were ready to go. It just wouldn't. We tried all the usual remedies, such as changing the plug and checking the spark. We even attached my carburettor to his bike. Nothing would get it going. We removed the tank and looked inside the engine. A rocker-clamp bolt had sheared off, and the others wouldn't tighten. No road-side repairs with duct tape would fix that problem. Hendrikus's bike wasn't going anywhere under its own steam.

We assessed our situation. Looking at the negative side ... There was absolutely nothing but wallabies and gum trees for the 125 miles to the next town. Hendrikus was a big man, and his bike carried heavy luggage, such as the tools and spare parts. I had a very painful shoulder. The road was heavily corrugated. Looking on the bright side ... We had lots of painkillers, one bike that worked, and a rope. I towed him.

At Burketown, people on the campsite were helpful. One "top-ender," as people in the north are called, had a device called an "Easy-out," enabling us to withdraw the broken remains of the bolt from the engine. Someone else suggested Helicoil replacement threads, and his friend had a friend who flew the supply plane so asked him to bring the Helicoil kit. Whilst we were waiting, someone else took us fishing for barramundi fish amongst mangrove swamp, where we saw no fish but plenty of freshwater crocs. Hendrikus's bike was mended and back on the road thanks to everyone's expertise and kindness. My shoulder was still extremely painful and had now gone black, blue, and green.

We went on again and slept out at Gum Creek. On waking, the first thing I saw was a cloud of sulphur-crested cockatoos flapping across a clear blue sky, inspiring an inadequate but succinct description in my diary: *"Nice life!"* I wrote.

It was so peaceful there we decided not to spoil it by speaking, so just for the fun of it, we used sign language and smiles as we packed up.

Monday 15th September 2003. The Gillies, near Atherton, Queensland:

> *"WHAM! Suddenly we were in a different country. Dry, dusty roads had vanished. Now we rode through green hills. I could hardly believe my eyes. Within a few kilometres our precious Outback had gone and we could have been back in Wales or Kashmir."*

I had the same "end of Guide camp" feeling and went into mourning for the three months of Australian Outback life I'd loved. It was depressing to see traffic lights and road signs and cars and people, and we both felt gloomy.

When we arrived in Cairns, Hendrikus wanted to stay there to work for a while. He was tired and, for once, left the accommodation arrangements to me. I bought a copy of the local paper to see if there was a cheap room to rent and looked down the ads. "Caravan to rent at Crystal Valley trailer park at Redlynch. $105 per week." A phone call to the proprietor secured it. It was perfect. An outdoor pool, room for the bikes, and our own caravan just outside Cairns.

It was clearly not the sort of holiday caravan site of my childhood Devon holidays. I soon realised the other campers were not having a week's break from work. These were static caravans, not tourers. I met a young mother with her baby in the laundry block. The child looked miserable; the woman was waiflike and had a black eye. She told me that her boyfriend had beaten her up, which was why she was here, hiding from him. We talked for a while, and I looked for her again, but she'd left. Perhaps he'd caught up with her, and she'd had to run.

On our first morning we awoke to . . . "Shut up!" "No, you shut up. I've heard it all before. Any more and you're walking!" "We won't be able to come here again." Our neighbours shouted at each other until they got into their car with their children, slammed the doors, and left.

Opposite us resided a family in a large static caravan. Unlike the woman with the black eye, this robust woman was unlikely to be beaten up by anyone. She had bright orange hair and wore red and pink clothes. She looked like a firework going off. She sounded like one too as she exploded at her sheepish little husband and their two children. All day, she shouted at her angelic-looking toddler, Tabitha, who blithely unaware of any ill-intent on her mother's part, was a smiley little thing. Having learned that "Fuck off" was a normal form of address, she frequently told her baby brother sweetly to "Fuck off" when he cried. The mother suggested that I take little Tabitha for a ride on my bike. I dared not refuse. She laughed and sang as I rode with her round the perimeter track. One morning there was a terrific row going on. Doors slammed amid shouting and swearing. They were leaving too.

After they'd gone, the proprietor of the site came and inspected the place and emerged fuming. The woman had sprinkled sugar on the ceiling fan, over the tops of wardrobes and kitchen units, and all over the carpet. Australia has thousands of species of ants and termites. It's a constant battle to keep them from devouring whole houses. The ubiquitous household sugar ants, true to their name, would be marching in as soon as they sensed the sugar. It would need an intensive clean throughout and was a non-violent method of revenge for being thrown out.

Another neighbour was a man whose caravan I had to pass every time I went to pick up fallen mangoes for breakfast. I found his countenance alarming but said a cheery "good morning" as I passed. "Where are you from, you plummy bitch?" His cigarette stuck to his bottom lip as he spoke, exposing a few brown teeth. He called me over and, after a short introduction, henceforth called me "You stuck-up, blue-eyed, Pommy bitch."

Subsequent chats with Spike revealed that he'd been in prison for murder after finding his wife with another man. He'd shot the man. He'd later done national service and fought in the Vietnam War and was living off his war pension. During the ensuing weeks, he treated me to Australian delights, such as filthy jokes involving Viagra and the Tower of Pisa, and an album of Kevin Bloody Wilson, an entertainer famous for bawdy songs such as *Super-Dooper Dildo*, *Grandad's Got a Stiffy*, and other ditties of a similar nature with no sophisticated subtlety or delicate innuendo.

I'd been a Samaritan volunteer for seven years in the UK and had heard it all so was used to not expressing shock or distaste. I'd also learned as a health visitor to not judge people by their appearance or demeanour. Everyone deserves a hearing, and I liked this unpretentious foul-mouthed man. He entertained me whilst Hendrikus was looking for work, typing CVs, and sending them to businesses in Cairns, some of whom were looking for his skills.

I'd heard the term *trailer trash*, and now I was part of it. For many, living in the trailer park meant they were at rock bottom, but for us it was luxury. Even though the pool was full of cracks and dried vegetation instead of water, we loved it there. Cairns provided opportunities to get organised. We went to a vehicle dismantler and found that a Toyota car headlight was the perfect fit for the Enfield. I bought new boots and extended my visa so I could conveniently stay as long as my bike could.

My shoulder was still black and blue. I could hear it grinding when I moved my arm so went to the hospital, where I was not surprised to learn, following an X-ray, that the collarbone was broken. "You must rest it," I was advised.

Things weren't going well for Hendrikus either. His Enfield's Carnet de Passage had expired, and Australian officialdom would not hear of renewing it or allowing him to import the bike whilst it was inside the country. The only option was to ship it out of Australia and apply to import it again. He kept trying to make the authorities see reason, but eventually we agreed to make the most of whatever circumstances befell us in our usual way.

Despite people warning us it was dangerous, we decided to have a short trip to Papua New Guinea (PNG) with his bike. He arranged the shipping, and we booked flights to Port Moresby, PNG's capital, about an hour's flight 524 miles north across the sea from Cairns.

All I knew about PNG was that its lush, undiscovered forests were home to birds of paradise. Some Australians knew it for its mineral resources and viewed its people with the same disrespect they viewed their own indigenous population. Present attitudes to them were disgraceful. I was reading a desperately sad book about their noble history and how they had looked after the land for over 40,000 years before Europeans came and hunted them for fun and ostracised them. The book, *Why Warriors Lie Down and Die* by Richard Trudgeon, made me cry.

With his bike in transit and whilst we were waiting to follow it, we went to the Tablelands above Cairns and attended a motorcycle event, where my bike won "The Furthest Travelled Motorcycle" category, as it had come all the way from India. There we met a couple who separated us, each propositioning us to go back with them to their house "for some fun." I ran away; it wasn't just the wildlife that was scary here.

At a vintage rally (a more refined event) we met Andy and Julie. I liked them immediately. She hailed from Margate and he from Germany. Both were open, friendly people who asked us back to their traditional Queenslander house near Cairns, not far from our trailer home. They did not want group sex with us, and we became good friends with them.

Andy and Julie offered to care for my Enfield whilst we were away. I would have taken it with me but learned that it would not have been allowed back into Australia. I was surprised at all the rules. I'd been told Australia still had the pioneering spirit and was a law unto itself, but they were not so keen to bend the rules as we'd imagined. Just as I found on my arrival three months previously, this was not Asia, where anything is possible.

We packed up and left the Crystal Valley Park. Before setting off for the airport, I went to say goodbye to Spike. He gave me a hug and, rather embarrassed to be so emotional, shoved a present into my hand. I still treasure it. It was a cassette tape of Kevin Bloody Wilson.

11
Papua New Guinea to Australia

More Running Away. Who's afraid of who?

Where does fear come from? Is it inbred, or do we learn it? People warn us about other people. They say they threaten our safety and possessions, our way of life. After years of meeting these "dangerous others," I'd learned to find out for myself.

Not everyone we spoke to said we'd get eaten by cannibals in Papua New Guinea, but enough people told us "it's dangerous, the people are primitive, tribal, and violent" to ensure we were slightly apprehensive about going, despite our own experience that most people were more hell-bent on helping than harming us. Whatever perils awaited us, we set off to meet our fate.

Port Moresby did its best to uphold its poor reputation, with potholes and gaping gutters like oblong open mouths, ready for unwary or inebriated pedestrians to drop into. Mangy dogs wandered around looking apologetic and miserable amongst the barbed wire and shuttered shops. With metal grilles instead of windows, customers were served from a small hatch.

Early sixteenth century explorers cruising round Melanesia named the island. Papua means "curly hair." The people were reminiscent of those from Guinea in Africa, hence Papua New Guinea. I saw people out and about and wanted to dump our stuff and go and meet them, but when attempting to leave our hostel, which was festooned with razor wire, I was stopped by the security guard in the watch-tower, who forbade residents from going out after dusk. Were the Aussies right? Were people here a lawless horde as we'd been told? The ones in the hostel seemed nice enough, and local people weren't hostile when we went out the next day.

Hendrikus's Enfield arrived and had a trouble-free entry, whereupon we immediately arranged to have it shipped to Lae, further round the coast. We couldn't ride it there, as there were no roads on this fractured landscape with its mountains and deep valleys. This isolation is also the reason for PNG having over one thousand different languages. Each tribe has its own. People spoke to us in Tok Pisin, a Pidgin English, which made sense once you said it how it was spelt. For example, New Guinea is spelt Niugini.

Two of us on one Enfield necessitated minimal luggage. I was used to travelling light and had little but the jeans, boots, and long-sleeved T-shirt I wore all the time. I'd packed waterproofs to keep me dry and water-colour paints to amuse people with silly poems and cartoons; and (a surprising find on the book-swap shelf at the hostel) a study book on Shakespeare's *The Merchant of Venice*, the story of racial and religious intolerance. After all the warnings of tribal violence, I'd wondered about packing bandages and antibiotics for wounds from teeth and spears but settled for pain-killers and a few plasters. I always carried my diary; it was a daily ritual to write in it. I'd memorise things to record as we rode along; things that amused, shocked, and interested but also my feelings when Hendrikus was increasingly distant and irritable.

During the wait for our flight to Lae, I found a physiotherapist at the local hospital. My shoulder was still very painful. I had two sessions with her that helped considerably. She gently massaged, exercised and heated it, gave it ultrasound and provided much-needed sympathy all for the equivalent of £3.40.

With Hendrikus's Enfield out of Australia, he could now apply to take it back in. The online application was winging its ethereal way to the DOTARS as we flew in the opposite direction, 200 miles north for forty-five minutes over forested canyons and high hills to Lae, where there were onward roads. Here we saw a different, gentler PNG. We learned that in a week's time there was to be a huge festival. Many of the tribes that make up PNG would be there. I was thrilled, if a little concerned; if all the reports of disharmony amongst the tribes were true, unresolved feuds could cause a bloodbath.

We booked in at the Kamkumung Guest House. It had no razor wire or guards, only friendly owners and an outside bar where we could cool off with South Pacific lager to help us cope with the heat and humidity.

We paid for a day at the outside pool of the posh Micronesia Hotel. People under the umbrellas and on the sun-beds were mostly Australian or Chinese. Many Chinese people have come over the years to harvest timber, coconut, cocoa, and valuable minerals. A little local boy with his coiled springy hair was fascinated by a little Chinese girl with long, straight, sleek hair. He, being born by the sea, was a good swimmer. She was so encumbered by buoyancy aids, she hardly got wet. He played with her hair, stroking it and watching it sway as she moved. They were unable to use a common language but, unhindered, were inseparable for hours.

At our guest house, new residents arrived for the Lae Show, all from the same tribe. The men invited us to join them outside and secured a dartboard to a tree. The official tournament distance between thrower and dartboard is 1.73 metres (5 foot 8 inches), but the men exhibited impressive accuracy from distances of about half a cricket pitch away. Even in the semi-gloom of dusk they were throwing bulls'-eyes! Innate skills perhaps; they have been hurling spears at each other for millennia, possibly helped by Lae Navy Biscuits that proclaim on the packet that they make you "bigpela and strongpela." Our fellow guests confirmed that tribal feuds are common with much "tit for tat" killing, their way of sorting out their differences.

We visited the nearby Uni-tech, PNG's University. Within the grounds was a small zoo containing a "saltie" crocodile, a few kangaroos, and the highlight . . . an echidna. The size of a large hedgehog, it snuffles along the ground searching for ants and termites. Like the duck-billed platypus, this mind-bogglingly odd, long-snouted creature defies definition. Females lay eggs and, in the absence of nipples, suckle their young through milk patches. Echidnas have no teeth but have a beak like a bird, quills like a porcupine which are arranged amongst its fur, and a pouch like a kangaroo. They also host the world's largest flea, and if all that weren't enough, females have two vaginas and the males have a four-headed penis. The caged birds of paradise were astoundingly colourful and beautiful, which is unfortunate for them, as their feathers are used extensively in tribal finery. They all do elaborate mating dances; the males of one species hang upside-down from branches and flap their wings to impress the females.

By contrast, Hendrikus no longer tried to impress me; previous pet-names now a thing of the past, he didn't call me anything, not even my own name. He worried whether his Enfield would be allowed back into Australia.

I spent my time designing an illustrated congratulatory poem for Abby, who had just been promoted to captain in the army. Now to find the post office. I approached people and used sign language by miming licking a stamp and pointing to the top right corner of the package. Getting things posted is, in many countries, quite a time-consuming experience when there are no familiar signs. Hours can be spent looking for an "invisible" post office only to find that it's the humble little premises already passed three times. They can be tiny and look like somebody's front room or big, busy places where queues are long at each of a dozen counters. You may join the wrong one and end up in the bill-paying queue instead of the weighing and stamp queue or the one for domestic, not foreign post and then have to start all over again. Presents, poems, and heartfelt wishes are at the mercy of the post office. Words written, pictures drawn and painted with love can go astray. Tales abound of parcels being stolen and stamps being removed to resell. In Calcutta I had packed up a parcel for despatch. It was quite a flat package, and as it rested on the scales, an overhead fan pressed it up and down making the needle fluctuate wildly between several different price levels.

The vessel bringing the Enfield docked, and with time before the festival to see what PNG's roads were like, we bought a map and rode towards coastal Madang. We crossed Markham Valley, a wide-open flat space (unlike most of PNG, which is thickly forested). Swimming and snorkelling was pleasant at Madang. I watched a brightly-coloured anemone with ten spidery "arms" waving in the swell. Afterwards, we went to a local café and overheard a conversation amongst the mostly Australian men. Even though two of the group were men from PNG, the Australians referred to local women as monkeys. I was nearly sick.

That night, Hendrikus was displeased with me for some reason. He zipped himself up in the tent. Despite the rain, I slept in a garden gazebo of the hotel garden where we were camping, keeping dry except when I had my tears licked by friendly dogs, whose affection cheered me considerably. Next morning, he was normal again, leaving me confused and upset.

We returned to Lae for the show, staying at the same comfortable guesthouse as before. More of "our" tribe had arrived, so now it was full. The show was the following day. How lucky for us. At 6:30AM, I stumbled out in a dream and had that "I'm in a documentary" feeling. In front of me I saw bare-breasted women wearing shells and face-paint. They were being preened and painted by other women. Feathers stuck out from their hair. They wore finely plaited twine and fur skirts interwoven with red feathers. The strands hung from a waistband to mid-calf, attached at the front and rear with open sides. Everyone was enjoying getting ready for the day's "sing-sing."

Birds of paradise in their hundreds must have been slaughtered to adorn them. Long, dark blue and green feathers decorated the head-dress. Red parrot feathers decorated the forehead band. Tattooed faces were enhanced with painted designs. Arm-bands of intricately-woven grasses and fur were pushed up arms. Around each neck at least two huge kina shells hung like half-moons. These shells give their name to the currency of PNG, being the equivalent of coins. They clack together when the women dance; anklets of bone and shell jingle during the dance, which is performed in rows, the people in each row passing on news to the one behind by head-shaking gestures, waving the plumage as if birds were dancing. The men were equally as beautiful. They anointed each other and prepared their feather headdresses and loincloths. They looked magnificent. Their pride shone like their coconut-oiled bodies.

My mouth hardly closed all day. Apart from the tacky American-style marching bands and Australian commentary, the day was really about the wonderful displays put on by the tribes of PNG. There were drums, bows and arrows, and spears. I covet pictures I took of this spectacle as being some of the best I took during my travels. How could any picture go wrong? Of the estimated eight hundred tribes in the country, at least forty-four of who are not yet touched by the outside world, thirty tribes took part.

Some were painted black with red and yellow feathers; another tribe wore hats like admirals' hats. One tribe smeared their bodies with mud and wore large round mud "helmets" like deep-sea divers of old. I liked the story of these . . . long ago, they'd been in retreat from a stronger tribe. Hampered by a swamp, they staggered and fell, emerging coated in mud. When they saw them, their pursuing enemies became so afraid they ran away from what they thought were ghosts. The mud-men then chased them with their axes and won.

Fear is a powerful thing. Fear of looking foolish stops us trying someone else's language or asking directions, fear of other people who might rob or injure us stops us approaching strangers or travelling to experience other cultures, fear of the unknown prevents our going to see different things, fear of change. Fear of loss or being alone keeps people in relationships they should leave but cling on to hoping they will improve.

The Lae event was sponsored by Coca-Cola, which seemed as ill-fitted to a celebration of tribal life as it had in the remote mountain areas of Pakistan, where people were cooking on open fires and carrying firewood on donkeys. The sponsorship money might have been better spent on providing decent toilet facilities for the performers and spectators. Awash with human waste, the toilets were unable to cope with the numbers and were by far the worst I've experienced anywhere (and that's saying something). There were stalls selling food and drinks and one that sold a juice that, they claimed, cured AIDS. Hendrikus said that all day he could feel fingers trying to get into his pockets.

With my head still buzzing from the overwhelming Lae Show, we rode again up the Markham Valley, this time turning left and heading into the Eastern Highlands. Food in PNG was tasty and fresh, with vegetable and rice dishes. Passion fruit, so expensive in western shops, were so plentiful and cheap that I almost became tired of them, buying a string of twenty at a time for a few pence.

We stopped at a restaurant in Kainantu, 105 miles from Lae, where surprisingly, cocktails were on the menu. A lunchtime cocktail would be a treat, so I ordered one. Instead of something fruity and alcoholic in a glass, what came was a plate of chicken rear-ends (parson's noses as they were called when I was a child). I enjoyed them anyway. A man we'd been talking to at the restaurant contacted some Indian friends of his, who insisted we stay with them.

Asim and his wife had a luxurious home. They had the sort of bathroom one dreams about; hot bath, white fluffy towels—that sort of bathroom. An hour's soak was followed by a steak dinner with our hosts and their friends. Next morning, Asim showed us round his coffee processing plant. Local growers supplied the beans. He told us they tried to fool him by making the sacks heavier, adding stones and wet sand. I bought some roasted beans to send back for my family.

Near Kainantu, there was a small town consisting of six-hundred American missionaries, who were translating the Bible into PNG's languages. As we were white, we were allowed to enter the gated and guarded compound where the missionaries lived in special houses. I felt like I was visiting GCHQ. They employed local maids, gardeners, and guards. They bought food flown in from Australia. I didn't see them at market stalls or in local restaurants eating local food, never on buses. All the worthy and no doubt well-intentioned Americans looked rather stressed. We sat outside their supermarket at a picnic table eating hamburgers. At midday, a whistle blew, and they streamed into the shop. I was surprised to see that they had to hand in their bags to the security guard and collect them when they'd paid for their shopping. Surely they could be trusted not to shoplift.

They go to the villages to learn the language and spread Christianity. This is nothing new, of course. Missionaries have been coming there for centuries to convert the "heathens." Many were killed (and reportedly eaten by some of the cannibalistic tribes) or died of malaria, but eventually they got a foothold and the country became officially Christian, represented by Lutherans, Seventh Day Adventists, Presbyterians, Anglicans, Methodists, The Assembly of God, and a variety of other church groups.

Missionaries had not yet been successful in quelling the "pay-back" system of justice. During the time we were there, we heard of several, despite the missionaries' best efforts to spread their "turn the other cheek, forgive thy neighbour" messages. I spoke to a policeman who had a tribal shield on his wall. "They don't use these nowadays, of course," he said as he tapped on the sturdy wood and tree-bark shield. I assumed he meant that the tribes were now more peaceful, but he said, "No, they have replaced them with lighter, corrugated iron ones." Tribal killings were the number one crime there. With all those languages, it is little wonder there was no way to talk things over, make compromises, or offer apologies.

The people of PNG originate from the earliest inhabitants of New Guinea. There was a land bridge from Australia that led settlers from the Malay Archipelago and prior to that, Africa about 70,000 years ago. Crop-rotation gardening is thought to have originated there. I noticed that vegetable gardens were commonplace in villages in clearings amongst the trees. Everyone looked healthy and happy.

Nowadays, Malaysians and Japanese are raiding their forests for valuable trees. Other people are telling them they must believe in a God over whom "civilised" nations fight (or use as an excuse to fight). They are told to wear clothes to cover themselves and consume the same foodstuffs that are making us ill in the western nations. They seemed to have been doing quite well on their own for about 70,000 years before the outside world came and told them they were doing it all wrong.

There was not yet any response from DOTARS, so we continued northwards to Goroka, in the Highlands. The weather changed to a wet and gloomy "I want to go home" kind of day, so we went to the museum. We learned that this area was mined for gold in 1933. Early prospectors found an estimated one-million people living much as they had in the Stone Age. Black and white photos showed everyone proudly wearing traditional dress and holding spears. Nobody, except people with white hair, was allowed to wear white shells, a respectful symbol of wisdom.

We stayed in a comfortable hotel room with a balcony. Skulking about was an enormous spider with a big juicy body and about six to eight inches from leg to opposite leg. I was happy to watch it from inside the room, wary of the diverse spiders in this part of the world. As I hovered there I overheard our Muslim neighbours on their balcony saying, "We must have a centre in every village." My heart sank as I foresaw not only tribal feuds but religious differences causing trouble. I just couldn't see that this sunny tropical place with its natural people could be a place where women would have to cover themselves completely. The white man had already told them their "sinful" breasts should be covered. What next, head to toe clothing?

There was a frieze around the town's community centre wall depicting a ceremony for a young woman's right of passage to womanhood at her first period. She was depicted full of joy and anticipation as she linked arms with two girlfriends and saw how pleased people in the village were for her. I thought of how girls in my culture were too embarrassed to tell anyone; certainly not an event to be celebrated publicly. We are embarrassed about the human condition and want to deny our stages of development. We wash away our natural smells and replace them with artificial ones. Pheromones must be blotted out at all costs.

The rain cleared next morning, and the mountains all around showed themselves. Hendrikus went to check emails and came back with good news from DOTARS and fresh produce from the market. We had the perfect breakfast of strawberries, avocado, coconut, passion fruit, pineapple, bananas, and nuts whilst marvelling at the view. The plants were unusual, with species I hadn't seen before. Some trees had flowers like massive carnations on the ends of their branches. There were hibiscus, bizzie-lizzies, and poinsettias so big they sprawled over houses and huts. There were bright yellow spikey bushes and black toilet-brush trees. A scented, fresh smell filled the air that was bursting with the sound of cicadas.

The Inn Goroka, where we were staying, was run by Lillian, a friendly woman, who invited us back to her home for a traditional PNG meal. We met her husband, Leslie, who dealt in gold, and Rachel, who as well as running a local bar was also his other wife. Tapioca, cao-cao, plantain, two types of leafy greens, rice, and coconut were stuffed into a wide section of bamboo and put over embers. The flavours mingled as they cooked, making a delicious vegetarian dish for all of us, the group having now grown with their combined offspring and Leslie's mother, "Mamma." In the light of the fire, Mamma sang a lovely lilting song that tugged at the heartstrings with its emotion and beauty. When she had finished, I asked what the song was about. "It's a family song about when Leslie was drunk and drove his car into Rachel's house. Another time, Lillian was cross with him and she hit him over the head with a stone." The song was whisperingly tranquil, belying the turbulent subject matter.

We'd been invited to visit the village of the owner of our Lae guesthouse, where after a very difficult and steep valley-crossing on small footpaths, we were welcomed like royalty by the whole village. I was given valuable necklaces of boar tusks and sea-shells from the inaccessible coastal regions. The residents helped us push the bike back over the half-destroyed bridge to the road.

We descended the mountains back towards Lae and stopped when we saw some tribesmen. I bought a bow and arrows, which I watched being made from entirely natural materials. The bark from some bamboo was stripped, the ends inserted into a thicker bit of bamboo that was then heated in a specially lit fire. Priceless; it cost about £1.

Back in Lae, I bought a string bag (bilum) and a wooden mask. PNG is the only place I'd been where I felt compelled to buy such items. I'd have loved a rug from Pakistan, a metal lantern from Syria, some silk from India, or Burmese furniture but had to learn to admire, rather than possess them. Some things I sent home disappeared. I had to accept that I might not see things again and didn't expect my treasures from PNG to arrive. It seemed such a hit and miss affair, but about six months after I'd posted them by sea-mail, they arrived.

I thought about my daughters and wondered what was happening in their lives. My contact with them had diminished since reaching Australia; there just weren't the Internet cafés or phone signals (there was no Skype, Twitter, or Facebook then). Distance and time were having an effect. I was losing touch. I missed them and wanted to go home and nurture relationships. It was late October, and I decided to fly home for Christmas.

We'd been in PNG for four weeks and had experienced no violence, aggression, or ill-intent from the people. Nobody had stolen anything or tried to cheat us or ask for money. I didn't need a single thing from my first aid kit.

Fear is often unfounded and works both ways. For all the warnings about how scary PNG would be, we were not prepared for what happened during our excursion to Madang. We had been advised not to ride at night due to potholes and "rascals" so had to look for a resting place. In the late afternoon we came to Walium village. I was driving; Hendrikus was pillion. As usual, I was wearing sunglasses, with my scarf over my nose and mouth to avoid dust and sun-burn. Both of us wore helmets. I approached a group of young people to ask if there was a guesthouse. They scattered. I rode up behind a man, and he too, on turning to look, ran away at such an incredible speed I could almost see the adrenaline coursing through his arteries. I looked at us, at what they would see . . . a large ginger-bearded man behind a woman wearing a helmet with her face and eyes covered. I supposed we and the motorbike did look a trifle unusual as we approached at twilight, but were we that frightening? I removed my scarf and sunglasses and asked some other people, who directed us.

Apart from waking in the night to the sound of a cat rummaging through one of our plastic bags in our "mattress on the floor" room, we slept well until awoken by raucous laughter downstairs the next morning. We were told by our hosts that the man who had hared away was a friend of theirs and had just been in to tell them what had happened. All the people we had scared were genuinely afraid. Stories were circulating that foreigners were capturing people for their internal organs or injecting them with syringes of the AIDS virus. They were terrified of us and were running for their lives. Violence did seem to be a way of life there. A friend of the guesthouse owner had been shot dead recently by a "rascal" who thought he might have money.

Later, as we left and tried to pay, we all had a right old laugh as it turned out this wasn't a guest-house at all, we had just assumed it was, and these lovely people hadn't liked to turn us away. The kindness of strangers was humbling, and it was we, not them, who had caused alarm.

On our return to Australia, we stayed briefly in Cairns. Hendrikus went to Townsville to collect his bike and look for work. I enquired about flights home for Christmas and told my family of my plans. I hadn't seen them since I left to be reunited with my bike in Pakistan back in February 2002, twenty months previously. Once I'd spoken to my family, I couldn't stop being excited. My tummy lurched every time I thought about it: I was going home. "Home."

Usually a place, a building where one's "stuff" is. I didn't have one of those. To me, home was where my daughters, my brother, my mother, and my friends were.

Hendrikus's parents invited him to join them for Christmas in Haiti. I hoped that once he had some money he'd be happy again and we could be like we'd been before. I didn't want to see that things had changed. He was busy sending off his CV to various places in Australia and making a website for a local businessman. He made it clear he didn't want me or my Enfield around, throwing spanners about if I needed his help with a job I couldn't do myself. So I looked at my map and decided I'd ride up the pointy bit in the north east . . . towards the Cape York Peninsula.

With no particular destination in mind, I said, "See you soon," to Hendrikus and our friends and set off up the Captain Cook Highway, sleeping wrapped up in a groundsheet at the edge of a field for my first bedroom. Mosquitoes and the moon kept me company. I had a little meths stove for making tea and porridge.

Unlike Asia, there was little public transport; people used their own vehicles and stayed I knew not where. Consequently, there was not the variety of hotels or hostels everywhere, so unless I felt it unwise, I usually accepted offers of accommodation. Hence on this journey I would share a boat with an artist, a concrete floor with a dive instructor, and a caravan with a man who panned for gold. To meet and stay with people who live there was part of the journey. Yes, the question of exactly where I was going to sleep came up, but as one of them said delicately as he made up a spare bed, "If I'm not invited to the picnic, I won't ask for a sandwich."

I was forty-six miles from Cairns when a massive old nail punctured my rear tyre. I knew I wasn't far away from Mossman, so I took out the wheel and stood hitch-hiking with it and a spare inner tube at the side of the road. It was half an hour before anyone stopped. Car after car went by. Lorries and flatbed trucks ignored me. This would not have happened in India; someone would have helped immediately.

Eventually, a man driving a pick-up truck nervously asked me if I needed a lift. On the way I asked him why nobody had stopped. "We're not supposed to pick up hitch-hikers. I think it's illegal, but I thought I'd risk it." I paid to have my new tube fitted and the repairman kindly gave me a lift back to my bike and watched me put the wheel back in. When he'd gone, I had a swim in a nearby river to cool off, assuming crocodiles wouldn't be this close to town.

At Port Douglas, I stopped to look at some paintings in a park. After a conversation with the artist about his oddly fey pictures featuring kangaroos, I accepted his offer of a spare bunk on his boat for the night. To earn my keep, I varnished some picture frames for him and left him painting more hovering kangaroos the following morning.

At Daintree, in the Cape Tribulation area seventy-seven miles from Cairns, there was a walking trail in Mossman Gorge. A little bird delighted me by not only guiding me to its nest but patiently sitting there on her little orange eggs, posing whilst I fumbled with my old film camera, now on its last legs after these hard years on the road. The astounding wildlife picture I'd hoped for didn't happen.

Later, when I stopped for fuel, I was told the road ahead was very bad. It certainly was a bone-shaker. I crossed the two foot deep Broomfield River ford at Wujul Wujal. On the other side, I felt a serious jelly-steering problem, as if I had a front tyre puncture. I got off to investigate and found that the front down-tube part of the frame had sheered where a crash-bar fixture had been welded in Malaysia to prevent it swivelling and damaging my legs again. I would not be able to ride further.

There was a local Aboriginal community. I found some people outside the shop and asked if there was a mechanic or welder anywhere. "Someone comes once a month," they said as they leaned on the shop porch. I wondered when he was due. Did he come yesterday, and I'd be here for a month? I tentatively asked when he was next expected. "T'morrrah." I had grown quite used to miracles like that. However, I was not going to flaunt my good luck and miss this welder so didn't look for anywhere to stay, in case he just breezed in and out. I managed to push the wobbly bike and slept beside it outside the heavily secured yard.

During the night, I awoke to baying dogs. They got closer. A pack of them was heading straight for me, howling and panting. They might tear me to pieces. With no time to get a knife or shin up a gum tree, I rolled myself up in my groundsheet as they approached. I imagined yellow-eyed hounds from hell, slavering with tongues lolling, but they ran straight past me and I went back to sleep.

In the morning, I was up and ready when the young welder came. He examined the damage and explained that it had been a bad weld, which had affected the metal. He did a stronger, more reliable one. He would accept no money, saying it would be good for his karma to help a traveller to keep on the road.

The onward journey presented an area of breathtaking beauty containing species unique to this locality. An information board said that within a four square-mile radius lived a species of frog that lays eggs, as do all frogs, but with this one the young hatch out as frogs, bypassing the tadpole stage, like no other frog in the world! It was a special Aboriginal place too and very wild. Reading that some people went in there and never came out, I rode on.

I got to Cooktown and didn't need to go any further.

The diary entry for 11th November reads:

"I have quite fallen for this place. I have not had that "I could live here" feeling for ages but it feels right."

It was unpretentious with the "end of the road" feeling I'd imagined when I thought of Australia before I arrived. What it didn't have appealed to me more than what it had. Not built up and selling itself, it was happy just being what it was. I was happy too; alone, totally free, relaxed, and excited to be going home.

Mary's Caravan Park was perfect. Nobody else was there. Whispering paperbark trees offered companionship in the coastal breeze as I slept amongst them on my groundsheet. I could read in my sleeping bag propped up against my Enfield, which also supplied power for the reading light attached to the battery terminals. A bandicoot, a ratty little marsupial, visited at night, helping itself to my food to supplement its usual diet of berries, nuts, and seeds. When I shone my torch on it, it looked most put out and shuffled off to the bushes with my breakfast roll.

Cooktown developed because of the gold that brought early settlers there. Now far fewer, the present residents were rather miffed at being left out of the 2000 Olympic Games in Sydney and had devised their own torch-bearing ceremony, carrying a torch by four-wheel-drive (or "ute" . . . short for utility vehicle) and having their own games that included "Watching the grass grow" and "synchronised beer-drinking." Neither game would be short of teams in this one-horse, no-traffic-lights town.

I learned more about the history of Cooktown and the man for whom it was named at the museum. In 1770, Captain Cook had washed up there when his ship, *Endeavour*, had run aground on the Great Barrier Reef. It took two months to repair. There was a bit of nasty business involving the aboriginals and the rightful ownership of turtles from the sea, after which they had no contact with each other. On the second voyage, his sister-ship, *Adventure*, was captained by Tobias Furneaux. There was a Furneaux Street, and I had my photo taken by the street sign. I like to think I am a descendant of his.

A dopey old hippy insisted on talking at me all through the England/France rugby match on TV at the Returned and Services League (RSL) club. The town did have a laid-back feel to it, however, there was a dispute about the fee at the campsite, so I left and slept wild for a couple of nights. Then, when I enquired in town about a dive trip on the Great Barrier Reef, I met Richard, who offered me a space on his floor which I accepted, because even though I had yet to see a police officer, there was a huge fine for wild campers.

Richard, from Singapore, was one of those fortunate people who knew from an early age what he wanted to do. As a boy, he'd dismantled and reassembled the family hi-fi and thenceforth was determined to design the best speakers in the world. After completing the relevant university degree, he spent twenty years working for Wharfedale in Bradford, because they led the world until they were bought out by Sony. Where does one go after Bradford? To the wilds of Australia's York Peninsula, of course. I went for a scuba dive on his friends' boat, but the visibility was limited and wasn't the anticipated dive of a lifetime, although I did see huge clams with deep purple inside the lids, looking like treasure chests lined with velvet. I was told it was the wrong time of year and that the weather had been rough. I accepted that I couldn't be lucky all the time.

Often, when I left the bike parked for a while, I'd return to find people looking at it, all with an opinion about where it came from with its strange number plate, TN 09 7257. Sometimes, for my own amusement, I'd stand nearby and listen. It bore no stickers, it was just a plain black Enfield, by this time rather scratched and dented. No longer shiny, it was engrained with dust from the road, heat-stains on the exhaust pipe, and worn paint where my knees rubbed the tank. It had a snapped-off clutch lever, due to dropping the bike so frequently. The chrome was peeling off the crash bar. The luggage racks were bent from many falls.

"Of course . . . ," one man said, " . . . it's not a real one. It's an Indian copy." I could feel protective indignation rising and, hands on hips, burst out with, "Excuse ME! That's MY bike you're talking about, and "real" or not it has brought me here all the way from India, and I'll thank you not to talk like that in front of it." Then I smiled, and we all laughed.

With a soft-toy kangaroo for a second cousin's newly-born baby and Christmas cards to aunts, uncles, and cousins stamped and posted, I came out of the Cooktown post-office and found a wiry man strolling round with his hands in his pockets, staring at the bike. "This yours?" he asked in an American accent. "Come back to my place and tell me about it over a cup of tea."

I'd met Stuart Owen Fox. I followed his car, riding the bike up Grassy Hill to the most superb home I'd ever seen. It was open on the side that faced the sea, the mouth of the Endeavour River, the forest beyond, and the bay where Captain Cook would have limped in in 1770. Stuart gave me jasmine tea and biscuits and told me that he was a photographer of world renown and a pioneer of flat-scanner imaging. Wondering at first if they'd be like the pictures of people's bottoms on the office photocopier at Christmas office parties, I was staggered at the quality of these images. I was not allowed to call them photos or pictures. They were poster sized and three-dimensional images.

Many of his subjects came from nature. Flowers, butterflies, even fish. He had a sense of humour too, and with some dead specimens from the local tropical fish dealer, with whom he had a deal, he created a "going with the flow" theme. To deal with the "dead-eye" look of the fish, he touched them up with a computer programme to make them sparkly and life-like. It seemed you could make a picture an *image* from anything.

He had left the US before the Vietnam War, living for many years in Denmark before coming to Australia. He'd ridden a Honda 400/4 from Perth to the East Coast, on the way rescuing a baby kangaroo from its dead mother's pouch. He made a cloth bag and hung it round his neck until the joey was big enough to fend for itself.

Stuart's thinness was due to yet another often lethal Australian creature when living further south. The Australian parasitic tick (*Ixodes holocyclus*) usually feeds off the blood from koalas, bandicoots, possums, and kangaroos. But one fed from Stuart Owen Fox and nearly killed him. He recovered but, heartbroken, had to leave his home and his friends so great was the risk to his health.

Like Richard, who couldn't bring himself to make second-rate speakers, Stuart had found refuge there in Cooktown. He was a sad man and, like some of his salty subjects, was like a fish out of water, with sorrowful eyes that needed digitally touching up a bit to make them sparkle again. He was going into hospital for a prostate operation, and I had to head back to Cairns to finalise my flight home and rejoin Hendrikus, who'd told me by email that he was now living in a large tent in Andy and Julie's garden.

I took a westerly route via Lakeland. That night, as I brewed some coffee over my campfire somewhere off-road forty-three miles away, I was watched by some roosting black cockatoos in the branches of the eucalyptus trees. They offered no advice to my queries about the meaning of life, but they occasionally nodded agreement to my suggestions before, like me, they settled down to sleep.

Stopping for fuel at the Palmer River Roadhouse, I met James, an interesting chap who lived in a caravan and made a reasonable living by panning for gold. Driving his faithful, rusty "ute," he took me past gnarled old trees struggling to survive the dry season to to his favourite spot; a bend on the river where he brushed and collected the dusty soil from around tree roots to be sifted, soaked, and swirled around in a pan, whereupon little sparkly bits might present themselves. When he got enough, he sold it. I wanted to try my luck, imagining digging up Australia's biggest ever nugget in my first spadeful. I dug into the topsoil and got excited when I heard the sound of metal on metal. James was delighted with my find. The rusty pliers had been lost for years. I did find a few specks of gold.

That evening, in addition to introducing me to the theory of the New World Order of which I had previously been blissfully ignorant, he treated me to a country music session that included *Scarlet Ribbons*, a song I remembered from childhood. In the morning before I left, James kindly added to my few specks of gold and presented the little collection to me in a tiny jewellery box with black velvet to make the gold show up.

The ride back to Cairns was outstanding. Hardly a soul used the road. I stopped by the McCleod River to explore on foot. I came back to find a motorcyclist with a BMW looking at the Enfield. I approached and said, "It doesn't matter how long you stand and stare at it, I'm not going to swap!" We had a chat. He ran a nearby campsite, but I was moving on. I had a mission, and nothing else mattered. It felt so right to fly home.

Back in Cairns, reunited with Hendrikus, Andy, and Julie, I paid for my flight and went to check my emails and received a huge surprise. My ex-husband wrote that our daughter, Claire, had got married to her boyfriend, Peter. Not emotionally aware enough to think that she might have preferred to give me this joyous news herself, his message preceded hers asking me to phone her as soon as possible, as she had something important to tell me. Grinning with delight, I phoned her to give her my congratulations and hear the whole story. Then, calling in at the off-licence for two bottles of Tasmanian champagne, I found Andy, Julie, and Hendrikus on the balcony of the local pub, where we all happily toasted them. Claire and Peter had told only Abby and a few very close friends, invited the bell-ringers to be witnesses, been to Raymond Blanc's restaurant for lunch, and told everyone before they went on honeymoon to Austria.

"Stop the car!" I shouted to Andy, who was driving me to Cairns airport. Mangoes were for sale at the roadside. I recalled a childhood Christmas when the postman had staggered up the meandering steps to our house with a box of oranges from my mother's friend in Australia, a rare treat. I would replicate this special gift, but rather than send them, I would bring a box of sunny mangoes with me on the flight back home. I imagined the joy.

I'd got used to brash, rough, loud, boastful, don't spare your feelings, call a spade a spade Australia and again found a huge contrast in Tokyo, where I had an overnight stop. People were quiet, polite, gentle, and stylish. The food on the plane was delicate and intricate, but for once I was tired of making observations and comparisons. I was all "travelled out," and I was going home.

12

HOME FOR CHRISTMAS
AND JAPAN

I composed myself as I waited for my things to appear on the carrousel at Heathrow, so that I wouldn't hurl myself at my daughters as soon as I saw them. Aware of previously over-exuberant welcomes, I didn't want to cause embarrassment and create a distance the minute I arrived; that was the last thing I wanted. As I collected my luggage containing Australian Christmas gifts, I held my joy in rein and went for a more sophisticated approach. "Decorum, Furneaux, decorum."

Christmas at Claire and Peter's was traditional and lovely, with family, friends, and partners, but despite everyone's best efforts, I felt out of place. I didn't have the right clothes, had lost confidence in the kitchen, and was unable to join in the talk about TV programmes or recent news items.

Still in a travel bubble, I couldn't understand why people weren't interested in what I was bursting to tell them; like the difference between a saltie and a freshie crocodile, the amazing tribespeople I'd seen in PNG, or what a broken collarbone feels like, but nobody listened, and I felt out of place and silly. The mangoes weren't a treat either. By then, mangoes were available all year round in Britain, unlike oranges in the post-war 1950s.

I couldn't get interested in their world, either. Computer games and the activities of celebrities, most of whom I'd never heard of, left me cold. Surely my world was real and the world they were interested in was made-up, a smokescreen for what was really happening? But I learned to shut up and tried not to be a bore. I explained how out of touch I felt. "It's a pay-off, Mum," said Claire as, manoeuvring an iron for the first time in years, I pressed her delicate designer clothes. "It's you who is missing out." I couldn't expect to have both the travelling life and be involved with the day-to-day goings on of my family and their interests.

At this time of extravagance, I didn't have as much money as I would have liked and felt, as usual, like the poor relation who'd always worked hard but felt unrecognised. Although tired, I'd worked nights to earn extra when our daughters were small. I'd been weary and wish I could have been a more tolerant mother, but there was so little money, so much to do, and such little time in the day when I'd been working in a hospital all night. But my training in frugality was useful. Hendrikus and I travelled on a shoestring. He was always skint. So many times he'd stormed out of restaurants, as if the prices were a personal slight to offend him, after I'd already chosen what I'd have and started salivating. Meekly, I would follow, not wanting a scene. I'd come home for Christmas, the most excessive season. Although I didn't rush out muttering about the prices, I panicked at the cost of everything.

After Christmas lunch, we played games and went for a walk. A little four-year old girl, Peter's niece, put her hand in mine when we were walking to the village adventure playground. I felt awkwardly out of touch and out of place, but little Tiggi knew none of this and held my hand unbidden, and by so doing satisfied my longing for acceptance that wintry day in an Oxfordshire village playpark.

A shock was in store for me when I went to see my mother. By then nearly ninety-six, deaf, and totally blind, she didn't know who

I was, and there was no possibility of telling her anything about anything I'd seen. At the nursing home Christmas party she sang, knowing all the words to every carol as I, unable to join in for the burning in my throat, wept silent tears. I hoped the fairy lights were dim enough to hide my tragic face. There would be no more "Tell me about the Golden Temple again, dear." In a way, I'd felt I was doing her travelling for her; writing long letters and sending audio tapes when she became unable to read. Now it would be useless to do even that. She had "gone." I was grateful that we had already made time to express our thanks, apologies, and farewells, talked about the past, hugged and cried together. It's something not everyone has the chance to do. My devoted brother, who unlike me, had not gone gallivanting to Asia, had seen a gradual slipping away. For me, it was distressingly abrupt.

After Christmas and New Year, everyone's working life resumed, and I went to Bristol, working at the backpackers' hostel with my friend, Martin. I earned some travel funds and looked forward to being reunited with Hendrikus, my bike, and our travelling life. He had spent Christmas on holiday with his family in Haiti, paid for by his parents. We had kept in touch by email, and he gave me every indication that he was as keen to get back on the road as I was; everything sounded promising according to the tone of the typed word. First, however, I was going to take advantage of an unmissable opportunity. On my return ticket to Australia I was allowed a week in Japan.

At a bus stop in Bristol, I met Rupert, a poet. When I told him I was going to Japan, he advised me to buy a Japanese rail pass before I went as he had done for visits there to study haiku poetry. I liked the suggestion. £154 bought me a week's unlimited and speedy (200 miles per hour) rail travel anywhere I liked.

It is noticeable that my diary of the week spent in Japan is tidier and more neatly written than any others. The writing is smaller; the sentences more succinct. Things I stuck in my diary are trimmed rather than torn, and I used scissors, not my teeth, to cut the sticky tape for attaching them. Within the paragraphs are observations of equally well-ordered events. I wrote of getting lost occasionally, but as if the good people of Japan did not want any untidy loose ends, I was swept up and guided wherever I went.

I was not expecting the same levels of hospitality I'd found elsewhere in Asia, but surprisingly, a young Japanese woman on the airport train-link to Tokyo city invited me home with her, until I explained I was going straight on to Kyoto. As soon as I arrived in Tokyo rail station, I exchanged my voucher for the Japan Rail Pass.

I attempted my own haiku poem to describe my first impressions on arrival:

Vending machines deliver.
Orchids blossom.
Automatic cash machines evade.

Four hours later, at 11:30PM, the train pulled in to a dark and cold Kyoto. I was tired and really pleased that I had, for once, been organised enough to do some research and select a hostel, "The Cheapest Inn," quite near the station. When I emerged from underground, I was so glad not to have to traipse around . . .

All the subways and buses had stopped. "Never mind," I thought, " . . . I sat on a plane for twelve hours, then a train for another four. The walk will be good." I found the street, but a soup restaurant was where the hostel should be. The owner had never heard of it. Then some customers got involved, phone calls were made, and a taxi called. The driver didn't know the elusive hostel either, but nobody wanted to give up, so we all (except for the chef) piled into the taxi and trawled up and down the street asking other taxi drivers and pedestrians. At 2AM, when I would happily have slept in the gutter, everyone admitted defeat. Expressing my gratitude to all, I booked in at the same hotel as the diners, thus messing up my budget. It was like any hotel room anywhere, so the next morning, I asked at the tourist information office for somewhere more authentic.

An easy bus-ride took me to Gion and its temples, shrines, parks, and gardens. I booked in at a typically Japanese hotel. It was perfect. A finely woven tatama mat and futon on the floor for sleeping, sliding "paper" windows, slippers, a cotton kimono-style dressing gown, and a thick wool jacket for my comfort. A low table had on it a tray with kettle, cups, tea bags, and a dear little blue and white china teapot. I would have liked to have stayed in my room all day, but even though it was cold and dull outside, I thought I should go out. I bought some sushi and ate as I walked around the park, following an uphill path to a monastery. Ravens were clattering about in the bare branches, and little birds were "peep-peeping." At the entrance was a rank of vending machines, making me think how incongruous they would look outside a British church. I bought a tin of coffee that heated itself upon opening.

Unable to resist the call of my hotel room any longer, I returned to explore the spa-bath. My guide book informed me that many of these in Japan are communal and to be sure of the rules before stripping off and wading in. Some allowed nudity; some were one-gender only. Some were mixed. Nobody at the hotel spoke English, so I put on my costume and went into the deserted, large indoor hot pool, delicious after so little sleep and the cold outside. I ate noodles in my room and watched David Attenborough on TV, head resting on the traditional Japanese pillow of wood.

I had to be phoned to come for breakfast in the morning, as I overslept. Food came to my table in tiny containers like a doll's tea set with small bowls of soup, rice, tofu, and fish. There were mushrooms with diamonds cut in the caps, their stems dipped in beetroot juice to make them pink. A pot of hot water arrived, in which I cooked something and then fished it out with a miniature net. It was delicious. Reluctantly, I packed up to leave, and upon asking the manager where to stand for the bus to the station, he walked with me, crossing the road to ensure I got on the right bus. Some women in traditional Japanese dress were walking outside; socked feet in wooden sandals, huge hair done up in rolls and scrolls, kimonos with the "cushion" at the back.

The stations were like underground towns where one could live without needing to go up into the light. Everything was available there (except cash machines that hid shyly from me). The platforms had numbered sections at the edge corresponding with the carriage number on the ticket, so passengers knew exactly where to stand. Exactly on time, the train arrived, and the door needed for the allocated seat opened in front of the designated spot on the platform. The Shinkansen trains looked and sped like bullets—unlike my own un-streamlined Enfield Bullet, waiting for me in Australia.

The railway staff looked like air-stewards. The ticket inspectors gave a short speech upon entering the carriage and bowed on their way out backwards. The toilets were both squat and sitting type. Notices were in Japanese, English, and braille. Refreshment trolleys went back and forth.

My next destination was Ibusuki, on the Satsuma Peninsula. I chose to go there because it was as far south as I could go by train, not because Satsuma citrus fruits originate from round there or because it is a popular spa resort with natural hot sands where people are buried up to their necks in the summer.

After enquiring at the station tourist office, I stayed in a room at the home of a professor of calligraphy who spoke no English. He showed me his studio. With a brush like a pony-tail, he sloshed water on a block of solid ink in a tray and offered it to me. He showed me how to hold the brush without putting pressure on it. His work was displayed all over his minimalist home with its sliding paper doors and fine matting. I expected to see Madame Butterfly at any moment. I made two inartistic attempts, one saying "I love Japan" and the other "Love." I wrapped the watch I had brought from England for Hendrikus's birthday present in the second one.

I left and boarded a train to Kanazawa, capital of Ishikawa in the north-west. Disembarking in the evening a kind young woman at the tourist office told me that the YHA minibus was due and waited with me. An over-ground journey to a hilly area just outside the city was lovely. It had been snowing, and everything looked pretty. As much as I would have liked to stay longer in my room, with its own hot-tub, I looked at the map and saw that I was still some way from Tokyo for my flight back to Australia.

A quick walk up and down the snowy road the next morning had to suffice before catching the bus back to Kanazawa centre. I stowed my backpack at the station left-luggage depot and went to explore Kanazawa's famous gardens, castle, and Omicho Market where any food one could want is available; fresh ingredients, fish and meat or ready-cooked meals to eat there or take away.

I bought a print in an antique shop. It showed a young woman having her hair prepared by her maid. I didn't realise then that it was a Geisha being prepared for her evening's guests. I was still a feminist in the making at that stage and feel somewhat guilty now at my choice, but it serves as a reminder of why I am now a fully-fledged feminist. I walked to the castle gates and meandered round the famous Kenroku-en, "The Garden of the Six Sublimities," one of the three most famous gardens in Japan. It was snowing heavily. Peaceful, despite many tourists, it was beautiful, and in a few weeks all the trees would be in flower. I had wandered quite a long way from the station and on checking the time was alarmed that my train would soon be leaving, so I ran, collected my backpack, and just made it.

Shizuoka was my next destination, chosen so that on leaving in the morning I would have a view of Mount Fuji on the way to Tokyo. I wanted to sleep in a capsule hotel but was not allowed to, as it was male only, so stayed in a sterile hotel, where there was a men only hot bath. I stole a hotel kimono/dressing gown. It was cotton and had the hotel name stamped all over it. I think it's the only thing I have deliberately taken since I developed a moral conscience and gave up pinching sweets from a shop in Weston-super-Mare High Street when I was about ten.

I saw Mount Fuji as I shot past the next day. It had snow on the top and would have been truly beautiful had it not been for the industrial scene in the foreground that is never shown on postcards.

I spent an hour or two in the vast emporium, Tower Records in Tokyo, amazed at the nine storeys of music, far too overwhelming for me to make a choice. My next stop was the airport, and thankfully I arrived early. My passport would not swipe at the check-in desk. The Australian immigration officer at Cairns airport had been wrong when he said I could re-enter Australia on my current visa. The superbly efficient Japan Airlines representative hastily arranged an electronic visa for me. I thanked her profusely and got on the plane to Cairns.

On arrival at 4:30AM I was questioned for two hours in a back room by a pompous bully of an immigration officer. who was convinced I had come back to Australia to work. Why else was I in and out of Australia like a boomerang? "I'm travelling around on a motorbike" sounded feeble. My backpack was searched for work-related documents. Photocopies of my credit cards were taken, and I felt like a criminal, which was probably the intention.

Hendrikus was there to meet me, curled up asleep on a chair in the arrivals lounge. We were both tired, so it wasn't an emotional meeting. Neither was the journey back to Andy and Julie's garden where he was living in a large tent. I had only three months to stay there now. I assumed that we'd be making plans to move on to New Zealand together. He said, "That's nice," when he opened his birthday present of the watch wrapped in my own "Love" calligraphy paper and then, "What's next?" as he put it to one side. The next day I saw his muddy footprint on the paper on the ground, and the watch was lost. In a temper, he threw a spanner when I asked if I could borrow it. But still, even with spanners being thrown at me, I thought it would improve. What was WRONG with me? Why did I persist in this increasingly abusive relationship, driven by the continued hope that once we got on the road again all would be well? But it was by no means the first time. He had "come right" before. Surely he would, again?

13

AUSTRALIA TO NEW ZEALAND

LOOKING BACK WITHOUT A MIRROR
OUTBACK REFLECTIONS

My homesick father's plea to his mother in 1912, to let him come home from sea at the age of fourteen, was met with "You've made your bed, now lie in it." Whether or not he endorsed this view I don't know, but when this was related to me as a child I absorbed it and thenceforth felt I let everyone down when I gave up on anything. After years of piano lesson misery, I was finally allowed to give up, but the freedom came with the price of condemnation and failure. My parents, although distant with each other, had stayed together, despite several severe hiccoughs. I had to stay with Hendrikus. If he wasn't being nice to me, it must be my fault. I wanted things to be good again so tried harder. In the past, when he'd left me to go and do what he wanted to do, I coped perfectly well, but I couldn't make that break myself. I wasn't dependent on him, so why did I behave as if I was? I'd been prepared to travel alone when I returned to Pakistan. Why not now?

Five weeks of my precious remaining three months Australian visa were spent waiting for Hendrikus, who was always "just finishing" a website or some maintenance on his Enfield. After dignified Japan, it was fascinating to see drunks toppling off bar-stools and falling down steps in Australia. Rapidly adjusting to life there I had a few "stubbies" too many myself and posed inelegantly for a photo on my bike in my underwear, in which I'd been swimming in a creek with Hendrikus, Andy, and Julie. I enjoyed the bawdy freedom of Australia. There was plenty of room for it, unlike Japan, where space is limited for such uninhibited behaviour. I was amused by company names like "Mind Your Own Business" a computer programme for the self-employed, a mouse-trap called "Dead Easy," and "Down to Earth" for a demolition company.

Hendrikus was no nearer to being ready to leave as he had been when I'd returned. We'd talked about travelling down the notoriously tricky Birdsville Track. I yearned to do more travelling together, but he suggested that I leave on my own. He would catch me up in a few days, bringing with him the tent and stove and all the tools and spares. He needed to finish building an online dating website for a woman in Canberra.

Distressed at his indifference to my presence, but shying away from conflict, I looked at my map and set off on 3rd April. With no suggestion to the contrary, I continued to believe that Hendrikus and I would go to New Zealand together. He'd instructed me to keep checking in so he'd know where I was. I'd make slowly for Birdsville, 1,045 miles south-west of Cairns. As I turned to wave goodbye, only Andy and Julie were still there waving back.

An off-road wooded area near Mount Garnet, 111 miles from Cairns, was my first camp. It rained, and I missed Hendrikus. I slept on the bike under the waterproof cover. I almost turned back but at 5:30AM when the rain stopped, the sound of birdsong and an enamel mug of tea made on my campfire gave me the heart to carry on. My large enamel mug was cooking vessel, cup, and bowl. I did some yoga in the road and felt I was being watched. A little wallaby was seemingly spellbound at my "Salute to the Sun."

The Australian roadhouse, few and far between, is like an oasis in a desert. It has everything the Outback trucker and traveller needs . . . food, fuel, showers, shops, and quite often, a campsite. I stopped at the aptly-named Oasis Roadhouse and had just switched off the engine when I was approached by a driver, who touchingly gave me five dollars to go towards petrol so I could enjoy Australia. Overcome by his gesture, I only just stopped myself from filling my water jerry-can with petrol.

A few road trains were parked up. "Just get off the road if you see one coming," I'd been told, " . . . they won't slow down for you." I wondered if I'd have time to find a safe place to pull over if they go so fast but discovered that the dust cloud created by these massive trucks can be seen from miles away. There was plenty of time to get as far away as possible, not only to avoid an accident but also the aftermath of being covered in dirt. With no rain for three years in some places, dust hovered in the air for ages after a road train passed by. I was in awe of them and would have loved to see inside one.

No matter how small, each Outback town is famous for something. Atherton had its massive curtain fig tree, Greenvale (my next stop) is famous for Stan Coster, a country music composer, and also for its Mozambique sausage tree. It had a phone, too. I got through to Hendrikus to tell him where I was. Oh—joy! He was getting ready to leave. I'd be seeing him in my rear-view mirror soon, and we'd be travelling as happily as we'd been before. Just beyond Greenvale, I shared my wild campsite with several million grasshoppers with powder-yellow wings. They sounded like pebbles tumbling with a withdrawing wave on a shore.

Ever since Stuart Owen Fox told me about being foster-parent to a baby wallaby, I'd hoped to find a travel pet and started to examine recently dead kangaroos at the roadside for orphaned joeys in pouches. Suddenly, just in front of the Blue Water Springs Roadhouse, I found my pet. An apostlebird, hit by a passing road-train was flapping about in the road. I'd come across these birds at the campsite in Mataranka; grey/black with a displeased countenance, they busily forage for grubs and seeds in groups of about twelve (hence the name).

It looked like one wing was broken. As I picked it up, it looked cross rather than frightened but made a dreadful racket until I put it in my bike cover bag. Apart from its wing, it looked robust, so I decided to adopt it, envisioning it travelling with me, sitting on the handlebar and eating out of my hand. The roadhouse had some bird seed, and I rode on with a growing love and sense of responsibility towards this injured creature.

The campground at Fletcher Creek had picnic tables and a group of birdwatchers, who I hoped, would give bird-care advice. But they were unimpressed with such a lowly bird and not a little disgruntled that I had seen some rare Great Australian Bustards on the way that they had spent days searching for, so they ignored my request for advice, dispersing and settling round their campervans like waterfowl on a billabong. My bird took a drink from my little finger dipped in water and ate some seed from a coffee jar lid. It was calm only if its head was in the bag. My sleeping spot was between a picnic table and my bike. I tied some string to the bird's spindly leg to keep it from wandering away, securing the other end to the bike.

As usual, I slept like a log after some apple and cinnamon tea. In the morning I remembered the bird and sat up. There was a scattering of feathers but no apostlebird. The string was still there, and attached to the end was my poor bird's leg. I cried out in horror and dismay. Something had come along and eaten it. A snake? A hawk? A dingo? I'll never know.

I felt guilty for my lack of diligence and went for consolation to a sympathetic couple, Jan and Bob. They were touring the country in their campervan and had given me some of their pot-caught crayfish (or yabbies) for dinner the previous night.

When they left, I talked with another camper, Mike. Fifty, divorced, and on anti-depressants but able to see the funny side of things, he'd bought some land for investment, which utterly useless, had remained unsold for ten years. Finally someone offered him a truck in exchange, the truck he lived and travelled in now. He found my bird story morbidly funny. He asked me to stay, but Charters Towers was calling.

What a grand place. At the museum, I learned that in the 1800s this once thriving town had 32,000 inhabitants in its gold mining heyday compared with the present 9,000. It had its own grand stock exchange and assay office with many elegant old mansions and was such a contrast to the unassuming little towns I'd passed.

The bike was running well, doing fifty-two miles to a gallon, but it was using oil. When I went to buy some, the mechanic chatted to me about the Enfield. "Why on earth . . . ," he asked, "has the bike had three new sets of piston rings?" Hendrikus had included regular decarbonising as proper maintenance, but apparently the carbon should be left on to make a good seal. From then on I'd happily leave it alone.

At the cinema, I watched a thriller before settling for the night beside the bike at the town campsite. I started reading Joan Lindsay's novel *Picnic at Hanging Rock*, a story of the mysterious disappearance of a group of schoolgirls in 1900. Tense and sinister from the beginning, the combination of the story and the film I'd just seen evoked scary imaginings. Something was digging and scratching nearby (someone trying to get out of a coffin?), hopping kangaroos were thumping (a zombie coming for me?), while occasional car headlights lit up the neighbouring trees making a ghostly monochrome scene. But sleep overcame the fear for ten hours until I was awoken by a trail of ants marching over my face.

I went into town for supplies and to post letters to my daughters. Outside the supermarket on the community notice board I saw childcare classes advertised, interesting to me as a health visitor. I was amused to read of the "Beast-feeding support group."

A similarly uplifting message came from Hendrikus. He missed me. I was waiting, travelling only sixty miles a day and telling him where I was whenever I could, hoping in my rear-view mirror to see his fully-loaded Enfield complete with his red jerry cans tied on the crash bars coming up behind me in a cloud of dust. I was still only 372 miles south of Cairns.

On the Flinders Highway, six miles out of Charters Towers, I turned down a track and found a camping spot amongst some trees. It had become my routine to ride until the sun was three fingers above the horizon and then look for somewhere to spend the night, light a fire, have something to eat (rice, sardines, and dried peas were my favourite), get my "bed" out, and read. I scrutinised the bike as I lay next to it ready for sleep, as early as 7:30PM, checking for loose nuts and bolts before dozing off. The moon was so bright it woke me up. A sugar glider floated down to the ground and scampered away. I loved this way of life. How lucky I was.

Diary-writing and looking at the map were morning activities over a cup of tea made by reviving last night's embers. I marked my route on the paper map which despite, being bought many months before, was in remarkably good condition, because once that day's destination was chosen it could be put away, there being no other way to go. Even I couldn't get lost . . .

Diary entry 8AM, 19th April 2004:

"I'd better write this down quickly so the people who find me will know how I died. Lit a fire and siphoned water from the jerry-can for my morning tea. As I sucked, I felt something other than water enter my mouth and bite me and immediately spat it out. I watched a spider give itself a shake and walk away . . . a little brown one about the size of a 5 cent coin (not a red-back or a black widow, then!) it must have crawled up the tube for moisture. Then I noticed a tingling on my tongue. I will continue to write this so that my family will know how I spent my last few days but before I die I must say that I love you all and thank everyone for letting me know and love you. I have had a happy life full of fun. I am happy to die now. Hope I last long enough to enjoy the tea!"

I recorded that I could see the marks on my tongue where the spider bit me. *"Stings and tingles a bit."* Obviously I lived but held my knife ready to do a tracheotomy if required. There was no further swelling, so I packed up and left. Sleeping in the places I picked might well result in my bleached bones never being found by anything but kangaroos.

I rode on through sparse, shrubby, flat land on hard-packed dirt track with occasional holes and troughs. There was nothing outstanding to hold my attention, and my mind started to wander into the past. Wondering why I stayed in circumstances that made me unhappy led me to review a period of my life I had barely considered for over forty years. This was no isolated episode of introspection, which seemed to be getting stronger, perhaps feeding from something in my desolate surroundings.

Pentland is famous for its 1867 gold rush. I met a plump shopkeeper with dry, wrinkled skin, looking like she'd been in this hot, dry country for too long. She sold stray hub caps on which she'd hand-painted pictures of kangaroos. Lack of space on the bike excused my reluctance to buy such things and had prevented offence dozens of times. But I was happy to buy a beetroot sandwich. There must have been a glut of beetroot that year, as beetroot sandwiches, a favourite of mine, were often for sale. I don't think she had much custom, because she wouldn't let me go without a discussion about how everyone is getting like Americans, everybody suing anyone for anything. She'd heard that some Australian parents, whose son had a harmless cherry stone fly into his eye at a party when the boys became boisterous, demanded money for medical bills and even recompense for psychological damage. The safety pin struggling to fasten her blouse strained as she grew increasingly heated.

Prairie, with its population of 103, is "Where the mountains meet the Outback." The hotel is famous for serving a "feral plate" of camel, kangaroo, emu pâté, and goats' cheese. The shopkeeper in the only shop was embroidering a huge picture of the "Four Horses of the Apocalypse," scaling it up by an alarming four times its intended size. She too sold me a beetroot sandwich, which I ate while she discussed the royal family. I'd been surprised when Australians voted to keep the monarchy, but she said, "Oh no, we love the Queen and everything she stands for."

In these vast spaces of the Outback wilderness, I found the only place to go was inside myself. Alone, really alone, for long stretches of undistracted time, I peered into the attics and cellars of my past looking for clues to help me work things out. By then, the Enfield was imbued with a wise personality and was so much more than a means of transport. I talked to it as I would a confidante. "Why didn't my mother accept me for myself, instead of wishing I was like my brother? Was I unlovable?" Recalling childhood occurrences, as if some supernatural projectionist was showing me a film, I felt them anew, recognising reactions I'd had at the time but had no words for. "Feelings" were an unknown language. I could not have expressed my feelings even if I'd known I had any. I was told I was a naughty child, a tomboy. That was my label. I was curious and, therefore, always in trouble. My fearless curiosity led to my frequently getting lost, and I was made to wear reins to stop me running off.

As I rode on endless Aussie tracks, more forgotten scenes from the distant past played themselves in front of me. Freud would suggest they were distorted, that my memories were false, but my recall was detailed and real. I must have been quite a strange little girl. I ate little at family mealtimes but sometimes got up in the night and went to the larder, eating things I didn't think would be missed and then making myself sick; it would be called an eating disorder now. I didn't know why I was doing it, but I knew it was odd because my brother didn't do it. In the kitchen drawer there was a bottle of "Dabitoff," a solvent that removed stains from clothes and smelt nice. This was years before glue-sniffing was recognised. I remember frequently sitting with the bottle under my nose and did the same with my father's petrol lighter. Nobody saw a problem with it, and eventually, I must have stopped doing it. Perhaps that's why I was so naughty and didn't comply with expectations. I was high.

And my brother? I loved him so much his pain was my pain. He rarely got admonished, but I cried if he ever was in trouble. I felt sorry if I beat him at cards. I followed him like a puppy. He must have found me tiresome, especially as we got older, but he never, ever made me feel I was a nuisance. I was not only told to be like him, I *wanted* to be like him. He was everything I wanted to be. But he was clever and academic as well as loving the outdoors. I just liked the outdoors bit and was considered "not good enough." Not until I started going to friends' homes and saw their parents being affectionate and loving did I realise something was amiss with mine. They were not like that. They were both strict about table manners. If I giggled at the table I got a sharp smack across the knuckles with a stick Mum kept in the drawer. My brother never got smacked, but I was hit all the time. I concluded that my mother didn't like me.

As I rode the Outback roads, I felt sorry for the little girl I'd been. As I approached thirteen, I believed I'd been adopted, so out of place did I feel. But it was probably just a stage of growing-up, and perhaps most children feel like that. Nurse training, marriage, and motherhood made me settle down at last.

I rode on in the never-changing landscape, mesmerised by what was appearing in my mind's eye. Mile after mile of little change was like a meditation, and things came to the surface unbidden. Absorbed in self-pity for a while, I then a looked at my parents' own backgrounds and understood them more. They didn't know how to be parents any more than I did. My mother had a severe upbringing with a rigidly religious father. Little wonder she'd had a force-field of unapproachability round her when I was growing up, unable to be tender because she didn't know how. Perhaps she wanted to be cuddly and to say loving things, but the words were too timid to come out. When she became much older the barriers started to crumble and she would let me hug her, but as a child I'd felt an invisible wall, and there were those awful, awful silences. Yet, I had been given every material need, and best of all, for which I shall always thank them, my parents provided me at birth with my wonderful older brother.

Riding was less dreamy when I came across corrugated tracks, I had to be more mindful and try not to add to it by ruminating on my own bumpy ride of the past. I bedded down that night in a nice spot but couldn't sleep. My mental monsters were awake, and they would not let me get away with feeling sorry for myself. They presented me with my own misdeeds. Bitter regrets from the past were awakened. My affair, the lies and deceit, and the ending of my happy family, as I'd perceived it. I saw the mistakes and the choices I'd made but could not undo them.

I continued on the unremarkable road to Hughendon, which didn't announce it was famous for anything. I found it to be a little town with a disproportionately huge entertainment centre. It was Easter Saturday, and a country music festival was in full swing. People were milling about with huge Queensland hats, checked shirts, jeans, and guitars. Broken hearts and Jesus were being crooned about on stage.

I was welcomed by a woman whose husband had an Enfield. She took me home to meet him. He had an immaculate 1949 Enfield twin and didn't think much of mine. Another beetroot sandwich was my lunch back at the festival, where I met a couple who had left Northern Territory because they couldn't stand "the blacks," believing "they get everything for doing nothing." Uninformed of the facts, I kept quiet, privately thinking, "But they were here first!"

I decided to give nearby Winton a miss, even though it is where the lyrics of Australia's unofficial national anthem, *Waltzing Matilda*, were written. Oh well, you can't see everything.

I spoke to Hendrikus, who was vague but said things were going well and that he'd catch me up. As if I'd taken drugs, I was euphoric again and laughed out loud at a pair of alarmed emus running across the road in front of me. With their great feather boa bodies and human-like legs with the knees bending the wrong way, they looked ludicrous—even though they can outrun a kangaroo.

On the long road to Muttaburra, through endless prairie land, a notice warned of 12 miles of bulldust. I fell afoul of the hateful stuff, nosedived into a deep trough, and crashed heavily. The only damage was a broken rear view mirror and a severe knock to my knee that displaced the joint; both disabling and agonising. It had happened before, so I knew to just get on with it and straighten my leg to click it back into position. There was not a soul about. After many expletives to cope with the pain, including some Dutch ones I'd learned, I dug a hole with a tyre-lever beside the rear wheel for it to fall into, which made righting the bike easier; then rode on.

As for the rear-view mirror, I didn't need one anyway, as what I was looking for wasn't appearing. So, I did my own reflecting. What I wanted to see was Hendrikus's Enfield approaching, but all I could see when I looked back was my own cloud of dust and memories; with my mind fixed on the past, I was able to envision them as if they'd only just happened. Moreover, I had no control over the film clips playing in my head but was being made to watch them by some great force.

I smiled ruefully at a sign for Upsan Downs. Someone with a sense of humour must have named it, but I was certainly going through mine. My mind drifted to my equally up and down relationships. I was reminded of the glow of happiness when my mother said something nice to me, and the crushing despair when I'd been naughty and received the silence of disapproval, ignored as if I weren't there.

My relationship with Hendrikus reproduced the same elation and fear; Everest high when Hendrikus said he missed me and was coming but the deepest of lows when he didn't. My marriage hadn't been this way, more like softly rolling countryside than an alpine landscape. But the highs with Hendrikus were like a drug, and although increasingly rare compared with our initial travelling days, a simple "I miss you" would restore the emotional peaks.

Regardless of my unease that something was wrong, I made excuses for Hendrikus. He couldn't travel without working as I could with my regular small income, and he must have felt I was pushing him; but an uneasy feeling that he wasn't being honest with me kept nagging. What he was telling me didn't match up with what he was doing. A week later, my location was less than 621 miles away. He still didn't come. But he missed me, so that was alright . . .

Muttaburra, population 106, swelters in a subtropical climate: one pub, one shop, one church, one dinosaur. Yes—a dinosaur. In

1963, local grazier Doug Langdon dug up an almost perfect skeleton of a forty-foot long, 100 million year-old dinosaur from the Cretaceous period. Predictably, its name is the Muttaburrasaurus Langdoni, and a scale model of it stood in the middle of the little town. The camp ground was closed, so I set up home on the free rest area on the main street not far from the Muttaburrasurus, hardly my usual discrete hideout.

The Enfield and I were as much on view as the nearby celebrity. but unlike the vegetarian dinosaur, that night I ate steak cooked up by a truckload of workers who'd "come by it" when on a job. They pulled in for the night and also shared sausages for breakfast. Free hot showers from a sulphurous bore turned my silver jewellery brown. An enthusiastic local pensioner showed me the museum hospital and an original pioneer's home.

Liz, who worked at the Exchange Hotel, where I had fish and chips and a couple of pots of XXXX beer, offered me a book swap. When I visited her home the next day, she suggested a novel about Aboriginal folklore. She showed me her photos of when she used to drive heavy plant machinery to lay pipelines and cables, having left home at fifteen. Six years before, she also did cattle-mustering, chasing cows by motorbike, grabbing the tail, falling off the dropped bike, and tying the legs of the beast before securing it to a tree. Now she had a lovely home, chooks in the garden, and was happy with her job at the pub. You'd never dream she'd have such a past.

Liz came to visit me at the rest area, bringing with her a wing mirror with the compliments of Doug Langdon, the grazier who had found the Muttaburrasurus. I left beer money for him at the pub, as he was not at home when I went to thank him. I don't know why I have no photos of Muttaburra. I had such a great time there and met some interesting, kind people, but the only photo I took was of a three-legged cat I saw at the petrol station.

The replacement mirror made no difference; I still couldn't see Hendrikus in it.

An advertising board on the way to Longreach announced the Welcome Home Hotel "where the beer's colder than a mother-in-law's tongue." The road was long and straight, but the seventy-two-mile journey was made more interesting when I came upon a woman who was changing a wheel on her truck due to a puncture. The wheel she had just fitted was also punctured, so we took that

one off and fitted a third; an easy job and a nice opportunity for
mè to help someone else for a change. She was so grateful she gave
me her address and told me to phone her when I got to Longreach,
saying that she and her husband were staying on her sister's sheep
station and I'd be very welcome. I knew I wouldn't make it without
an overnight stop and looked for somewhere to rest for the night.

A shaded hollow called Deadman's Creek looked aptly sinister
and smelt of Eau de 'Roo. On investigation, I found a horrible,
inexplicable sight; two mutilated kangaroos with severed tails and
heads, entrails abuzz with flies. I moved on. The next place down
the track had a dead dog and sheep skulls. Between the bushes were
spiders' webs that wound round my face, as elastic as a bungee cord
and as strong as tensile steel. The huge spiders had lozenge-shaped
bodies.

It was getting dark and I really didn't like it there, so I went
on to find a free campground, where I met a friendly couple and
contributed red wine to a "bush oven" meal. On losing their jobs,
they'd bought an old bus and were travelling round looking for
work. He gave me some of his homemade "single malt" whisky. I
think it was flavoured ethanol, as he had other essences for rum
and brandy which he added to the same base substance. As I lay in
my sleeping bag, another couple came to see if I was OK and said,
jokingly, "Mind the snakes!" I didn't sleep well, snakes or no snakes.

It was a depressing place. I could hear the cattle in the yard of the
nearby abattoir in obvious distress. Only a couple of nights ago, I'd
eaten steak. How could I? In the morning, the snake people invited
me over for coffee. She had no front teeth. He'd had eleven children
but left his wife when she'd become a born again Christian. Two
children had died; one from illness, another was murdered. This
candid couple had met at a rehabilitation centre. It was generous of
them to befriend me and give me coffee. They had so little. People
were always kind to me everywhere and I was touched by it. A
huge insect resembling a eucalyptus leaf walked across the path as
we were talking. I picked it up and put it on a gum tree, where it
instantly disappeared. Nature's conjuring trick.

I spent the afternoon at the excellent Stockman's Hall of Fame
museum and then phoned Jan, the woman with the puncture. She
came to guide me to "Dundee," the sheep station where her sister
and brother-in-law kept six and a half thousand merino sheep

for their high quality wool. Instead of my Enfield as a sleeping companion, now a ginger cat shared my bed on the veranda. I spent a few days with the family in their spacious single-storey home with gracious gardens and tennis courts. I marvelled that the sisters would flare up at the men and each other, but as soon as the words were said, they continued as normal with no aftermath of silence.

There had been tragedy here. Two young male members of the family, including their son, had died in auto-gyro accidents. I thought about the people I'd met and how different all our lives were as I helped around the place. Their aerial needed securing, so I was happy to repay their hospitality by going onto the roof and passing the cable underneath the panels; a satisfying and fun job using an electric drill. Jan's sister showed me round some of their vast estate, family picnic spots by billabongs, and endless grazing land. It takes a professional shearer three minutes to clip the fleeces from a sheep, and they are shorn twice a year, most of the wool being sold to China. Before I left, I showed the "Dundee" family how to do the yoga "salute to the sun" in the hope that it would encourage calm.

Back in Longreach, I phoned Cairns and spoke to Julie, who said that Hendrikus was still there and may have found work. I was shocked and confused. Wasn't he coming to join me?

At Windorah there was a dear little camping ground. I met the Sevenoaks brothers, who could trace their family-history back to Kent, then some Jehovah's Witnesses on motorbikes arrived. The first pair of gentlemen provided food, beer, friendship, and amusing anecdotes, whilst the second pair provided alarming information about the forthcoming Armageddon.

The Enfield's clock showed I had travelled 1,625km since leaving Cairns. I checked my emails at a library. A message from Hendrikus told me he hadn't yet left but still wanted to catch me up.

I set off for Dion's Lookout in a state of intense confusion. It was windy up there, and I felt I could see all of Australia as the wind flapped my bike cover like an uncontrolled sail, reminding me of lashing storms and panic. Far from the Straits of Malacca, I was now south of the tropic of Capricorn. Julie must have been mistaken. Hendrikus would be on his way soon. I awoke at dawn, ate leftover garlic bread toasted on my fire, and tightened a loose nut on the front wheel.

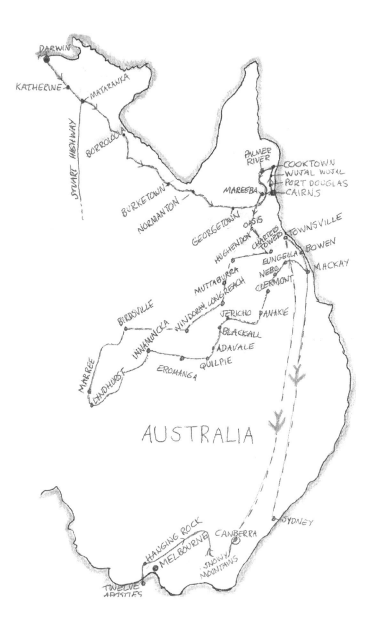

When I got to Birdsville I found commercialism such as I hadn't seen since Darwin. An outpost on the edge of the Simpson Desert, many people restock there, and every business was out to reap the maximum from them and the plentiful tourists—it isn't called Birdsville for nothing; it's a birdwatchers' paradise, as several tributaries converge, forming lakes in national parks. No free camping there. The bars, restaurants, campground, and filling station were clamouring for every cent. The filling station wanted me to pay for the forecourt space I'd use if I did an oil-change, even if I bought the oil there. In a scene reminiscent of India, I was watched by a group of men on the campsite as I took the front wheel off to tighten the nut properly.

I checked in with Hendrikus. This is where we were going to meet if he hadn't already caught up with me. I went cold when he said he wasn't coming. The website for the dating agency woman was going well, but he couldn't yet set off. Thrown into disappointment and panic, I did the oil change in tears at the campsite. I talked to Hendrikus again before I left. He felt everyone was using him, was jealous of my freedom, and wished he was on the road again. Claire wasn't in. Abby reported that she was happy to be stationed by the sea at Gosport, had a good adjutant, and was going to The Gulf in November. My heart sank further. My daughter was going to war.

With Birdsville behind me, I entered South Australia with a worried heart. The first 114 miles of the 372-mile Birdsville Track was not bad at all. It was mostly compacted with sand and fine gravel, sometimes banked up in ridges with pebbles or sharp stones. Nothing but pebbles and the odd sand dune of red and gold, this was once an inland sea. Then it became desert, followed by another period of sea, and now desert again. At 6:30PM the sun went down. I lit a fire between two trees, worried and as lonely as the landscape around me.

It was getting colder as I rode south, refuelling at Mungerannie Roadhouse, and it was midday before I could feel any heat from the sun. Camping wild, I saw few people. At one stop my only company was a dog who jumped up and sat on my seat. She watched whilst I stripped off and had a swim in the clear, brown water in the creek. I slept badly because of the cold and read a book as I warmed up by my fire. On to Maree Roadhouse to stock up and, then after passing Farina, I rode to Lyndhurst.

I'd completed the Birdsville Track, but I didn't feel a sense of achievement. It hadn't been difficult. I phoned Hendrikus to tell him where I was. He wanted me to go back to Cairns, but "There would be things to iron out," he said, implying I had faults that needed addressing. Feeling like a naughty girl again, I didn't know whether to be happy or sad but agreed to go back. We could ship the bikes to New Zealand from there. I'd wanted to see Sydney but was unlikely to go there now.

Instead of retracing my steps, I decided to take the Strzelecki track from Lyndhurst to Innamincka and then find other roads going further to the north-east in the general direction of Cairns. There were no roadhouses or towns on the Strzelecki track, so I filled up with petrol and left at 2PM, saying farewell to some other motorcycle travellers on "proper" off-road bikes who wanted to join me but could not carry enough fuel to make the 293 miles to Innamincka. Good old Enfield. With the jerry-can holding an extra 1.32 gallons (totalling five) I calculated I could get there.

After sixty-two miles, I found a really lovely place to stop by a dried out river-bed. Raucous galahs, like pink parrots, were squawking and having high jinks amongst the gum trees. I oiled the Enfield's drive chain, tightened up the loose studs on the seat, and checked the clutch oil and the tappets. I always turned the bike to face the way I'd come for a quick exit if required, ready to follow my tyre marks out. Eucalyptus leaves, smelling so beautifully fresh, made excellent kindling for a fire to cook baked potato and sardines.

I fell asleep but woke up when a log fell outside the stone circle I had built round the fire, lighting the eucalyptus leaves on the ground in all directions. I could have set fire to the whole of Australia but managed to put them out by stamping about like a frenetically dancing madwoman. On leaving my charred resting-place, the bike got marooned on a ridge of roadside gravel, which necessitated unloading the bike and digging it out. A hot water bore further on provided a natural washroom and foot-soak. Heaven.

It was that "three fingers above the horizon" time. I should look for an overnight retreat. I could have spent the night undisturbed in the middle of the track, for there were no road-trains, trucks, or other traffic. I considered an area under a tree within sight of the road, but it didn't feel right so, although wary of bulldust in the approaching dusk, went on, unsure why I was doing it. I raised my head and shouted, "OK . . . If there IS a God up there, I'd like a roast dinner, good company . . . preferably female, and a comfy bed somewhere nice, please." I hadn't seen anyone for two days. I finished with "Ha—there's a challenge for you." I'd probably have my usual sardines and rice and sleep under another tree somewhere further on.

Blast! No more trees. I admonished myself for passing the one tree for miles. Ahead were some white boxes in the distance. They became portable cabins as I approached. "I'll hide behind those." A woman emerged from one of the cabins. "Crikey!" she cried. "Another woman—can you stay? I'm cooking roast chicken and vegetables for us all."

Ruth and her husband ran an earthmoving business using enormous machines making roads to nearby oilfields. That night I had my roast dinner in good company, including my request for a woman to talk with. I contributed some wine, which I always carried. The cherry on the cake was a night sleeping in a cosy road-train cabin. I didn't know what to think. Not only had all my wishes been granted, I had the extra treat of a night in a road-train. Hmm— was there a God? Outback gods having fun? Or just coincidence? I was in awe, whatever the reason.

Nearing the Strzelecki Desert, the track started to get very sandy and I fell. I had just removed the luggage and was about to get the bike upright when along came a couple in a four-wheel-drive. She was a photographer and he an Anglican vicar visiting some of his parishioners. His parish covered over two THOUSAND square-miles. They were the only people I'd seen all day and as so often happened, came along at just the right time with some welcome help. Strange things were afoot in the Australian Outback.

I was proud of my Enfield. Petrol leaked from the petrol cap each time I fell, but it still did 250 miles, mostly in low gears, before I topped up from the jerry-can just prior to reaching busy Innamincka. Rain started to pour, and the track became an uphill, bumpy ice-rink with slithery mud over hard-baked earth. Soaked, I made it to the roadhouse having fallen twice, while other travellers had to push abandoned cars off the track. With so many people stranded at the roadhouse, all the accommodation was full, so I slept on the floor in someone else's room. It rained all the next day, and I read the book I'd been given in Muttaburra. In the story, an Aboriginal wrongdoer was informally sentenced to death, not by any white-man's law but by having "a tribal bone" pointed at him. He died. In this land of magic, I could well believe that such things are possible.

The flooded airstrip was unusable, but the pilot of a small plane used the track as a runway and off went a handful of people to their next destination—a very expensive holiday. Other people played pool to pass the time, waiting for the flooding to subside. An Aboriginal man was employed by a drilling company to advise about avoiding sacred places. Well paid, he bought all stranded people drinks. The rain stopped, and a few of us went out to survey conditions. Eagles and crows were feasting on fish stuck in pools, unable to swim against the frantic Cooper River. I caught one with my hands. I posted letters, phoned my daughters, and finally set off on a slithery, flooded track. After sixty miles of green pastureland the road became very welcome bitumen that I had quite forgotten existed.

Eromanga. Population 30–40. Famous for cattle, sheep, oil wells, opal mines, and for being "furtherest from the sea." Now back in Queensland, I stayed in a tiny room at the pub for ten dollars, joined in with some jackaroos who had come to town for the town barbecue and booze-up (raising funds for the Royal Flying Doctor Service), and watched an Aussie Rules game on TV. After all the beer they'd drunk, the first for three weeks, it was more loutback than Outback, and there was an inevitable fight amongst the ranch hands. One was still missing the following day. An emergency team went searching, but he hadn't been found by the time I left. Someone kindly took me home to use their washing machine; it was my first change of clothes in a month. I left lovely Eromanga after a drink with some locals who liked the royal family. "All except that Duke of Edinburgh . . . ," said one lady, "I met him once and he eyed up my daughter."

I saw no vehicles for the sixty-five miles to Quilpie, which was closed for a bank holiday. Adavale was 62 miles further, and I could reach it if I pushed on. I shouldn't have been riding at dusk; kangaroos come out to feed, and although they run away when they see you, they can get in a panic and run straight back.

So, I arrived at Adavale with an injured kangaroo that had launched itself at my rear wheel just after it had run away. I'd scooped it up and done the "this is my pet" thing again and rode up to the pub crying out for help with this creature. "Let me deal with that young fella for you," said the kind man at the pub as he took it round the back. I heard a shot, and my pet was dead. The tears wouldn't stop, and I had to be given several beers. I felt so guilty. "Shouldn't have been out at dusk, should have gone slower. I've killed another creature." In the morning they said that they viewed kangaroos as vermin, and mine would have grown to a full adult, much too big to carry on a motorbike. Again, I said to myself, "But they were here first."

The population of Adavale is twenty "when everyone's home." One chap took me to the tip to show me old rubbish, undisturbed for eighty years. Bottles had started to opalesce from the silica in the soil, and I found an antique Bovril bottle to take back for Julie, who collected such treasures. The road onwards became diverse again with soft, grassy floodplain, trees, bushes, and outcrops of rock. I tootled along until, an hour or so after leaving Adavale, I had a strong feeling to check my sleeping-bag. It wasn't there. It could have dropped out at any stage. There was no choice but to go back and look for it. It was only 100 yards back; the Outback gods were looking after me again.

Blackall, the next place on the map, was famous for once having a black stump that was used as a marker for surveying Queensland and "Beyond the black stump" is an expression to mean the "middle of nowhere." I chatted to the caretaker of the museum there and snuggled down that night near some old ploughs.

The next day, I arrived in the charming little town of Jericho, so irresistible that I stayed for a few days. A family who were home-schooling their daughter, Bonnie, befriended me on the campsite. Kerry baked some potatoes on the campfire that I slept beside at night and gave me her old "Jackaroo" hat. In the town there was a humorous clay model of all the houses and people who lived there; the policeman who returned from a shift one day to find someone had put a camel in his garden, a man who had so many animals in his house he had to sleep out in his yard, a woman who made cakes. Another model showed the walls of Jericho being blown down by Joshua's trumpet, but nobody could enlighten me any further about why this little settlement had been given its name.

Also living on the campground was John, a tall and gentle man, fitted with an artificial voice-box after his had been removed through cancer. He kept a few horses and was teaching Bonnie to ride. One day I went with them. All went well until I saw a black-headed python. My horse spotted it too. I'd seen such scenes in *The Lone Ranger* so knew what to expect. The horse bolted. I just had time to grab its mane and flatten myself against its neck to avoid overhead branches until it stopped. Jericho was another place I could have stayed forever, but saying farewells to the people and horse, I saddled up my far more controllable Enfield and rode on to Anaki and Sapphire.

I thought I had come across an art gallery at Anaki, however, on entering found it to be a church. I was invited in while a service, unlike any other I'd attended, was in progress. The ecumenical preacher was a very attractive woman who looked like Dusty Springfield. She talked about love and kindness without reference to any deity. Somehow, I ended up sleeping at her house that night, a bewitching home with a cottagey feel to it, made and designed by Denise and her husband.

She told me the next morning that she was a Catholic but also a witch. The mixture didn't seem too odd until she gave me some leaflets about Buddhism and Gnosticism too. Another amazing Outback woman. On my way out the next day, I passed an area of little shacks used by people fossicking for sapphires. Denise had found many and gave me some uncut ones. Not so long ago, someone had unearthed one of the biggest gems ever found.

I saw a pimple-like hill and went to investigate, leading me to ride over hummocks, long grass, and ridges. The Enfield got stuck on one and toppled over in another area where spiders lurked in the corners of their stretchy webs. Luggage off again. The bike wouldn't start, and I envisioned a few nightmares that night if I had to stay there. Cleaning the plug and appealing to the now familiar Outback gods worked once more. I got out and back to the safety of the track alongside a busy railway.

Intending to treat myself to a comfy room there, Nebo, a busy mining town, was full. At that point I really didn't care where I slept as long as it wasn't with those spiders. So when the only place to stay turned out to be a toilet in the showground shower block, although ashamed at the depths I'd sunk to, I was really grateful. The toilet was clean, warm, and dry, and in the morning I showered in my en-suite accommodation.

I phoned Hendrikus. He said he would ride south to meet me and to keep telling him where I was. Hope blossomed again. Work, he said, was going "really, really, well." I was now only about 186 miles from the South Pacific Ocean. I'd ride through Eungella National Park and go up the coast, where Hendrikus and I would meet somewhere. How lovely.

The deserted narrow dirt track through Eungella ran up and down, round and between the hills—perfect all-day Enfield country. The afternoon became evening, and soon the bike was tootling happily along the track to a deserted campground. I'd just lit a fire and was drawing a picture for Abby when a red camper van drew up next to me.

A lone Maltese/British man introduced himself as Michael. As dusk approached, he started bringing out some strange things in cases from his van and assembled an enormous telescope. After sharing our food and wine, he showed me the Moon, Jupiter, and Saturn. So powerful was his telescope, and with no light pollution there, I could see the rings around the planets and the craters of the moon. I was astounded to see how quickly the moon was moving, and the telescope had to be altered every few minutes to find it again. "It's not the moon, it's us," Michael laughed. We stayed up late comparing travel experiences. I slept beside the fire, waking in the early hours, watching the moon again before dawn and making tea. We exchanged contact details. He was heading for the coast, too. He was the first non-Australian I'd met since leaving Cairns.

I felt emotionally "wobbly" at Broken River. I'd been trying to contact Hendrikus. Julie said that, even though his things were still in Cairns, he was nowhere to be found.

It was the same when I reached Platypus Bush Camp at Finch Hatton. I felt a crashing sense of desolation, even though surrounded by other travellers and sighting a duck-billed platypus.

I couldn't cope with silences between people, crashing like a wintery hush when snow has fallen. I had a fear of them, having developed an ability to pick up on any sort of atmosphere in my childhood home. No-one shouted or accused or blamed. No words needed to be said. I just knew there was trouble. I'd be in a state of fear and confusion, trying to work out what it was I'd done. Now, confronted with the silent treatment by Hendrikus, I reverted to trying to work out how I had upset him. It was like entertaining an old, but unwelcome visitor. Like once again wearing an old garment that you thought you'd thrown out but found again, and although you didn't like it, it was familiar so you put it on. I fell into self-blame every time.

I realised my sojourn in the Outback was over. If a place can be harsh and soft at the same time, the Outback is it. I'd so much enjoyed its huge spaces and its people, large in generosity, living in isolated conditions, unimpressed by luxury and opulence; it was paradise for me.

I left a message on Hendrikus's mobile begging for contact. Days went by with no message from him. So, I made a rash decision: I would go to Sydney.

A kind family, friends of the bushcamp owner, allowed me to keep the Enfield at their home in Mackay while I flew to Sydney for six days, just long enough to see the fantastic aquarium, zoo, and the iconic opera house. Unlike the Taj Mahal, it didn't overwhelm me to tears, but it did make me smile because of its familiarity. I met a friend I knew from Malaysia. We walked over Sydney Harbour Bridge and visited the observatory, pertinent for me having just seen some planets quite close-up. We had a swim on Manley Beach.

Then I flew back to the lovely family who had stored the Enfield. Her father worked at the tip. He rescued discarded washing machines, repaired them, and sold them again. Most needed only filter-cleaning or hose unblocking. People just threw them away and got a new one.

I had my mobile phone with me (Abby had chosen the *Mexican Hat Dance* for my ringtone when I was last home—it always made me laugh), but Hendrikus remained silent.

I had reached Proserpine going north towards Cairns and was staying in a little pub. Early in the morning of 24th May 2004 the *Mexican Hat Dance* awoke me. It was Hendrikus. Overjoyed, I asked him where he was; "I'm in Canberra." What was he doing in Canberra? He was supposed to be riding from Cairns to meet me. "I've got something to tell you. I have fallen in love with someone else."

It was the woman who had the dating agency. I said all the right things like "I hope you'll be happy. Thanks for everything." That was that, then. I hadn't realised it at the time, but our travelling days together had ended when we arrived at the trailer park in Cairns. I could not allow myself to be bitter. Seventeen years my junior, I knew this wouldn't last forever, and the four years we had together were beyond my wildest dreams. I could allow myself no regrets, but I was devastated and sorrowful all the same.

Although I realised all the signs were there, I hadn't expected that. But at least I knew where I was now. The catalogue of mixed messages in the three weeks since I'd left Cairns, being told he was going to catch me up, then he wasn't, then summoning me back to Cairns with a review of my behaviour in the offing, the gradual feeling of devaluation, the psychological zigzagging; he'd been playing with me. The end was a relief.

After a few days on the coast at Bowen in the company of Michael, the Maltese moon-watcher, who I met up with again, I went to Townsville and arranged to ship my bike to New Zealand.

I was emotionally rescued by Sue after we met at a backpackers' hostel. I was leaving because of some frightening and ill-mannered male German guests just as she arrived on her motorbike to visit a relative. She took me home, gave me emotional comfort, and shared Milo, her very relaxed cat, with me. Her lovely home contained films and books and words of wisdom pinned to the walls. It was just what I needed. She went away for the weekend, leaving me with "Do whatever Milo does. When he stretches, you stretch. When he eats, you eat. When he sleeps, you sleep." I stayed for a week, left the bike with the shipping agent, and then was invited to stay in Canberra with Stuart Owen Fox, the photographer I'd met in Cooktown.

Stuart appointed himself as my guide, in more ways than one. He drove to creepy Hanging Rock in Victoria, where I saw my first koala bear, to the Twelve Apostles rock stacks in the sea, and to the Snowy Mountains, where we slowed down on a quiet road to let a wombat cross, which then hid its face in its paws imagining we couldn't see it. Whatever I had left unexamined during my Outback self-analysis, was completed by Stuart during weeks of psychoanalysis. Stuart took me apart and examined every piece of my past, suggesting things about me that I hadn't even considered. When he'd finished, he introduced me to his friends, who also thought I was fair game and had a go as well.

One, a brilliant water-colour artist, concluded that my mother resented my arrival, because without me, she could be seen as just another lone mother who had lost her husband in the war. I was born in 1950, and in those days of social respectability, she couldn't get away with having an illegitimate child. Unable to marry because my father's existing wife would not divorce him, she changed her name by deed poll and brought my father into her household (and it was always *her* household). Instantly, she changed from being an independent businesswoman with a fatherless son to a "wife" with a family. They were not the happiest of couples. Perhaps she blamed me.

Then, Stuart's Tibetan monk friend helpfully made an analogy comparing the men I went into relationships with and a recipe for sponge cakes. Although I wanted to change and make rock cakes, i.e. kind and loving men, I always chose the same ingredients and made the same old sponge cakes with men for whom I must spend all my time trying to please.

When my analysis ended, I felt something had been achieved. I could understand why I was as I was, why I did what I did, and why I felt how I felt. I'd been in my wilderness, like some ascetic in the desert finding the meaning of my existence, and now it was time to go forth armed with this new insight. I was going to New Zealand as a new me. But one old thing would be with me, my one constant companion; my beloved Enfield Bullet, and it would be there waiting for me.

At Canberra airport, I phoned Julie to thank her for her generosity and friendship. She told me Hendrikus was getting married. It all became clear why I'd been dumped. He wanted to stay in Australia. I laughed and got on the plane.

14
NEW ZEALAND

SWEET AS

"New Zealand . . . 994 miles from tip to toe; 1,118 miles of coastline. Landscapes range from coastal beach and broadleaf coastal forest to estuarine swamps, vast inland plains, podocarp-covered hills, sub-alpine ranges, and mountains capped with snow. There are thermal regions and volcanoes. It has minerals, unique forests, and wildlife." So said the guide book. I was to have all this and who knew what else?

It had cost £271 to ship the Enfield from Australia. This included crating, shipping, agency costs, Government Sales Tax, customs clearance, and biosecurity inspection, plus mysterious extra charges for devanning and forestry. Even though I'd been warned of mugging, theft, and murder in "dangerous" places in Asia, the only place I'd ever had anything stolen was in Australia, where an entire pannier bag was pinched from the bike in Townsville, so I needed to replace spare parts and manuals.

The Royal Enfield dealer in Auckland assured me by email that they could supply everything. Trevor and his business partner, Frank, couldn't have been kinder. Disillusioned by constant strikes, they had quit the UK with their families in the 1970s. Trevor collected me from the airport and showed me some of the sights of Auckland, despite my reeking of alcohol, having thrown wine all over myself on the flight. He took me to a backpackers' hostel, and when my Enfield was ready for collection, Frank took me and a trailer to the docks, loaded it, and took it to their workshop, where it had some professional maintenance. I painted it, careful to preserve the original hand-painted gold stripe on the black tank.

I liked Auckland. It had a crisp but friendly feel with its bridge and clean harbour full of sleek seafaring yachts. Smart business-people hurried around, a noticeable contrast to relaxed Outback Australia. I missed morning birdsong. Auckland was quiet and, of course, there were no kangaroos.

As a film addict, I took full advantage of the Auckland Film Festival, often accompanied at the Civic Theatre by Maya, a big, loud and lovely German midwife who was staying at my hostel. My favourite film was *Ae Fond Kiss*, a Ken Loach film set in Glasgow. It was a touchingly funny story about a Pakistani man and an Irish Catholic woman in Glasgow who fall in love and struggle with religious and cultural difficulties. The theatre was spectacular in itself; had it not been graced with Buddhas, it might have been a splendid golden palace in Morocco with its prancing horses and green-eyed panthers. The auditorium had an ever-changing cloudscape and stars on the ceiling.

When I had the bike back, I stayed just north of Auckland with Margot, the daughter of Margaret, a remarkable seventy-two year old potter I'd travelled with in Laos during my year backpacking. She'd said, "If you ever come to NZ . . . ," so I'd sent a post-card from Australia saying I was on my way and to put the kettle on. When Margot, a sculptor/stone-carver replied, she told me of her mother's death the previous year, "But do come. Any friend of Mum's . . . " There was a fridge magnet declaring "Fish and guests go off after three days," but I was made so welcome I overstayed by a week, helping around her home and garden in a secluded dell with her cats and dog and huge stone-carvings as I acclimatised to my new surroundings and being single.

The army surplus store in Auckland provided two ex-military bags, a perfect fit for the Enfield's racks. For the first time in my life I had matching luggage. Smartened up and revived, the bike and I set off north to explore the "top end"—with a mobile phone at Margot's insistence.

Outside Auckland there was little urban sprawl. It was August, the equivalent of February in Britain, and although there was no snow in what is deemed "the winterless north," it was too cold for sleeping out, even though the trees were in full leaf. I was puzzled until I learned that New Zealand's indigenous trees do not lose their leaves.

The first place I stopped was at the Kauri Museum at Matakohe, eighty-seven miles north of Auckland. As it was a tree museum I was reminded of Joni Mitchell's song, *Big Yellow Taxi*. A dear little caravan was for hire at the motorcamp for twenty dollars. It was perfect. Also staying there was a group of young women, one of whom, the enchanting "Princess Itka," was inspired by my mode of transport.

"You're cool."

"Oh—I don't want to be cool."

"That's REALLY cool."

She wasn't really a princess, but for one so young, Itka had wise advice about choosing men who would not manipulate me. I went to look at the museum. A drainage pipe made by connecting empty tin-cans together end-to-end demonstrated the innovative methods of the early explorers. A man approached; "They certainly knew how to make do with what they had in those days, didn't they?"

Don't visit a museum or art gallery with me. I have a high tolerance level for explanatory labels and leave only when I am brain-numb with information. Therefore, I was in the Kauri Museum for some considerable time and kept bumping into the man who had spoken to me. I was reading how Kauri trees were felled almost to extinction from the 1800s, before they were protected, when I noticed him looking at the exhibit from the opposite side. If I went to look at something else, he'd be there too. He made me laugh. And that was it.

Paul and I had coffee in the café when the museum closed, dinner in the restaurant when the café closed, and came back for breakfast the next morning. Any heartache, regrets, or dwelling on the past were swept away with his whirlwind arrival. He coloured, enriched, and influenced my experience from the minute we met.

He told me his story. Once a mechanic and dairy farmer, he'd spent the last seven years fighting a legal battle against another farmer to whom he had leased some cows and who then refused to return them. Paul had lost two farms, his marriage, and most of his money. The police did not support him, and subsequently, he considered the New Zealand justice system to be corrupt. When he could no longer pay lawyers, he represented himself in court and made his own prosecutions. He would not rest until he received justice. To some, it would be a fuss over nothing. To him, it was his life's work. What did I think about it all? It was none of my business. It wasn't that I didn't care, but quite a bit of me didn't believe that such a thing could happen in pristine New Zealand. I couldn't decide if he was a madman or a hero.

Despite his troubles, he was radiant and enthusiastic about life. I liked and admired him but being newly light of heart and spirit, didn't want to get involved. I was going north, but he invited me to call in to see him at his home in Edgecumbe, in the enticingly named Bay of Plenty, on my way south in a couple of weeks or so. He gave me his cousin's address and suggested a visit to the family on my way north. As I was to discover, this sort of open invitation to someone else's home is common in New Zealand due, I supposed, to the sparsity of people and places to stay in the harsh days before tourism. They had no phone, so I couldn't ask if they minded a complete stranger staying with them.

A ranger cooked me curry after I booked into a warm cabin in beautiful Waipura Forest, even providing after-dinner whisky cream liqueur. Travelling alone certainly had its advantages. I was meeting people and having fun.

The next day I gasped at the size and presence of Tane Mahutu, New Zealand's largest Kauri tree, forty-six feet in circumference and a hundred and seventy feet tall. Just imagine.

Many of the roads should have had signs warning of forthcoming stunning views, because I ended up on the other side of the road and nearly fell off the bike at the brow of a hill approaching Opononi. Then the couple in the car I almost ran into invited me to stay at their home. The land slid into the blue sea below me. Inland lakes sparkled in the sunshine, surrounded by forests. Everything I'd heard about New Zealand's unspoiled beauty was true. This was where Paul's cousin lived.

Had I accidentally wandered into a film set? A cart-horse with a smile came to greet me at the farm-house, followed by a waggy dog. A cat jumped from the ground onto my shoulder. An elderly man dressed in a full-length brown tunic and wool cape was at home. He had a long white beard and was kindly in a wizardly way. His story was intriguing. Studying at an Anglican theological college, he switched to Catholicism just before the end of the course. He married, and he and his wife brought up nine children over twenty-six years there, living off the land. Still curious about philosophy, he taught himself Classical Chinese so he could translate the *Tao Te Ching* ("The Power of Nothingness") the sixth century B. C. philosophy of Lao Tzu. He then wrote a book about it, which I read whilst I stayed there.

Amongst many other things, I learned that I should "have without possessing" and that "the only useful quality is weakness."

The family welcomed me as kindly as if I were a happily anticipated guest. The whole place, the people and animals, gave it an enchanted feel. With no electricity and untouched by materialism, Cathy and Joseph lived and worked with love—love for each other, their children, love for the land, animals, neighbours, and their God. "We cannot do anything without God," they admonished when I suggested they were self-sufficient.

They lived simply on home-grown food and milked their cows by hand. We ate purple maize porridge with fresh milk and cream from their cows and tangerines from the garden. Prayers were at 7AM, announced by a bell. Each family member contributed a prayer, a reading, or an observation to be grateful for. All seven children were home educated. Joseph said of school, "It's a capitalist training scheme. You put children in at one end and out of the other come money-needing capitalist consumers. We prefer living like this." Two of the children had been to university and travelled to Europe but came home to the farm. Cathy cooked all meals on an open fire.

The children collected wood and helped with growing food and caring for the delightful animals. A cat named Bert, disabled through being trodden on by a horse as a kitten, staggered around as if drunk. He had to fend for himself but couldn't manipulate his head into the porridge pan for the leftovers, so I scooped some out, and he ate from my hand.

One of the children was ten-year old Clarence, who was also disabled due to a near-drowning incident. I loved him immediately and didn't even mind, when with concentrated effort, he dribbled into my tea when he carried it to me. All the animals had personalities, and I felt I was amongst characters in a children's story. A pet dog was so loving that it accompanied me to my bed and even out to the field to the deep drop toilet. I would have stayed longer, but after two nights felt I'd better go. "Those who flow through life as life flows feel no wear, feel no tear, need no mending, no repair."

I left with this from Lao Tzu: "There is no greater evil than not knowing what is enough; no greater fault than wanting to acquire. For when you know that enough is enough there is always enough." As I re-joined the rest of the world on the main road, the sun came out and the sky was suddenly full of rainbows.

The bendy roads enabled me and the Enfield to do some flipping-flopping, a treat I hadn't had in Australia. The bike was in fine form, and I had to hold it back once or twice when there were knee-scrapers of bends. It was one of those "the bike and I are one" rides. I was enjoying it too much to stop for anything. Even when it started to rain I donned waterproofs instead of sheltering. I was happy.

The many warnings about riding up Ninety Mile Beach and photos of stranded cars didn't deter me.

Diary entry for 24th August 2004:

> *"I am sitting on a hill in Apihara in the warm sunshine and can see Ninety Mile Beach disappearing into the distance. I am apprehensive about riding it tomorrow as there are rivers running onto it and soft sand where vehicles get stranded."*

But I was calm from my Taoist learnings, and after a night of dreams featuring my mastery of thick sand, I believed the bike and I would handle it. I set off when the tide was low enough.

> *"Full of bacon and egg and with my helmet off, I set off under a cloudless blue sky. Rode onto the beach and shrieked for joy! No problems at all. Slowed down to cross a stream and sped up the other side yelling aloud from sheer pleasure!*

Stopped to talk to some people who were digging for tua-tua
shellfish."

I was very aware that if anything had gone wrong with the bike
and I couldn't move it, I would just have to watch the tide wash
over it. This element of risk added to the excitement and sense of
achievement. At a bluff there was a section of beach covered in a
thick layer of pink and white shells: *"A bit slidey but they made a
nice crunchy noise under the tyres."*

Whooping and grinning with pleasure at this hours-long,
stimulating journey, I left the beach and rode a track to the
lighthouse at Cape Reinga, where a signpost by the lighthouse told
me I was almost 125,000 miles from London. I was content to be
alone like the lighthouse. Except that I wasn't always alone ... Why
is it that when you stop for a discreet wee, someone or something
comes along? With nobody about for what seemed like ninety
miles (fifty-four miles, actually) a herd of a dozen curious wild
horses surrounded me.

Te Paki Stream is at the end of the beach and a challenging
way on and off it. It is a bit of a legend for off-road vehicles. I
wanted to test myself but dropped the bike at the start. I must
have been getting stronger, because I picked it up with the luggage
on. I got to the top of the sandy stream and dismounted. Massive
sand-dunes rose on my right. I climbed up one then slid down on
my bottom. My Enfield did Ninety Mile Beach AND the Te Paki
Stream.

It started to rain heavily. Cold and wet, I headed south, stopping
at a shop to buy some food. Not only did the shopkeeper give me
some avocados, she also gave me the name and address of someone
to stay with when I got to the Coromandel Coast.

The ride was chilly. A hot drink was called for. I called into a
pub for a quick coffee but ended up staying for three days. There
was a warm welcome at the family-run Waipapakauri Hotel. "You
should stay for the Annual Possum Hunters' Duck Dinner," said
Delwyn temptingly. In Australia possums are protected. People
welcome them into their gardens. In New Zealand they are hated
with a vengeance. Why the different attitude? Possums are eating
New Zealand. They are munching crops, forests, rare trees, and eggs
of rare birds. They spread bovine TB and eat the flowers from trees
that the native birds need for nectar. They were brought there for

their fur, like cane toads brought to Australia to keep insects under control, but it was a huge mistake.

It was Friday night, and so after settling into my comfortable room containing a bed with an electric blanket, I went to the bar with its open fire. People were playing cards, and at least three raffles took place during the course of the evening. Everyone was getting a bit tiddly.

I was befriended by a huge Maori woman called "Luvvie," until she was told to leave me alone. Someone who had travelled in England told me she'd often been invited to stay at people's homes during her stay, so I didn't feel too bad about accepting hospitality in New Zealand. "Gosh—you're brave. Good for you, girl!" people exclaimed. The admiration I received was hardly justified. Bravery is doing something frightening, but I was having a great time.

At the Possum Hunters' Dinner I met Malcolm, a millionaire with a yacht moored in nearby Rangaunu Bay. He'd made his fortune by breeding bees and sending disease-resistant queens all over the world. Would I like to go for a sail tomorrow? I'd vowed to never get back in a boat again after my Malaysia to Indonesia experience, but this time my bike was safely ashore. I enjoyed the day watching blue penguins and admiring the scenery; sailing wasn't too bad after all. Rows and heaps of dead possums were proudly exhibited by hunters the day I left. "Run over as many possums as you can," I was urged.

Emails to and from Paul were warm as I travelled south and closer to Edgecumbe.

I arrived at Russell via a ferry and "grass growing in the middle' roads." My hitherto rosy opinion of the police had been affected by the things Paul had told me, so when I was asked for my documents by an officer in Russell, I was apprehensive. As my documents were scrutinised, I thought it best to say nothing. All correct, they were handed back without comment. My tank was nearly empty, but the petrol station had closed for the night.

A couple who had seen me pull into the forecourt shyly invited me to stay with them, so with a "Follow us!" I rode behind them but noticed that the bike spluttered when going uphill. Should I alter the float? Was it bits in the bottom of the tank clogging up the fuel-pipe somewhere? Was it engine-trouble? Had water got in the tank when I'd hosed the salt off after Ninety Mile Beach? I followed

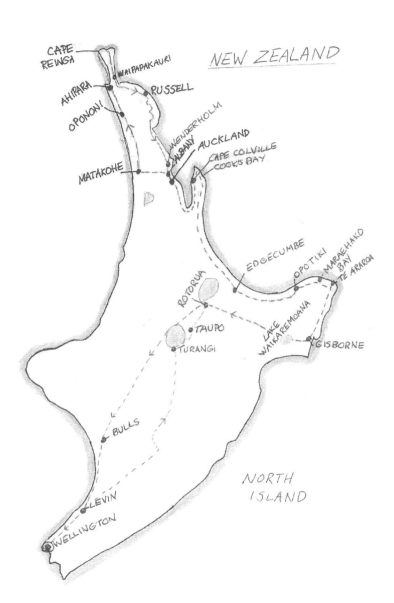

NEW ZEALAND

CAPE REINGA
WAIPAPAKAURI
AHIPARA
RUSSELL
OPONONI
WENDERHOLM
ALBANY
AUCKLAND
CAPE COLVILLE
COOK'S BAY
MATAKOHE
EDGECUMBE
OPOTIKI
MARAEHAKO BAY
TE ARAROA
ROTORUA
TAUPO
LAKE WAIKAREMOANA
TURANGI
GISBORNE
BULLS
NORTH ISLAND
LEVIN
WELLINGTON

them in the dark to their garage, secured the bike, and the three of us went off . . . in a canoe.

At high tide their house was reachable only by boat. It was a large canoe and held the three of us, their shopping, and my luggage. What a treat to hear paddles lapping the water by moonlight and feel the surge of forward movement with each stroke. Linden and Brenda had built their house themselves in the days before strict building regulations had been imposed. It had no electricity, and inside, once the fire and lamps were lit, the round room took shape. It was arranged so that the kitchen area had the fire for cooking. Separating it from the rest of the room was an elegant French chiffonier. Further round was a dining space, study, and a sitting area. A spiral staircase led to the bedrooms. For such a small room it had a surprising amount of space. Three children, all home-educated, had been brought up there.

There were other buildings outside the house. The guest room was a "sleep-out" wooden shed reached by a path of white shells shining the way in the moonlight. The outside compost toilet had a shovel for earth instead of a water flush. In the morning, I saw that their home was like an upturned jelly-mould covered in tiles reaching to the ground with gaps for doors and windows. The spectacular bathroom was an extra building made from stainless steel and Perspex. It contained a bath, shower, and washbasin.

The whole place was solar-powered. What an idyllic *Swallows and Amazons* upbringing those children must have had . . . building boats, playing in the forest, and keeping pets. Linden, who had owned several English motorbikes, listened to the Enfield with his ear to a piece of wood placed against the engine before I left the next morning and declared it to be well.

As I neared Auckland, I fancied a bit of mud-riding before returning to Margot's, so dived down a "no exit" track. After a few miles it terminated at Wenderholm motor camp. Covered in mud and a grin, I wanted a photo so approached the only person there.

Keith told me I was beautiful and proposed to me, but I'd learned from Tao Te Ching to pursue an ego-less existence, so the flattery didn't go to my head. Keith lived in a minimalist large square box on an old Morris Commercial flat-bed truck and spent his life touring round New Zealand practicing naturism whenever he could. Once a high-earner with an expensive yacht, he quit sailing following a serious storm where he, together with many other sailors in the flotilla, lost his yacht and was rescued by the French navy. He now kept on solid ground and painted greetings cards and landscapes for a living.

Returning to Margot's was like going home. She had four cats and a very tolerant Staffordshire bull terrier. My favourite animal was Stinky-Minky, a cantankerous moggy who resented my presence because where I slept was her bed. She spat at me and growled when I pulled back the covers to get in before she slunk off somewhere else. Then there'd be a fight as she ousted another cat from its bed for herself.

Various jobs like tappets adjustment, oil-change, getting spare keys cut, and having a dental check-up needed doing. In Auckland, after seeing a dentist, I found a posh area where hundred year-old houses had wrought-ironwork like lace hanging from the eaves. Gardens were pretty. These were Auckland's oldest dwellings.

I had a phone call from Claire. "I'm off to Moscow!" (Where three-hundred people had just died in a terrorist attack.) "I was almost a widow at the weekend when Peter had a racetrack accident (unhurt), and Abby's going to Iraq, but then you're not a worrier, are you Mum." ARGHHHH!

Then I had a text from Abby saying how excited she was to be going to Iraq. In a few words she told me everything I wanted to know. She said, "If I die, you were ace, and I forgive you for making me eat liver!" She also admonished me for smoking marijuana in Thailand. That text meant everything to me. I didn't want her to go to Iraq, but it was her choice and she'd been brought up to make her own decisions, so I wished her well. Like my racing-driver son-in-law, there was little point in saying "be careful," was there?

It was hard leaving Margot's, but everyone had advice about places I must see. The Coromandel Coast, east of Auckland, was one of those. All along the coast I saw little wooden houses. It is quite popular to own a bach, as they are called, for weekends. I stopped to look at the map and checked my phone. Bad news from Paul. His truck had been impounded to pay for court costs.

As I stood by my bike, a couple originally from Northern Ireland drew up, gave me their address, and invited me to stay with them. New Zealanders were so generous. It was a most thrilling ride along a track by the side of the sea, milk-frothy from storms as it whisked onto me. I was blown towards the boiling foam as the wind bounced off a hill and tried to shove me into the waves. It was so exhilarating that at Cape Colville I turned round and did it again before finding Liz and Herb's lovely home in a kauri forest. A fire was lit, a casserole on, and wine ready.

Years before, they had travelled to Pakistan on a BSA so understood what a relief it is to be offered accommodation and friendship after a day's travel. Apart from the bike spluttering again, life just couldn't get better. They were surrounded by forests of rare trees and beautiful beaches with views of the islands. Most trees grow looking like they will when mature, but not the bizarre lancewood. Until it reaches about twenty years, its stiff, leathery serrated leaves, about a half-inch wide by a yard long, droop downwards from a single thin stem. When it gets older, the stem starts to branch out and the leaves get wider, shorter, and softer, looking nothing like it used to and resembling a normal tree of sorts. Tui birds and fantails displayed and sang in the garden. I was worried that I might get beauty overload.

Liz and Herb suggested places to visit when I got to South Island, including the Molesworth track, open only in January due to rough terrain and weather conditions. It was September; plenty of time to get there for when it was open. Liz took me to her yoga class. The view of the sea from the studio was rather better than most cheerless village halls where I'd practiced before. Unable to do a particular pose accurately because my Pakistani-repaired leg stuck out at an angle, the teacher came along and tried unsuccessfully to correct it.

Sunny spring weather shook me out of this comfy spot and away from this generous couple. At Cook's Bay I imagined the *Endeavour* moored here whilst Captain Cook's astronomer monitored the passing of Mercury across the sun in 1769, thus helping to determine the earth's distance from the sun using the cutting-edge technology of the time . . . a sextant.

The bike continued spluttering. I raised the needle in the carburettor to its highest setting to increase petrol flow.

I settled into Paul's rented home for the month of October. He filed off the shoulders of the carburettor casing to allow the float more movement. He also overhauled the choke. The bike was still difficult to kick-start, but I didn't mind, as the weather was still cold; it warmed me up. Paul and I became increasingly fond of each other. I was torn. I liked him because he was kind and funny. We both liked the outdoors and motorbikes. He also liked my cooking and my Enfield. He drove me in his van to show me his nearby previous farms when he was a well-off farmer, before the expensive legal battles started. We had a balmy, joyous day with views of the Bay of Plenty and Whale and White Islands.

I wanted to stay with him but to see New Zealand too. Sadly, he couldn't come with me. He had court appearances to attend and letters to write. Again, I was in the situation where I was free but in love with a man who couldn't or wouldn't travel with me.

As quite often happened when I couldn't make a decision, an event decided things for me. The ski resort at Mount Ruapehuis advertised as being "fun for everyone," but that is where I dislocated my elbow; which wasn't. The wonkiness of my leg meant that one of my skis crossed over the other, upending me and sending me plummeting head first in the snow. My elbow hurt a great deal. Paul dug me out, someone phoned for mountain rescue, and a very short time later I was strapped into a blue body-bag on a sledge and taken ignominiously, rapidly, and bumpily to the medical centre, where I was told I had dislocated my elbow. Two shots of Pethidine made me feel drunk and enabled a sharp pull of my arm by two gorgeous young doctors, who needed to lean back with their feet on the bed before the joint was relocated and a plaster of Paris backslab applied. I paid about £40 for this marvellous service and after three hours was discharged. So, I had no choice but to stay with Paul until I could ride my bike again.

We went camping in his van. He showed me all the varieties of trees, spotted nests in branches, and holes in trunks where moths lived, while glow-worms caught their prey using glistening adhesive threads with enticing lights on the end, like wreckers on the Cornish coast. I was learning more about attitudes to Maori culture, noticeably different from the attitudes to Aboriginals in Australia. New Zealanders may not have liked it (and lots didn't), but even though Maoris had been here only six hundred years before the first Europeans came, they had much more political clout than the Australian Aboriginals, who had looked after the land for at least 40,000 years but were not revered for it at all by the European invaders.

I phoned Abby, as I was getting anxious about her going to Iraq. There had been an early family Christmas for her, as she was soon to depart. We said our goodbyes.

Before we went back to Edgecumbe, Paul took me to visit some friends. This family lived on a remote farm, where we stayed overnight. It was docking day, and we ate barbecued lambs' tails for dinner that night. In the morning, someone rattled the pig-food bucket outside. The pigs lived in the woodland on the other side of the river cutting through their land. Wondering how they would get across for breakfast, it was charming to watch mummy pig lead six babies across the river, oinking and squealing to each other as they piggy-paddled across.

I felt like a hindrance to Paul, and as soon as I could pull in the clutch, I left him to his work. My elbow was still painful, but things were hotting up for him. He'd been thwarted by a judge who made his evidence inadmissible. Documents were mislaid, and his witnesses not allowed to attend. He remained dignified but would not be put down. Was it an obsession? He'd been light-hearted when we were travelling, now he was back in the throes of what he saw as his moral duty.

As anyone who has been to New Zealand will tell you, it is a visual paradise. Although I'd had to tear myself away from Edgecumbe, I didn't want to miss any of it and went straight to the East Cape. At Maraehako Bay Retreat I narrowly missed riding into the sea at the end of their steep, downhill drive, so close was it to the water's edge. I went kayaking, saw a seal, and ate freshly caught crayfish the size of a lobster. Fabulous place.

From the map, the Te Araroa coastline looked like a broad sweep of clear sand, but it was bleak and inhospitable and strewn with driftwood piled up like the skeletons of everything that had ever been alive in the world—all washed up on this seemingly endless stretch. The desolation was even more pronounced because of the salt sea-spray, which like a shroud, covered the distance in mystery like smoke in the aftermath of devastation. It was a huge contrast to the pretty scenery elsewhere, so I stayed in a cabin there.

The chain-guard on the Enfield broke in half, and I was directed to a female welder, who also provided a new screw, missing from the carburettor. I'd lost count of how many times the poor thing was taken apart and adjusted over the years. I discovered at last why my bike was spluttering. Small amounts of water were getting into the carburettor by running down the outside of the pipe from the petrol tank. The rubber cover had a little tear. A bit of insulation tape . . . problem solved.

After eight days apart, Paul joined me. At the agreed meeting place, I hid in the branches of one of the largest pahutakawa (bottle-brush) trees in New Zealand and called out to him when he parked. It was silly and childish and entirely suitable. We were dotty about each other. Two days chasing steers around on quad bikes with dogs on another friend's farm was fun, but once again, we had to part; he to his court stuff and me to Gisborne on the south of the East Cape, where I had been invited to stay with Brownie, a friend of Margot.

Suddenly, there were traffic lights and pay-parking. Brownie was welcoming and liked rides on the Enfield. Paul rang to say he'd been humiliated in court, with court officials laughing when he'd had crippling fines to pay. He would have to move house, as he could no longer afford the rent. Brownie was also having problems with the law, and several of her friends who I met were too. I was amazed. I'd never heard of such things happening in the UK. Did they?

Extra help was needed in the vineyard where Brownie worked. She showed me which leaves to remove to allow the sun to ripen the Chardonnay grapes, we chatted, and I met another of her friends who grew exotic shrubs in her garden; she picked and boxed them and sent them to florists in London.

A text from Claire informed me that:

"Abby has been out of the base giving armed cover, out on the roof of a Land Rover." But I'd believed that in the Royal Army Medical Corps she'd be safe in a hospital compound on a base. My blood ran cold.

I went on . . . Paul joining me when he could as I moved slowly south, gasping at views and the generosity of people who gave me addresses of friends as I went. I wrote an article about my journey for a motorcycle magazine and was invited to stay with the editor in Levin on the way to Wellington.

I practiced saying Waikaremoana on the gravel road leading to the lake and motorcamp. I'd been able to manage Indian and Thai place names but was confused about where to put the stress on Maori names, which was never where I expected it to be. It was funny to look at the map and see names such as Whakatane and Pukekohe mixed with Thames, Hastings, and New Plymouth.

I'd seen no-one for hours as I rode in Urewera National Park, but just as I stopped for a wee, right on cue, a man with four horses came into view. When I got to the park accommodation, Paul joined me there. I wanted to be with him so much that, after a couple of lovely days, I abandoned my trip south and rode back to Edgecumbe with him to help pack up his home and move in with his friend Morris in Rotorua.

Life got darker. At Morris's house, most of Paul's clothes and possessions were crammed into our room. I stuffed stray items into overflowing cardboard boxes, as if by this futile effort it could seriously tidy things up and sort his life out like a fairy with a magic wand. We helped around the house and paid some rent. Paul did odd jobs in town, wrote reports, and studied legal books. It was dismal, but Paul remained optimistic.

When the Enfield tappets wouldn't adjust, we found that the rockers and valve caps needed replacing. The exhaust one had a nasty crack, and the inlet one was worn. I asked Trevor to send new ones from Auckland. Whilst I was at it, I bought new front forks and replaced the ailing odometer. Since I'd bought it new in India, the Enfield and I had travelled 30,194 miles together. Paul secured my loose exhaust pipe. So many people had bashed it to make it fit the corresponding lugs on the frame that the end was telescoped in on itself. Touchingly, he welded a heart to my side-stand to prevent it sinking into soft ground. The Enfield had a cylinder rebore, a new sleeve, piston, and rings. The engineer who did the job showed me that the cylinder had been at an angle and wondered that I'd had no engine problems.

Christmas was approaching. I sent paintings I'd done in Brownie's garden of the ferns and lemons growing there for Claire and for Abby, whose parcel went via the BFPO service to Shaibah, in Iraq. (I also sent a barking sheepdog soft toy as an antidote to some of the gruesome work she was doing.)

As if he didn't have enough problems, Paul adopted two dogs left by one of Morris's tenants. He had no money and now had these two pig-hunters to feed. One Sunday, we took the dogs, which we'd named Bullet and Fly, up to the top of a local hill. Morris's little son, Jamie, was visiting for the day. We had a good walk, the dogs off the lead, coming when they were called. A few hours later they were dead. Jamie and I had been playing ball with them in the garden. The mood turned ugly in an instant. Hunting dogs through and through, they attacked Jamie. I screamed for Paul to help me get the dogs off. Morris came and pulled Fly's jaws off Jamie's head, tearing his scalp. Paul drove them to hospital. I put the dogs in their compound, stroked them, and told them it wasn't their fault. They were bred as killers. On his return, Paul loaded his shotgun and shot them, which broke his heart. Remarkably unabashed, Jamie was fine after his scalp was stitched.

It was difficult living there. Our situation was hopeless. Things were bleak. I had to leave.

I let the days take me where they would.

As I was paying for petrol at a filling station, someone with a four-wheel-drive and an ego much bigger than his field of vision, reversed into my bike, knocking it over and breaking the side-stand. With the luggage on, I couldn't lift the bike onto the main stand. He could sense I wasn't best pleased. A welder was found, and the job done almost on the spot.

The hospitable editor of *Motorcycle Marketplace*, who had bought my article, put me up for several days. He let me ride a 125cc Suzuki farm bike, much lighter and more manoeuvrable than the Enfield. We had fun riding through forests, over fallen trees, and along the sandy beaches, but it was no touring bike.

On my way to the ferry to South Island I rode through a place called Bulls. The residents had amusingly used the name of their town to describe what the buildings were. The police-station was signed "ConstaBULLS," the antique shop "AffordaBULL CollectaBULLS," food shops "EataBULLS," and the fire station "ExtinguishaBULLS." So sweet . . .

All I wanted when I got off the night ferry at Picton, the South Island's ferry terminal, was a short ride to an idyllic motorcamp for some sleep. What I got on docking at 4:30AM was a puncture. Pushing the bike off the ferry in pitch black and cold was not in the plan. I took the rear wheel out and waited for daylight. A garage/ mechanic was half a mile away, so I walked with the wheel and waited for them to open. "We don't do punctures," said the snooty woman in reception, but I could see a tyre-removing machine in the workshop so called out to a mechanic, who helped me, albeit reluctantly. Even though I'd provided the replacement tube, I was charged a fair old whack for the job. I asked if someone could give me a lift back to the bike, but nobody could, so I staggered back to refit my wheel. It wasn't a good introduction to the South Island.

Then it started to rain. I stopped at a pub to ask about accommodation. At the same time, a swarthy man, the sort your mother warned you about, pulled up on a big motorbike. In a fringed leather jacket, he was tall with a shaven head and looked a bad lad. He admired the Enfield. I told him I was touring. "Where are you staying tonight?" he demanded. "Well, I'm looking for somewhere by the coast that's quiet and pretty and . . . " "You're coming home with me," he ordered. Remembering that "the only useful quality is weakness," I followed him. I had long since given up trying to be in control. We entered a small residential street and turned into a driveway. "What have I got into now?" I thought as Mike told me he'd been in prison three times for assault. He was a debt-collector "of the non-governmental type." With his two weeks' growth he looked like he could be mean and nasty. "Come and meet my mum," he said as we walked to the humble house, where eighty-five-year old June was preparing a Sunday roast. She told me that he was a good boy and had just got mixed up with the wrong crowd (didn't the Kray twins' mother say something similar?).

One of Mike's friends, who had been stripping bits off a wrecked car in the garden, joined us for lunch. The two of them were so polite, they even did the washing up. After that, I felt perfectly safe being driven round to various pubs all afternoon. Three glasses of beer later, I was so tired I went to the guest bed in the sleep-out whilst he, in a nearby chair, watched a film. He brought me tea at 6AM, as there was a film about Ned Kelly I must see before I go. I was warmed by the contact with him and his mum. The only sign of danger was in the snap, crackle, and pop of our innocent Rice Krispies at breakfast, before I tootled off to see what else South Island had in store for me.

The Molesworth Track, between Blenheim and Hanmer Springs, is 123 miles long. During most seasons, snow closes the pass and the track is prone to slips and washouts. Traffic causes stock disturbance, and in the summer there is extreme risk of fire. That's why it opens for only a month every year. I didn't know what to expect but didn't think I'd be distracted from my mission by pretty tea-cups on a tray and home-made scones and jam.

Had I not been so determined to ride the track, I might have stayed at Oak Tree Cottage with roses and hollyhocks round the door. The charming owner, Nicola, who had been inspired to open it after a visit to Devon in the UK some years before, brought out a Devonshire cream tea on a tray with a white lace cloth, and we sat in her cottage garden. She tempted me greatly, offering a job helping out when they had opera weekends. Even the pets were impossibly perfect. Two dogs, a collie and a Jack Russell, were "mothering a kitten." Sadly, I had limited time left on my tourist visa and had to move on.

Most people cover the distance in a few hours or camp at the recognised campsite, but taking my time, I second-geared it up a valley awash with blue flowers for as far as I could see. With the paints I always carried, I painted one of the viper's bugloss that was lovely enough solo but in swathes was unbelievable. With hot sun and blue sky all round, a gated track led me to another paradise of scenery so breath-taking I had to keep stopping. The track wound between mountains and hills with snow in the distance. Thinking back to passes in Pakistan, where conditions were so difficult that eighteen miles could take all day, I had no idea how long to allow.

This was a "No camping. No Fires" area, but I made the naughty decision to sleep out and make the most of it. The only other person I met on the track was a Belgian cyclist, so I wasn't observed going off-road to a dip and kept my little fire well under control when cooking my usual meal of sardines, peas, and rice. Marvelling at my good fortune, I sent everyone my love and best wishes as I lay under the stars and dozed off until the cold seeped sleep away at 4:30AM. All senses awake, I revived the fire and watched the fabulous stars as I listened to possums in the trees. A hedgehog, a rabbit, and a small brown bird heralded the dawn. On the 14th January, I wrote in my diary: *"Sun's up. Life's good!"*

Whilst life was good for me, Abby wasn't having such a good time of it. Trying to maintain order among clinicians with their own agendas was frustrating.

When I stopped at the top of the track, my wallet had dropped out of my day-pack, when seemingly, I'd left the zip open. I panicked and went to a house to ask if I could use their phone to ring the local police to report it missing. Kind people had already handed it in, and it was at the tourist office. What a relief. Tyrone, one of the people at the house, jumped on the back of my bike, and off we went to get it. Not only was a worrying situation resolved, but the incident led to another great experience.

On the way back to the house, where I was generously invited to spend the night, Tyrone asked me if I'd seen any sheep-shearing. I hadn't. "Turn off at the next farm," he said. He knew the farmer and asked if we could watch. I was invited to shear a sheep myself. The sheep was overturned, and I was handed the electric clippers as it lay and let me hack away at its fleece until Richard took over. I was rather good, I thought, if a little slower than Richard, the shearer, and what fun—all because I lost my wallet. The very next day I lost it again in the same way. What an idiot—I had put my email address inside that time but doubted I'd be lucky twice.

Someone had given me the address of their distant cousin, who, apparently, would be delighted to meet me at Kaikoura. I found the road but had to ring someone's doorbell to find the house. They told me the people I was looking for were away, but they had a holiday home by the beach that I could use. Jill and Wilson were complete strangers with absolutely no connection to anyone I'd met. They wouldn't hear of taking any rent and, after a cup of tea and biscuits, handed me the key and directions. Really?

At an Internet cafe I found an email with the subject "Wallet!" Someone had found it. It was waiting for me at Rangiora police station, further down the east coast near Christchurch. I stayed for a few days in Kaikoura, where the mountains came down to the clear blue sea, and of the available activities, I chose to go snorkelling with seals, rather than whale-watching or swimming with dolphins. I squealed with as much delight as someone with a snorkel in the mouth can when dozens of pup seals out for a laugh came like torpedoes out of the clear blue sea, swerving at the last moment to avoid head-on collision, smiling with wicked delight as they passed. An octopus the size of a cat changed from purple to grey as it blended with a rock. Amazing.

The news from Iraq was not good. Elections were approaching, and suicide bombers were blowing up police stations. I was horrified and couldn't eat anything all day.

Not wanting to take advantage of this lovely couple, who had even taken me for an outing to a friend's remote farm in the Kaikoura Range by the Clarence River, I carried on to Christchurch. New Zealand was just heaven.

Before I left, I had a phone call from Claire. The base at Shaibah, where Abby was, had just been the target of a suicide bomb attack. Claire and I wept together, frantic and powerless. Abby was unhurt and had rung home. I found a cabin to stay in that evening and shut myself in, not wanting to socialise with the drunks outside.

I collected my wallet from the police station and rang the people who had found it, thanking them profusely. I realised that the weight of the contents of the pocket in my day-pack had forced the zip-pullers apart as I rode; by just fastening it to one side, it stayed shut.

On my way to Christchurch, I learned of the recent tsunami in Asia. The devastating Christchurch earthquake was still years off, but I felt generally uneasy, distressed by the catastrophe and the danger that Abby faced in Iraq.

Tickets were scarce for the Black Caps vs FICA World XI cricket match at the Jade Stadium in Christchurch, but I managed to buy one for the very back and top of the stadium. Emerging at the top, with the sudden view of the cricket pitch below, made me gasp. I wasn't expecting anything so big or so overwhelming. Mexican waves and cheering in the packed stadium dissipated the awe I felt. Shane Warne was playing, but the man of the match was Stephen Fleming, who hit five sixes for the Black Caps.

The news in Iraq coloured my view of the next week, and I didn't find anything joyous in my explorations until I heard from Abby.

The bike was making a funny grinding noise, and I squirted chain lube everywhere I thought might be harbouring the problem.

At Geraldine I found an odd museum. The owner of a local knitting factory thought it would be a great idea to make a copy of the Bayeux Tapestry from hundreds of thousands of the tiny metal protrusions from obsolete knitting pattern plates, each one individually snipped off. He and his daughter had constructed it over twenty-five years. The finished result was impressive, with extra panels depicting William the Conqueror's coronation that don't appear on the original tableau. What on earth gave him the idea for such a zany project is unknown, but I was left with such questions as, "What did your wife think?" and "What are you going to do now?" Not only was he a mathematical genius, but he knew everything about the Battle of Hastings. Furneaux was the name of a noble family from France, who having fought with William, were given lands in Devon, where my father's family came from. Was I a descendant, I wondered?

At Burke's Pass the scenery changed. A range of mountains stretched across the horizon. I was marvelling at that when turquoise blue Lake Tekapo made the scene as perfect as it could be. Paul phoned, full of excitement to say he was on his way. I was glad he would be enjoying all this with me.

Quite expecting to find injured people, I rushed down to what appeared to be a recent road accident where a car had plunged into a ditch. Mostly stripped bare, the car had obviously been there for months. It still had the sun reflector on the back window, though, just the thing to insulate me from the cold ground at night. Later I slept out snugly fourteen miles along a track by a river with a view of Mount Cook, which looked like a big, distant tent.

As the rising morning sun coloured it pink, I watched rabbits from my sleeping bag and made tea. This is what I loved. I was born to wild camp. I bathed in the river and prepared to meet Paul further inland in Twizel, where according to my map, there were many rivers and lakes.

Paul had hitch-hiked 621 miles from Rotorua!

The weather was perfect, and he knew just where to go for wild camping. Stocking up with food for a few days, we set off on the bike to the Hopkins Valley, where ribbons of rivers flowed along a wide valley between mountains fringed with red beeches below and topped with snow. We were like wild people; swimming, fishing, making fires, sleeping at dusk, and rising with the dawn to look for trout.

One day we walked to where the raging Huxley River meets the Hopkins River. It was a heavenly spot with a rope bridge over it, and we felt greedy having it all to ourselves. There should have been nothing to spoil it, but Paul discovered a puncture and, more worryingly, a small lump in my breast. I didn't want to die. I was so happy but realised my life was not infinite.

We went to stay with Paul's friends in Oamaru, on the coast, where I had a biopsy. Some years earlier they had lost their son, whose body was never found, in a canoeing incident. Their unimaginable grief took form in a bitter conflict with their son's girlfriend over ownership of his record deck.

Whilst we waited for the biopsy result, there was a tiny place on the map that I absolutely had to go to. It was called Enfield, and, invited to bring the bike into the bar at the Fort Enfield Tavern, it posed for photos like a visiting celebrity.

The biopsy resulted in an "entirely benign" all-clear. This episode was another reminder to make the most of love, life, and interesting opportunities. Paul had been caring and supportive but, with an impending court case, had to return to Rotorua to pursue his own destiny, while I continued my tra-la-la way round South Island.

I was very lucky where the next puncture occurred. I'd just set off on the unsealed Danseys Pass in a late afternoon rainstorm, a silly time to start out. It happened right outside someone's house, the only inhabited place for about thirty miles. After a search, the helpful inhabitants found a foot-pump to inflate the repaired inner-tube.

From an altitude of 3,000 feet, some very scary descents took me down to a valley, and I was lucky to not slide off the sodden track into the steely river. The journey felt sinister and threatening in the gloom of the darkening cloudy sky. Having been alone on the pass, I was very glad to reach Naseby, an old prospecting town. Booking in to a cheery hostel, I watched *The Antiques Roadshow* by the side of a roaring fire and felt rather homesick.

Dunedin, according to the guide book, was founded by people with Scottish origins, and the way there certainly looked like the craggy, bald, brown-hilled Highlands. However, rather than the bagpipes heralding my arrival, all I could hear were strands of the clutch cable twanging as they snapped. To preserve what remained, I restricted gear-changes, not easy in the city traffic. There were two strands left by the time I limped into a mechanic's workshop. He made a new one, welding the nipples onto some sturdy steel cable as I sipped tea in the workshop.

I booked into a cabin at Waikawa, in the Catlins area, and wandered round the village. A handwritten note on the door of the museum invited enquiry at the house opposite, so I crossed the green to the single-storey wooden residence. A large glass of sherry and some lamb stew later, Jim Burns invited me to accompany him the next day to an air-show in Mandeville. "Those who flow through life as life flows . . . " Of course, I accepted and, for the first time in many months, had to set my alarm.

The event celebrated the flight of Herbert Pither, who flight-tested his Bleriot-style plane on the same beach Burt Munro used for his motorbike trials in the 1950s. A replica Pither had been made. Also exhibited were a selection of de Haviland aircraft (Dominie, Dragonfly, Tiger Moth, Chipmunk, Moth Minor, and Fox Moth), a Percival Proctor, a Beech Staggerwing, and a Piper Cub.

I got chatting to a pretty woman of my age, and before I knew it, I was co-pilot in her Gardner Minicab low-winged single-engine plane. What a thrill. It was a bit bumpy as we flew over nearby hills. Then she asked me via the headphones and mouthpiece if I would like to take the controls. Would I . . . ? I steered left and right, up and down, circling the airfield, hardly daring to appreciate the fantastic view from up there. Everyone was so generous. The least I could do was buy them lunch.

As I carried on along the south coast, I saw Hector's dolphins playing in the surf and, what I liked to think was, a rare yellow-eyed penguin.

With so many punctures in my rear tyre it was time to look for a replacement. Nineteen-inch ones are not common, but Invercargill had one at a good price, the dealer being as glad to get rid of it as I was to buy it. It had been on the shelf for a long time, but the rubber didn't look too crazed.

Every now and then, to save weight and space, some items in the luggage could be dispensed with and the remaining things reorganised. Extra space was created by removing the cardboard of my three-litre wine-box, leaving the inner "balloon" to lay flat on top of my other luggage, so that it took up less room than a quart bottle. Perfect.

Out of town, I pulled up by a compound to watch some of New Zealand's thirty million sheep having a rear-end trim. The farmer came across and explained that this procedure is to stop flies setting up home there. It didn't occur to me that shepherding might enter my travel itinerary, but I was invited to stay at Daryl and Angie's farm.

The next day, I accompanied Daryl on his quad bike and his five dogs to round up strays, left behind during the grand round-up the week before. We were out all day looking for pockets of escapees for the dogs to clear from their hiding places and join the rest of the flock back at the farm. Even though the dogs did all the work of herding them for miles across open country, we came back covered in mud. I had my first bath for months.

I rounded the tip of South Island and was then on my way up the west side.

Claire phoned excitedly to tell me the thrilling news that she had a very good new job with a world-renowned public relations company. Email and mobile phones made being a long-distance mother much better, I could share my daughters' joys and sorrows with a new ability. I began to feel more trusted and part of their lives again.

Everybody I met said I must see Milford Sound, but thinking that one can't see too many fiords, I first took a boat trip on Doubtful Sound, so named because Captain Cook wasn't sure if it was wise to take his ship up it, or so the story goes.

Overwhelming mountains rose from the blue depths, and waterfalls dropped in. I stayed at a motor-camp, where the owner had a varied collection of Morris Minors, my first car. Amongst all this beauty, poor Paul rang to say he'd be in court the next day.

All the pictures I'd seen of Milford Sound showed sun, blue sky, and mirrored views of the mountains in the clear, calm water. I saw fog—thick, damp, cold fog. I waited a few hours and then left it to the hordes of cars and twenty-two coachloads of people and instead, very pleased I'd seen Doubtful Sound, went to Gunn's Camp, where seventeen dollars bought me a night in a quirky old cabin with a coal range and fuel.

Norman, the possum-hunter, a shifty-looking bloke, lived in the cabin next to mine. He invited me to join him to bait the trees with irresistible peanut butter and to set the traps. The next morning, we went to see what had been caught. Turn away now if you are squeamish. He bashed them on the head with a hammer to kill them. The fur has to be pulled off immediately. He sells it for seventy-five dollars per two-and-a-quarter pounds, equal to fifteen to twenty possums. Spun with merino sheep wool, it is very cosy indeed.

Murray Gunn, the old gentleman who owned the decades old and unmodernised camp, had stacks of reference books about New Zealand. I asked him about Katherine Sheppard, who was featured

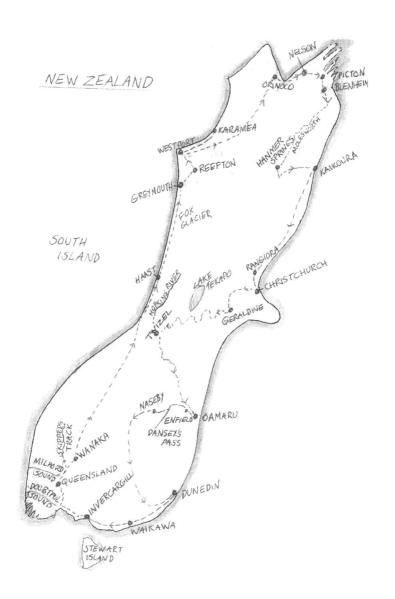

NEW ZEALAND

SOUTH
ISLAND

NELSON
ORINOCO
PICTON
BLENHEIM
KARAMEA
WESTPORT
HANMER SPRINGS
MOLESWORTH
REEFTON
KAIKOURA
GREYMOUTH
COX
GLACIER
RANGIORA
CHRISTCHURCH
HAAST
HOPKINS RIVER
LAKE
TEKAPO
TWIZEL
GERALDINE
NASEBY
ENFIELD
OAMARU
SKIPPERS TRACK
DANSEYS
PASS
MILFORD
SOUND
WANAKA
QUEENSLAND
DOUBTFUL
SOUND
INVERCARGILL
DUNEDIN
WAIKAWA
STEWART
ISLAND

on the ten dollar note. He got out several tomes to find her. She was a suffragette. Originally from Liverpool, she and her band of the Women's Christian Temperance Union got women the vote in 1893, thirty-five years before all women attained suffrage in Britain.

The next event was much nicer than seeing possums whacked with a hammer. I had heard that it was possible to put a motorbike on the Lake Wakatipu passenger ferry to Queenstown from Walter Peake Station, reached via a track from Te Anau. I waited in the sunshine to see what would arrive. Into view chugged the delightful 1912 steamship TSS *Earnslaw*. It was quite a sight. I wasn't allowed to ride the bike aboard, an easier method than two men having to manoeuvre it along the gangplank.

Off we went to Queenstown. A small band played gracious tunes from the 1920s as afternoon tea was served. I felt another surge of euphoria, realising how good my life was. I had wanted to look at Queenstown but, unbelievably, couldn't find anywhere to park. Too much of a contrast to my quiet pottering, I didn't stay. Instead, I enjoyed creek-crossings and "fall off the bike" views all the way to Glenorchy.

A woman I'd met at the air show had given me her number so I could meet her again when I got to Wanaka. Unfortunately, she couldn't be there, but she arranged for a key to be left under a stone in amongst the rhubarb at her friend's cottage. It sounded like something from *The Hobbit*.

I travelled up Arthur's Pass, staggered at the view at Coronet Peak. The notice at the top said, "No Hire cars insured on this track. Take great care. This track is very steep. Experienced drivers only." I mused, recollecting the tracks in Asia and Australia that I had done with Hendrikus and, later, others on my own. How bad could it be? I set off down the Skippers Track to find out. Down, down, down. Turning round was impossible. I was committed.

Early gold-miners had cut the gravel road into the valley by hand to access one of the richest gold seams in New Zealand. Today it was deserted. It reminded me of parts of the Karakoram Highway, with lethal drops and overhangs. I crossed a high, but mercifully flat, bridge where people pay to hurl themselves towards the river at the valley floor harnessed to elastic bands. Hundreds of miners and their families used to live there. Nobody lives there now, but the Department of Conservation had done a wonderful job of restoring some of the buildings and exhibiting old photographs. It looked quite a gay place and from the 1800s was thriving with picnics, parties, and cricket matches.

It must have taken days to get there then. There were plenty of places I could have slept out if I'd wanted to, but I indulged in a triumphal smile at the bottom and then rode back up in first gear. "Dangerous track" indeed.

I found the key amongst the rhubarb leaves and settled into someone's cottage in Wanaka. I started to think about staying in New Zealand. Paul was confident that he would win his battle soon. I'd be able to help him, and I dreamed we could travel together. I enquired about registering the bike there. The Enfield had a $125 bond that I'd need to pay, in addition to having a stringent test done on the bike.

The skies on leaving Wanaka looked grim. "I think we're in for a spot of rain, Bike." It pelted down practically all the way from Wanaka to Haast. Wind, rain, and poor visibility drove me onwards up the west coast and prevented me from looking at much. I could see grey bumpy things to my right that could have been mountains and flat grey stuff to my left that was probably the sea. There's nothing between there and the Roaring Forties, furiously blowing against the mountains, so little wonder it's rough.

The rain stopped long enough for me to walk up to Fox Glacier, now an hour from the visitor centre, as it has receded so much in recent years. I was enjoying myself back on the road, laughing every time an even heavier squall lashed at me, but I was shivering, and by the time I reached aptly-named Greymouth, I was going into coffee shops just to hug the hot food display cabinets. Fed up with being wet all the time, I went into a Salvation Army charity shop and came out armed with Wellington boots and thick PVC fisherman's trousers. I'd be wet no more.

At Reefton, I saw a huge old Fairlie railway locomotive, the last of its kind in New Zealand, it had been built back home in Bristol. I stayed at a pub, where construction workers bought me a beer. I was having a great time. Paul rang. He broke down in tears telling me about the court debacle. The judge and lawyer had ridiculed him and threatened bankruptcy. I did not realise the implications of that.

Asking for directions, I got chatting to a man of seventy-two who was trying for his twentieth child with a young woman, the latest of several partners, who had arrived as a backpacker and stayed. He had the "have no electricity/have a compost heap" smugness. New Zealand's population was only one million, but if he kept going . . .

I had been given the address of some friends of Herb and Liz. They lived in a tiny paradise called Orinoco, near Nelson, at the top end of South Island. I stayed with them for a few days in their beautiful single-storey house. I helped hurl logs around as they cleared the land. I slept well after all the exercise, just stirring in my sleep when there was an earthquake. I could feel the bed shake as it had in Pakistan when I thought Hendrikus was fooling about but wasn't. In my dozy state I thought, "Oh, it's just another earthquake," and went back to sleep.

Abby was home on leave from Iraq and was due back when I rang her. She was distressed and said she didn't want to go back. It was heart-breaking.

Back on North Island I stopped for breakfast. When I returned to the bike, a young man was staring at it. "Are you Jacqui Furneaux? I read your article in the *Motorcycle Marketplace*." I was tickled pink.

If I hurried, I could get back to Paul for my birthday. In heavy rain, I nearly got wiped off the road by an overtaking lorry towing a trailer on the notorious Desert Road from Waiouru to Turangi. At 3,524 feet, it is frequently closed by bad weather. It was, indeed, very bleak.

Then I was in Rotorua, the sun came out, and I was with Paul. My round New Zealand tour was over for the time being.

Paul found the cause of the squeak when he took the front wheel apart. A spacer made from a sardine tin lid placed between the speedo drive and hub assembly sorted it out.

There were choices to make. Some research revealed that if I wanted to come back to New Zealand (my tourist visa was running out) I must stay out the same time I had stayed in—nine months. I'd read somewhere: "Love and arterial bleeding, you know them when you see them!"

I was in love. I would leave the bike in New Zealand, wait out the nine months, and come back to stay with Paul. With my rose-coloured spectacles firmly on my face, I foresaw our future. He would win his cases, nail his persecutors, and we'd be free to travel the world together.

The *Tao Te Ching* may have hit a resonance with me, but there was some wisdom I wasn't listening to or chose to ignore . . . wasn't there advice about not getting involved in other people's matters or something?

15

HOME AND NEW ZEALAND

LOVE, LIFE, AND DEATH

As the National Express coach wove through heavy traffic, London looked ancient, robust, and grand after uncongested, new and fresh New Zealand. Sixteenth century farmhouses with gables and stone-tiled roofs could be seen from the motorway. Arriving in Britain in April, just as New Zealand was preparing for its cold season, meant I had avoided winter altogether. The English countryside was greening up with the promise of spring.

It felt good to be home with my busy family, thirteen months after my last visit. My mother, then ninety-seven, had shrunk so much the armchair she was hunched up in looked as if it was made for a giant; her white, candy-floss hair had been scraped into a severe bun. Largely unresponsive, she knew someone was holding her hand, but I don't think she knew it was me. She was very well cared-for, in no pain, taking no medication, and was enjoying her food. The reversal of roles was distressing when I fed her with spoonfuls of puréed food, as she once would have fed me.

It was too much to ask of family or friends to put me up for so long, so with no home of my own, Abby kindly let me live in her Scottish house in Kirkcudbright, near Dumfries, while she was in Iraq with the army. Almost immediately, I had a run-in with my neighbour, who spotted me putting my bag of rubbish into her bin by mistake. This was not acceptable. She made me think of an elderly Miss Jean Brodie. I snatched it out again with apology and trepidation, and when I had disposed of it appropriately, she invited me in, and we became regular chess-players in her home.

With a twinkling naughtiness, Muriel revealed parts of her past she'd admitted to no-one else, including private liaisons with gentlemen (following her husband's death) of which the churchy tittle-tattlers in this arty little town were unaware. This stately lady was slowly dying from cancer. "Well you have to die of something at my age!" She laughed with admirable sangfroid, passing me another shortbread. She was receiving palliative care from community hospice nurses, a service I already knew about but before long would know a lot more.

I bought an old bicycle for £5 from a charity shop and cycled all over the area. It was a glorious summer of wild swimming from the beautiful and unpopulated coastline and searching for wild food . . . wood mushrooms, watercress, and shellfish prised from the rocks. The limpets were a bit chewy, but the winkles were fine.

A local "Return to Nursing" course was advertised. Seven years had passed since I'd done any nursing, so a course to update me might validate me for a job when I returned to New Zealand. I met the criteria for the six-week course and was accepted. It was very strange to be going off to work in the mornings, travelling on the bus to Dumfries through "Scottish Calendar" scenery.

So much had changed since I'd last worked in a hospital thirty-four years previously. As soon as I'd qualified in 1971, I'd followed my passion and chosen the field of health promotion, leaving hospital nursing for good. Now hoists were in use; no more lifting and no scary ward sisters, either.

Much to my delight, as it was such a long way to come, Claire joined me for a weekend. After a long day at work followed by a five-hour drive, she brought with her the joyous news that she was pregnant. She'd come to tell me face to face, rather than by phone or email, and to prevent my hearing the news through a third party. A warm and happy glow poured over me. My daughter was to be a mother. My mother would be a great-grandmother. Abby would be an auntie. My brother would be a great-uncle, and I would be a grandmother.

A grandmother! If spoon-feeding my mother hadn't jolted me into accepting generational marching on, that news did. Gradually my exciting new role sank in, and I felt nurturing and caring towards my capable daughter. I dredged up words of wisdom from my own experience and my health visiting past but soon felt pretty useless. Mumsnet.com now had all the answers. We talked about the marvels of pregnancy, went for long walks, ate fish and chips, and I bought her a locally-made necklace to mark the event.

With the news, New Zealand seemed more than half the world away. There in Scotland I felt not only in a different time-zone but a different era. Paul rang to say that, because he'd been made bankrupt, the courts had frozen his bank account. With no access to his social security payments, he was now receiving food vouchers. I applied for a New Zealand work permit, imagining I'd need to support us both until it was all over. He still believed that would be soon.

One of the nicest things about having a temporary home was that people could visit me. Abby came safely home after her posting in Iraq and was based in Gosport until leaving the army. My brother drove up from Somerset, and I was happy to return hospitality to some of the people I'd met whilst travelling. Wendy, who had given me the job at the English language school in Islamabad, came; also Geoff, who Hendrikus and I had met on the Karakoram Highway in Pakistan. Both had returned to the UK and met each other whilst staying with me. Geoff brought Raymond, his friend from Tasmania, who he had met whilst in India. The random network of friendship was gratifying and is one of the best spin-offs of travelling.

With the nursing course completed, I took the ferry from Stranraer for a day-trip to Belfast, and just before I left Scotland, had a spiritual and blowy weekend on the island of Iona, where I stayed in a small hostel with two other guests; Elsa, an artist from

South Africa and Dieter, an airline pilot from Austria. We braved the violent weather and went for walks together. The wind was so strong I had to slither on my front to peer over the windward cliffs, where I was thrilled to watch the maddened waves hurling themselves against the rocks below. Elsa had gone out in a plastic waterproof cape, soon torn to pieces and whisked into the vortex of the ferocious wind. It was November, and I was wearing a poppy on my jacket. They asked me why I was wearing it. I could feel myself getting flustered like verbally clumsy Basil Fawlty in a "don't talk about the war" way but said that we wore poppies to remember soldiers killed in wars everywhere.

Full of love, hope, and enthusiasm to start a new life with Paul and believing that love conquers all, I returned to New Zealand.

If Paul had jumped into my travelling life on my arrival in New Zealand from Australia in August 2004, I most certainly jumped into his one-man fight with the law when I flew back from the UK in January 2006. Not only that, but I was in fear of drowning in it.

Bit by bit I settled in. I road-registered the Enfield, joined the library, and got a residents' season ticket to the outstanding natural hot-pool complex. Initially, I felt happily anchored, but after a few weeks I sank. Perhaps arriving back and living with Paul at Morris's house in Rotorua with so many expectations and having to share a house after living peacefully on my own was too much. There were two extra men living there. Morris had taken in a lodger, and Paul's grown-up son was staying too.

The dynamics were completely different. Paul and I were still as ardent about each other, despite the time and distance that had separated us, but I missed my family, feeling torn at leaving Claire just as she was pregnant and Abby just as she was leaving the army. I was in the wrong place at the wrong time. There were too many people, too much talking, and too little peace.

Morris wanted to sell the house. We would then be homeless. Paul did his best to make life enjoyable amidst the chaos and agreed to do some forestry for a friend. Ivan had a vast tract of land in a remote area near Opotiki.

We packed Paul's van with equipment and rattled along rough tracks to get there. Rather than being paid in cash, Paul preferred the bartering and favours way of doing things. The payment would be enough timber to build us a cabin somewhere picturesque. We spent our days felling pines and slicing them into planks at the sawmill, built and operated by Paul. Then we stacked them for seasoning.

I helped with the decrepit machinery, which broke down constantly, and learnt how to operate the tractor and digger, thoroughly enjoying dragging felled trees to the mill or perfectly balancing a few using chains from the raised bucket of the digger. If only we could have stayed in this wooded paradise with its lakes, streams, and panoramic views, living this pioneering life, but we left two weeks later when Paul and Ivan fell out. There would be no timber, no wooden house in the country.

For my birthday treat in March, Paul bartered the use of a kayak, and we floated down the Wanganui River, camping and fishing for a few days. Then we had to return to Morris's.

Paul became stressed as he resumed his legal work. I was there to stay, so I answered an advertisement in the newspaper for a community hospice nurse post. I put together a CV and sent it in. After an interview, I was given the job. The CEO offered to pay me as a registered nurse until my UK qualifications were verified.

Apart from experiencing copious deaths when working on the radiotherapy wards as a student nurse dozens of years previously, and meeting Muriel who was using the service in Scotland, I had little knowledge of terminal care and would shadow the other nurses until my registration came through. The work was full-time, with 9AM to 9pm shifts, but the "three days on, three days off" pattern allowed for planning of camping trips and looking for somewhere to live.

Rather than the hushed voices and reverence I was expecting, the hospice nurses were a cheerful team, kind and professionally efficient. The hospice had a secular, no-nonsense attitude to the end of life. The words *death* and *dying* were used. Euphemisms such as *passing on* or *going to a better place* were forbidden. Their remit was to encourage patients to make the most of the time they had left with skilful use of pain relief. Some people were referred to the hospice with months left to live, others with only weeks or days. Their death was discussed, not a taboo subject nor any pretence that it wasn't happening.

Morphine combined with paracetamol was the most effective medication for pain-relief. Local GPs respected the nurses' expertise and prescribed whatever they thought appropriate. Concerns about addiction did not come into it. These people were dying. Almost all patients died at home, surrounded by family. As soon as possible after the death, we removed tubes and medical equipment, so the family could more naturally support each other, relating happy memories as they sat on the bed, as if the dead relative was still taking part in it all, rather than being immediately whisked away by the undertakers. I remembered Muriel and hoped she'd have a death like New Zealanders do.

I thought of the many deaths I had witnessed during my nurse training. There wasn't one I could think of that was peaceful or loving. However, my experience had been on the cancer wards on extended night-duty in a dark Victorian hospital in 1970. It would be better now. Laying out patients who had died, ready for the porters to take to the mortuary, became my field of expertise as a student nurse. I'd grown fond of the patients whilst looking after them on the radiotherapy wards. I still remember some of their names and recall those night shifts, dreadful in retrospect, but as an eighteen year-old, I was unable to express the trauma and sorrow as I performed their last nursing procedure. Nobody talked about it until I worked as a hospice nurse in New Zealand, where we had weekly, sometimes emotional, debriefing sessions with the nurse manager.

The dying were not reluctant to talk about how they felt. Few were scared. They wished it wasn't happening but were resigned. I'd not seen my mother cry when her siblings died one by one but witnessed a short, terrible sob when my father died. To discuss death with people when they were dying was a macabre fascination.

I was asked by the manager to do a case study. I chose to compare two women in their early forties with small children. Both had been told there was nothing else the medical profession could do to cure them.

Ahora had been diagnosed with breast cancer. The large family had chosen traditional Maori methods to treat her. When we went for our first visit after her cancer had been diagnosed as terminal, there were branches of foliage around the door of the large, modern house and a notice pinned to the door demanding that nobody should bring any negativity into the house. We nurses were not welcome, as they feared we would disturb healing spirits. The doctor had visited and informed the hospice that Ahora was crying with pain, but the family was insistent she should have no morphine, as it changed her personality and that they would continue to treat her their way. This continued for weeks, until her pain became so unbearable that one night, the nurse on call was summoned to give her an injection.

Henceforth, we visited her regularly and did our best to make her comfortable but were always met with disapproval by the family. We wondered how much of her traditional treatment was her own choice. Her pain was preventing her from enjoying her last weeks with her children. Eventually, a syringe-driver was set up, enabling Ahora to control her own pain-relief, but we often found it disconnected and she would be curled up in a ball of pain. She died a few days later.

Her case was not at all typical of Maori patients, most of whom welcomed our involvement. Many Maori people live in the North Island, and it was interesting to experience Maori culture within their homes.

Annabelle, a New Zealander of European descent, had undergone extensive surgery to remove abdominal tumours but had become terminally ill and in an appalling physical state. She had moved back in with her estranged husband with their children so they could live as a family for the short time she had left. She embraced pain-relief, her final goal to prepare for her son's forthcoming eighth birthday party. Boxes of morphine were stacked in a locked kitchen cupboard for self-medication with medical approval. Well dosed up, she went into town with her son to choose party tableware, streamers, invitations, and presents. She made him a cake and was playing games with him and his friends on his birthday. She died a few days afterwards.

When my time comes, I'll go for the morphine please.

Although my bike was registered in New Zealand and could stay, I wasn't and so couldn't. My application to transfer my UK qualifications to New Zealand was refused. I would have to go on a lengthy and costly course to convert it, an expense the hospice was unable to support.

Without a job, I wouldn't be allowed to stay. I was fifty-five, too old for residency. I'd been working at the hospice for four months. I'd preferred being a health visitor, helping people shortly after their arrival, rather than a hospice nurse just before their departure. Not only that, it made me realise how short our lives are and that, once you hear the words "*I'm sorry but there's nothing else we can do for you*," that's it.

Even my three days off were not spent together with Paul, who was researching the law and writing letters to the judiciary, quoting how they had failed to follow correct procedures and ignored evidence in his favour. I tried not to feel abandoned again, as I had when my husband found a new and exciting job towards the end of our twenty-year marriage, and again when the man I lived with afterwards went away to work elsewhere for six months just as I'd moved in. Again, I was dispensed with when Hendrikus decided (without telling me) that he wanted to stop travelling and look for an Australian wife, whilst I thought we'd be travelling on together. Didn't anyone want to be with me?

In the midst of all this death and despair, there was new life. I wanted to be on the other side of the world, for I'd missed the birth of my granddaughter. Laurie's arrival had been difficult. Claire had been ably supported by Abby's presence and was not much helped by my lighting candles and sending messages of love and spiritual help across the world. However, Laurie was a perfect little girl, and Claire, although physically battered by the delivery, exclaimed her instant love for her.

The combination of having a new family member, nursing people who were dying, not being able to work as a registered nurse, and Paul's raison d'être dragging us both down had its effect. The likelihood of his release from bankruptcy and being free in the near future was remote. Even then, he would not cease until the justice system recognised that he had been wronged.

His travelling on with me was even more of a distant dream than it had been when we'd met two years previously. I'd hoped to be able to show him my world . . . The World. He was not ignorant of my needs but had no home, no income, and no plans to stop doing what was important to him. I could feel the tentacles of involvement reaching out from the entangled mess to get me. "Not getting mixed up with things is the supreme attainment of purity," Tao Te Ching warned. I had got mixed up with things, and someone else's things too.

One evening, Paul took me out for a meal. He told me that I should leave. To throw in the towel now would mean him pleading guilty to the crime of contempt of court, which he refused to do when he was innocent. He needed all his time and energy for his cause. As if our situation was my fault, I felt like a naughty ten-year-old and cried all over dinner. I am now quite unable to eat risotto for the memory of it. I had given it my best shot, but it wasn't working. I'd spent months trying but found, more often than not, that he didn't have time for us. And, I reminded myself, I'd given up everything precious to me to be with him . . . my daughters, my grandchild, my travelling, all that I loved so much. I had done the equivalent of pleading guilty for the sake of our love. There was nothing left for me to sacrifice.

Before leaving, I painted a large landscape in oils. My Enfield was disappearing out of the picture on the left. The front wheel of Paul's bike was appearing from the right. We hoped that one day he would catch up with me when his mission was achieved.

Abby was well aware of my situation. With three weeks annual leave to take, she suggested a holiday together somewhere in South America. It would be too cold in Chile or Argentina, so we settled on Ecuador, and I would ride on south afterwards. As if I was organising things for someone else, I went numbly onto automatic pilot and prepared to leave. I handed in my notice at the hospice. I rode the Enfield to a shipping agent in Auckland and booked us both on the same flight to Quito.

After saying farewell to Margot, Paul and I spent our last night in a little caravan, as we had done our first. The parting at the airport was calmly tragic. No tears, just quiet desperation as we had glimpses of each other through the various stages of my departure, mouthing words to each other through the security glass. Paul followed me until the last possible moment, me peering back to the terminal from the tarmac, searching every window for his face.

New Zealand is, to all who go there, a pristine, outstandingly beautiful country with good roads, a lot of sheep, and little traffic. Most visitors don't experience what I did by falling in love and working there. I had the privilege of peeping into other people's lives and deaths intermingled with my own loves, partings, and heartaches. There was nothing else I could do. Still unsure whether he was a hero or a madman, I was both heartbroken at leaving the man I loved and relieved to be continuing with my own mission.

16

ECUADOR WITH ABBY

WHO AM I?

A kindly air steward shuffled a couple of obliging passengers into different seats so that Abby and I could sit together on the flight from Houston to Quito. She, coming from London, had spent hours at the airport. My narrow margin from New Zealand meant I'd had just minutes to sprint through an airport the size of a town in order to catch the same plane. Hoping my backpack had also made the flight, I felt immediately relieved; our holiday together had started. After months of nursing dying people and living in Paul's cramped and edgy world, I needed pleasant times in merry, comfortable company before continuing to travel to Peru, Chile, and the rest of South America.

To demonstrate to my ex-army officer daughter how efficient I could be, I'd booked a room at the posh-sounding La Posada Colonial, a hotel in the old part of Quito. When we got there it was not posh at all, but it was comfortably adequate, and it had a shed for the bike.

We spent most of the first day at the airport arranging temporary importation documents for the Enfield, which had also landed. I scurried hither and thither with the paperwork, while Abby waited patiently with a book in the café. I was asked by various officials for "special" payments, but when I asked for a receipt, the matter wasn't pressed. I had learned quite a lot in Asia about "special" payments. By the time all the paper-shuffling had been done, the inspector had gone home, so the Enfield had to stay. It had five days of free storage, allowing us time for a short trip somewhere before returning to collect it.

Neither of us had been to South America before. It was neither an army exercise for Abby nor onward travel for me. We had a carefree holiday attitude as we sat outside a bar in the old town square with a couple of caiperinha cocktails and a guide book, planning our three week stay in Ecuador. First we'd have a short trip north to Otavalo to the centuries-old mountain market. The other destinations we picked were south, east, and west of Quito.

We spent the next two nights in a shed. Our guest house in Otavalo was a collection of brightly-painted, quaint wooden huts in a garden with hummingbirds and exotic flowering shrubs. The huge market filled the town square and surrounding streets. The people of the Andes wore canvas espadrilles, the men wearing white trousers and the women long dark wool skirts. Their hair was plaited, and some wore trilby-style hats. Strings of golden beads around the women's necks looked fetching against their frilly white flower-embroidered blouses.

For hundreds of years, even before the Inca colonisation of Ecuador, mountain people had trailed there from the surrounding mountains with their handicrafts and produce. It now also sells modern electrical goods and clothes from around the world for local people and caters colourfully for the many tourists it attracts.

Resisting the temptation to buy dozens of hand-woven ponchos and knitted jumpers for little Laurie, facing her first winter, we couldn't leave without a handful each of knitted animal finger-puppets and a rattle made from a huge seed-head. Generations of little Ecuadorian babies had likely been entertained with those, and I happily chose this authentic item over the plastic toys on offer.

Back in Quito with our stash of finger-puppets, I fetched the bike from the airport and was pleased that it stalled only once and that I didn't get lost on my ride back to the hotel half-way down a very steep hill, this being a land of the Andes and volcanoes. To avoid a difficult parking manoeuvre on the steep descent, I left the bike at the top and ran down to the hotel owner, who opened up the small shed where the bike would stay, as Abby wasn't at all keen to ride pillion on it. Chatting on buses and looking at the scenery would be a change for me, too.

With her army career now behind her, Abby had been on various "back to civilian life" courses and thought it may be useful for me to do an exercise that she had come across. Several weeks before, in an effort to help me sort myself out, she had emailed a Personal Life Plan questionnaire for me to complete. I was to consider how I saw myself and what my goals, strengths, and weaknesses were. What were my interests and needs, and what did I see myself doing ten years hence? I'd written that I liked travelling on my Enfield, enjoyed books, theatre, and films, liked people, was adventurous and that, by the time ten years passed, would presumably be settled back in Britain, possibly with some sort of job until I retired.

It had been fine when I'd prepared it in New Zealand, but although relishing the closeness with Abby, I became overcome with awkwardness when the next item came up. One of the things I had put on my list of hopes was that one day I would be guilt-free. What did I mean by that? Abby wanted to know. "Er . . . Well you know, how I feel about my affair and leaving you and Claire. I still feel terrible."

For the first time ever, we talked deeply about what had happened over thirteen years before. We both became tearfully emotional as she expressed the resentment, anger, and hurt she'd felt, especially as I had never apologised. I thought I had, but whatever I'd said had clearly been sorely inadequate. She said they thought I had acted selfishly, as if it was my right to do as I pleased. To top it all, I hadn't even met my granddaughter yet. I said that I had felt abandoned and lonely within my marriage. That old childhood "second best" feeling had crept from the depths, leading me to accept attention from another man at a time when I felt abandoned and useless. But I didn't tell her how I had begged their father to fall in love with me again and to give more of himself to me and our family.

She now knew that I had spent the subsequent years feeling ashamed and guilty, banishing myself, even though that meant also running away from the very people who meant most to me. I told her I was deeply sorry that I had been the cause of such devastation and distress. "Good—that's all right then," she said brightly.

It was acknowledged that I had paid a price for what I did. I had pleaded with God, Jesus, Mary, and all the saints, prophets, and gods I could think of to rid me of my guilt. But they all had their fingers in their ears, even the Hindu god Ganesha's big elephant ears were deaf, he the destroyer of obstacles. Neither did Durgha's terrifying face and necklace of skulls scare it away. I was still stuck with it. My condemnation of myself sufficed to serve for everyone else's too. Travelling about on my non-judgemental Enfield was a constantly changing distraction, a joyous and probably self-indulgent way to cope in places where nobody knew my past.

Somewhere in amongst this talk I was asked, "Do you have a personality beyond travelling with your motorbike?" Food for thought indeed.

Following this intimate talk, something shifted; I began to lose the hangdog self-image and started to behave more naturally. We played cards in cafés. Abby showed me how to do Sudoku, and I continued with the appliqué cot-cover embroidery I had started for Laurie but abandoned, because I didn't think it was good enough.

I'd bought the fabric in New Zealand when she was born. It depicted a big tree, and I planned to add various birds, flowers, and insects to it as I travelled around so I could give my granddaughter a home-made gift when I met her. Contrasting with the heavy business of motorcycle travel, I loved to work with tiny needles. Abby thought it was lovely, so I bought some Ecuadorian threads and worked at it with renewed enthusiasm.

Next stop was Riobamba, where we had a very comfortable room. I had picked up a shocking cold and felt most unwell. That night there was a silent candlelit street procession appealing to the Virgin to protect the town from the volcano Tungurahua (Throat of Fire). It had been acting up for more than a month and seemed to be preparing to erupt. Just before midnight, we heard the most terrific rumble and bang, discovering later it was the volcano, which although nineteen miles away, sounded like it had blown just outside our room. It was a lesser precursor to a major eruption a month later, when it really did erupt, destroying at least eight villages and killing six people.

We had planned to go to Baños, but the hotel manager told us the town had been evacuated, so we moved in the opposite direction towards Cuenca using the local scenic train via the Devil's Nose. Abby was tremendously caring and sympathetic, as I felt so rotten. We did the short train journey sitting with many other tourists on top of the train to 9,843 feet so we would see the best of the mountain views. Of course, the higher we went, the colder it got, but I was not going to give in. I wished I'd bought a woolly poncho from Otavalo.

In Cuenca, we had lunch at a smart restaurant, in an inner courtyard and somewhat different from my usual street-food stalls. It was nice to spend money on treats, and I began to feel much better. We visited the millinery factory where Panama hats are made. I tried on an enormous picture hat, so big it made my head look like a pea. Abby chose one for a forthcoming wedding. I had the opportunity to get close and fuss over her when she, too, became ill with my nasty cold. I was nursey and maternal to her. She responded with the hugely significant . . .

"Come home Mum. We need a mother."

I wish I could report that as soon as she said it the years of guilt and exile fell away and I had a golden flash, whereupon I fell on my knees and said, "of course I will, darling. I feel forgiven and wanted," but that isn't how it went. I must have responded but was so stunned by what she'd said that I couldn't cope with it immediately and mentally put it aside. It was too meaningful. Things like that had to be mulled over before being dealt with.

It was warmer having come down from the mountains as we made our way by bus to Manta on the coast. The scenery became more horticultural, and even the air must have been lush with nutrients, as air plants clung onto telegraph poles and wires. Various things were on offer on the bus, including musicians selling their CDs, other people selling sweets, fruit salad, coconut, and sesame seed biscuits, and even a bit of religion when preachers came aboard with Bibles.

A finger-wagging man in a dark suit shouted what we assumed were "fire and brimstone" messages at the passengers, who had no choice but to hear it. We were terrified, and we didn't even know what he was saying. In contrast, at a beach-bar in Manta that night, a Peruvian woman had to shout over the loud reggaeton music to invite us to her table for drinks with her and her New Yorker husband. A good evening ensued with tales of Peru, which I imagined I'd be seeing in the near future.

Next morning, we had a bad breakfast experience involving rubbery, cold plantain. Some soup we had later was worse. Fishing about in the bottom of the bowl, Abby's spoon emerged with an unappetising chicken foot.

The beach, which had been empty the previous night except for some half-built large wooden boats, was transformed into a temporary fish market. Eyed up by brown pelicans, the fishermen bringing in the catch was quite a sight. Wooden boats were being hauled ashore and the fish unloaded onto makeshift stalls. If that was the daily catch, the sea must be teeming with life.

Fabulous as a trip to the Galapagos Islands would have been, it was prohibitively expensive, so we opted for "the poor person's Galapagos" instead. However, we didn't feel at all poor on our return from Isla de la Plata. There were barely a dozen of us on the boat from Puerto Lopez for the twenty-five-mile trip, and before long, we'd seen four humpback whales' tail fins looping gracefully in front of us as we followed them towards the island. The area is on the migratory route from the cool waters of the southern tip of South America to the Galapagos and is where the males show off to the females, hence much leaping backwards, forwards, sideways, and any other splashy manoeuvres they think will impress.

A large floating turtle on the way gave us a look of surprise, as if it were expecting someone else; Charles Darwin, perhaps? After all, we were in the same part of the Pacific Ocean as the Galapagos Islands, and it may have been old enough to have met him. We considered the trip already worth the forty-five dollars US, even before we'd landed.

Water and cake were handed out as we clambered ashore this beautiful nature reserve for our walking tour. Creatures were so unthreatened by humans, we almost tripped over them. Male frigate birds puffed out their deep red chests as we passed. Large blue-footed booby birds did not attempt to get out of our way. They gave an apologetic and forlorn whistle through their long, pointed beaks, which Abby and I imitated and repeated to each other for the rest of the holiday.

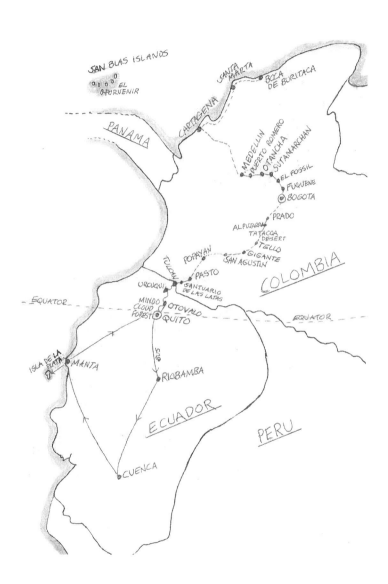

I took the opportunity for a snorkel off the rugged coast, where I saw many parrot fish. We were fed with sandwiches, more cake, and fruit and were delighted with the trip. But more was to come.

We were on the boat, making our way back to Puerto Lopez, when the skipper spotted some whales nearby and changed course towards them. We were beside ourselves with excitement as a whale breached and thrashed repeatedly, sometimes so close we could see the ribbing on its underside and even the craters in the barnacles clinging to it. Too thrilled to be alarmed, we all rushed from one side of the boat to the other. Like everyone else with their digital cameras I wildly snapped away with my old film camera, but not one picture showed the whale; only sideways pictures of disturbed sea where it had been.

We travelled by bus back to Quito along mountain roads the Enfield might have been made for. It was a long day's journey requiring snacks brought regularly onto the bus by vendors. When we got back to our hotel in the evening it was locked up and shuttered. We stayed at a better and cheaper one round the corner, so although I felt a heel for doing so, we made that our Quito base. I moved the bike out the next day when the owner returned from his day off.

We were now at the Grand Hotel, with a courtyard where the Enfield could reside under a fig tree whilst we went off for some luxury. El Monte, an eco-lodge in the middle of Mindo Cloud Forest, a few hours east of Quito, was our big treat.

An aerial runway double seat arrangement carried us over the river to get into the lodge parkland, where we were taken to our cabana, a little way from the main lodge. As much as possible, alternative energy was used. We ate organic food produced on the land and watched brightly-coloured birds in the garden. We drifted down the river in large inner tubes and saw a rare sun-bittern.

We became so keen on bird-spotting, we astonished ourselves by getting up before dawn to join a walking tour to see birds that favoured one particular tree when the dawn sun bathed it. We saw luminously bright birds and parrots of every kind, even a toucan. Later, a little agouti wandered contentedly among the lemon trees as we lazed in hammocks back at the lodge.

Our cabana was roomy. We had separate rooms and bathrooms with windows looking out onto the lush greenery. I could see the forest from my bath, which was almost in the open-air. I wallowed in the water heated by solar panels and wondered who I was. Naked and alone with nature, I had nothing on which to hang my identity—no job, no status, no address. I pondered the question I had been asked earlier as I looked out at the unencumbered landscape. It was a reasonable question. Was I just a woman with a motorbike? Who was I without it? I was left wondering; now that I had finally found something I was good at, i.e. motorcycle travel; if I was really Ms. No Personality? Who had I been before I went backpacking in 1998, anyway? I'd hardly left childhood at the age of fourteen when I met my future husband and hadn't really had time to find out about myself before I was in a permanent relationship, then doing my nurse training, and then married with children.

My bike didn't judge me. It sort of comforted and looked after me. We were a team. I concluded that, yes, for the time being, the bike WAS my identity and was happy with that.

And then it was all over, and I was sitting at the airport after seeing Abby off, feeling flat and lonely, and it was at that point, I felt my daughters needed further evidence at how sorry I was, so I wrote my heart out in a letter to them both. I wrote the long-overdue "sorry" and posted it the next morning. Abby had given me a chink in the wall through which I could see a way into being the mother she said they needed; I took the opportunity to knock out a brick or two.

I moved into a single room at the Grand. Having Abby with me had eased the heartache of leaving Paul, but it came back when she went. I stared at the map of South America. There was Peru and Argentina and Chile and Brazil. Why wasn't I excited about them? I'd developed a radar for doing things that felt right or didn't. I couldn't see myself there; I froze with indecision, apprehension, and loneliness. I felt sure I'd be back to normal after a few days so bought some oil from a filling station and set about an oil change on the bike.

This attracted some attention amongst other guests, who asked the usual questions about the bike and where I had been. The list of countries was growing, and like a memory game, I recited them in order. The bike and I had travelled together through India, Nepal, Pakistan, Thailand, Cambodia, Malaysia, Indonesia, East Timor, Australia, and New Zealand before coming to Ecuador. Eleven countries in six years. Correction fluid was near to hand, so I used it to write them on the air-box, thinking Peru would be the next one. How many more? What was I doing it for?

My wallet was stolen, and I found I was quite relieved that I had to stay put until a replacement credit card came. Luckily, my US dollars and passport were in the hotel safe. After two weeks, the new card arrived; a hotel clerk accepted it from the postman and promptly did a runner. I was using my other one so asked my friend not to send the second replacement until I had a different address. It was upsetting that someone at the hotel who knew me and knew I had already been robbed had stolen it. Apart from my pannier bag being stolen in Australia, I had never been robbed before. It affected the trust I'd always had.

Then I developed a rampant intestinal upset. I went to a doctor and described my problem with the use of a Spanish dictionary and by drawing a matchstick-person with rear-end hovering over a toilet. He had equal trouble explaining to me that he needed a sample, but we managed to understand each other with humour. The same day, a laboratory test showed I had a bacterial infection, and the appropriate antibiotic was bought from the pharmacy, all quickly diagnosed and treated at very little cost.

At the Grand Hotel I was now on the long-term rate and made friends with fellow guests. I shared cooking with a Chilean businessman, a trader in second-hand mobile phones from Peru, an Ecuadorian chef, and a travelling couple from America. A perky blackbird took shape pleasingly on Laurie's quilt, and I learned about Skype, the Internet communication system, hardly believing such a marvellous thing could exist.

New mother Claire sent me an email saying she wished she could have a fourteen-hour chat over coffee and that she missed me a lot. I wondered if she'd had my letter yet and worried that she was feeling low. And then I read an email from my brother, who found discussing personal matters really awkward. He wrote, "Everyone is missing you. When are you coming home?"

So much for my being a hardy, unfazed traveller. I was frozen by fear and indecision and could not contemplate moving on from the hotel. Neither did I feel in the slightest bit inclined to ride the bike. The longer I stayed, the more stuck I became. I felt stranded. I couldn't stay forever but couldn't summon the confidence to leave, either. So there I was . . . not only in a new country, but a new continent with a language I didn't speak, a motorbike I had suddenly become scared of, and my daughter had gone home. I'd been ill. I'd had to leave a man I still loved, and I'd been robbed, not only by a pickpocket, but by a member of the hotel staff who knew me.

A distant memory of Hendrikus using the Internet to get information about the countries we'd be passing through emerged from the mist. What was the website called? Oh yes . . . Horizons Unlimited. Perhaps I should have a look. Off I went to the Internet café and found the website. Sure enough, there were motorcyclists getting about all over the world and leaving messages and news, but I got swamped, unused to navigating around websites. All I could manage was to leave a feeble message somewhere on the site saying I was stuck and was anybody passing through who would like to meet up and perhaps travel with me?

Several days later, a message appeared in my email account. It was from Grant Johnson, who, with his wife, Susan, had travelled all over the world on their motorbike and had set up Horizons Unlimited to help other motorcycle travellers. He wrote, "Don't worry. We all get the collywobbles sometimes. Look at what you've already achieved—you'll be fine!" I was awestruck. The man, himself, had bothered to write back to me so kindly and with such reassurance, saying that even he had an attack of nervous apprehension sometimes. I felt better.

Another respondent, who called himself El Ray, had spent time in Quito and told me to go and visit some friends of his who ran a filling station in the city. I went there on the city tram and spoke to Andres and Pepe. Kindly, they reassured me and told me to bring the bike there, and they would look at it and see that everything was OK.

It was a monumental effort, but in a day or two, I started the bike, and having done the journey on foot first to make sure I knew the route and one-way streets (things that would never have bothered me before—I'd ridden blithely round Delhi and Bangkok, for heaven's sake), I set off to the filling station. I rode through the heavy traffic easily. The jinx was dispelled. The bike was given the once-over, a new plug, and a free tank of petrol. I was also given the address of some friends who ran an exclusive country hotel towards the border with Colombia.

I went back to the Grand Hotel, confidence fully restored. I could ride the bike again. The talk with Abby had changed things, too. Her "Come home Mum" meant so much to me. Claire said she missed me and was a bit low, and my brother was also gently prodding me.

I had reached a turning point. I realised why I'd got stuck. It simply didn't feel right to go south and further away from home. Once I'd acknowledged the messages and listened to what I was being told, everything did feel right. I didn't head south to Peru.

Confidently and happily, I turned the front wheel to the north.

17

To Colombia

Kidnap!

Wait a minute though ... go home? I didn't have a home. Where would I live? I'd have no income. What would I do? Everywhere I was travelling was cheap, enabling my survival on the interest on my savings, then at six per cent, high enough to yield £300 a month. The coffers were healthy after working at the hospice in New Zealand, but in the UK I'd be obsolete and unemployable as the health professional I had been eight years before. My ex-husband was receiving his pension but wasn't sharing. However, as usual, my heart confidently overrode my head. Something would come up. It always did.

Other travellers described feeling that once the return journey is commenced, the trip is over. Someone said it became limp and lifeless, try as he might to blow wind into its sails. But my return journey was to prove far from dull, for things hotted up in a "quite beyond my control" sort of way and continued to be as wonderful, serendipitous, and frightening as anything that had happened to me before.

It's true that it was different, because I now had a goal, but I was still travelling as I had always done, with eyes open to new sights, people, and experiences. There were times when everything seemed lack-a-day, but I'd soon reawaken the zest for my way of life. There was still so much to see in this new continent. Despite being on the road for over six years, I still enjoyed my nomadic lifestyle, even if my aimlessness had eventually become its own routine.

My goal gave me a warm glow. I almost wanted to rush towards it like a magnet, but I knew that if I did and gave up my travelling life before I allowed myself time to mentally adjust, I'd be at risk of feeling a huge anti-climax when I got there and resentment at being drawn back. So I stuck at the pace that suited my bike, which became increasingly important to me. In my diary I would write *"we"* rather than *"I."*

I wasn't the only one who was attached to it; my brother wrote that he was looking forward to meeting it, as it seemed like part of the family.

I'd had a taste of what Colombia may have to offer during a vibrantly loud street party outside the hotel during my last week in Ecuador. A lithe young Colombian man in a black leather jacket grabbed me, held me closer than surely was decent, grabbed my hand, thrust his thigh between mine, and moved me around to the exciting music. At first, I was affronted. "What are you doing?" but my feeble objection was drowned out by the music as he bent and swayed me this way and that to the music that ended rather too soon. He bowed and disappeared into the crowd.

Goodbye, Quito. No more processions through the streets with the Virgin Mary held up on a pedestal and a noisy band to accompany her on her tour. No more dollar almuerzo (lunch) of tripe soup with a bowl of dried blood as a condiment at my favourite corner restaurant. No more women street sellers calling out their wares, "cincuenta centavos!" fifty cents for a lottery ticket or some mandarins, laces, or insoles for shoes. No more shoe-shine boys asking to polish your footwear, even trainers, hoping for a few cents. I had, despite being robbed, had a good time in Quito.

Somehow, almost two months had slipped by. But I was ready to go. Andres at the filling station had hand-drawn what seemed a straightforward map and uttered the oft-heard, "You can't go wrong," but I got lost before I'd gone more than a few miles from the hotel.

I showed my map to a young man on a motorbike who had stopped to help. He roared off leading the way. I could swear he was an angel. Who says they can't have wheels instead of wings?

I was not prepared for the journey after he left. What had looked like main roads on the map turned out to be in the "back of beyond, dust, and desolation" category, full of holes and corrugations, in a quarrying area. With no-one to guide me, I was alone for the first time in months, not sure I was even on the right path descending many miles into a valley I'd mostly freewheeled down, leaving the engine running to take me through the sand and mud-patches. At the bottom, the bike stopped and, like a stubborn donkey, refused to go further.

I assessed the surroundings, thinking I may need to sleep out, as it was already mid-afternoon. My stores included a banana, a tin of sardines, and some oats. There was a nearby river for water. The bike and I were both hot and bothered, so in the shade of a tree, we cooled down as I gave the black, sticky spark plug a good clean. After a while, the bike started again, and with the hearty Enfield torque doing its stuff, it seemed to relish crawling up the other side of the valley in low gear.

Whilst I saw no more angels to put me on the right road, I did meet a priest in his dog-collar. I'd stopped for a wee, and with great bladder control, I hastily pulled up my jeans at the sound of the imminent uphill approach of a four-wheel-drive. The priest showed no surprise at my adjusting my clothing, having sprung up from a squatting position. He reassured me it was the right road. A miracle. I passed several pretty villages on my way to Urcuqui with its cobbled streets.

At the Hacienda San Francisco I was lucky enough to be a guest of the owners through an introduction by the Quito filling station chaps. I was shown to a suite, where I found a shower, soap, and shampoo and soft white fluffy towels. My day of divine interventions of angel and priest were completed by my heavenly room and a swim in the thermal pool under the celestial stars.

The next morning when I looked in my passport pouch, I noticed that I was very short of dollars. I knew I had stocked up before the journey in case I couldn't access any. Where had they gone? At least 175 dollars were missing. Then it dawned on me . . . I'd kept my documents, passport, and money in the reception safe at the Grand Hotel before I left. I realised with dismay that someone had taken my dollars. It hadn't been safe at all.

I enjoyed a few days being shown around the area by the hacienda owner, Maria's husband, who farmed protein-rich alfalfa animal feed. Roque helped me investigate why the bike's idling speed varied so much. It was also using oil. We dismantled the carburettor and found a piece of plumber's tape in the barrel. Somewhere in the past, someone must have used it to seal a thread, and it had found its way there. Its removal made no difference. The engine would tick over calmly and then race. It had no perceptible effect on the bike when we were moving, so I left Ecuador with it as it was.

Friends begged me not to go. The Foreign and Commonwealth Office website urged extreme caution. Should I survive kidnap by rebels, one of the fifteen active volcanoes might get me. All I knew about Colombia was that the singer Shakira came from there, that there was danger of kidnap by drugs barons, and that it produced great coffee.

The Horizons Unlimited website was optimistic. I had made good use of it and contacted a resident of Pasto, just across the border, to ask if I needed anything special before arriving there. Camilo, aged thirty, told me to display my registration number on my helmet and to prepare myself for the beautiful Colombian women. I told him of my gender and mature years. He and his mother then invited me to stay at their home. How kind.

With my registration number cut out from duct tape and stuck on my helmet so that the Colombian police wouldn't think I was a drug dealer, I set off.

The border-crossing on the 8th September took only two and a half hours. It was easy enough to enter Colombia, but I had no idea how I was going to get out, and had I been able to foresee the future, I may not have gone at all.

At 9,448 feet above sea level, the border control was very chilly. Then it started to rain, and the cloud had a "here to stay" look about it. I still had the thick PVC fisherman's trousers I'd bought in New Zealand so put those on, plus a fleece under my waterproof jacket, the first time they'd been unpacked for months. I borrowed some correction fluid and wrote *COLOMBIA* on the airbox, smiling with the usual thrill of achievement and anticipation when riding away from the last person to stamp the last document to say I was out of one country and into another.

Heavy rain danced on the dark tarmacked road. Lorries were different from any I'd seen before, looking with their black rounded roofs like covered wagons from the Wild West. Pleasingly, there was a hard shoulder for motorcycles, so the lorries and Colombian-assembled Renault 4 cars could overtake me as we struggled up the ascents.

The first thing I did was disregard my own rule about keeping to the Pan American Highway that runs from Ushuaia in Argentina to Prudhoe Bay in Alaska. The Karakoram Highway in Pakistan had not been the well-maintained three-lane motorway I'd imagined, so my expectations were more realistic here. However, even its whereabouts were vague and not marked on my map. It all looked pretty safe, so I turned eastwards to see Santuario de las Lajas, a neo-Gothic Catholic Church.

Well worth the detour, it looked like it had been flung onto the cliff face and stuck there. It, and the bridge it rests on, was built after the Virgin Mary's image appeared on a vertical rock-face high above the river below. Pilgrims, many with disabilities, thronged the area. The church has a reputation like Lourdes, with many visiting it to be healed. Crutches and walking sticks had been discarded on the path, and plaques describing miracle cures were set into the walls.

If I wanted to see it, I had no choice but to leave my bike with all my luggage outside a stall in the market and walk across the 150-foot bridge spanning the valley. I'd lost some confidence in the honesty of people. My emergency dollars hidden amongst the Enfield documents were gone, discovered missing during my stay at the hacienda. The staff at the Grand Hotel in Quito, who had helped themselves to my money and credit card put in their safe-keeping, had warned me about the thievery I could expect in neighbouring Colombia. But it was not fair to tar every South American with the same brush, and trust was restored when everything was just as I'd left it when I returned to the food stall. I had lunch there, thanking the people who'd kept watch.

As we ascended and descended the mountains towards Pasto, where I was to meet Camilo, I stopped to either take off or put on my fleece, the temperature changed so dramatically. The bike also responded to the variation, sounding rough and feeling jerky.

On arrival in the quiet evening city, I looked around for a phone box, hoping it would take cent coins, as I had no local currency. A kind man, who wouldn't hear of me using a phone booth, used his mobile phone to make the call for me and, having explained to Camilo where I was, waited with me until he came.

Camilo led me to their home, a luxurious sixth floor apartment under the shadow of the volcano Galeras. They had a monitor in the kitchen to warn them of any activity. All was quiet. Whilst they were well-prepared for any seismic activity, nothing could have prepared them for the sudden disappearance of their younger son a year back when Camilo's mother, Maria, a Supreme High Court Judge, was overseeing a case involving some pretty nasty drugs traffickers. Knowing he wouldn't get parental permission, he had sneaked off to Bogota to see a Guns 'n' Roses concert. They thought he'd been kidnapped, a common occurrence there. He returned a few days later to find them beside themselves, waiting for a ransom demand. They must have been through hell.

Maria gave me a recipe for cocaine.

Ingredients: Coca leaves, petrol, ether, chalk.
Method: Soak coca leaves in petrol for a few days until they become a slimy mess. Add ether to remove petrol. Add chalk and make a paste. Dry off moisture to make a powder. Serve.

Camilo's father was a shadowy figure, who when I did see him, barely acknowledged my presence. A devotee of Marx, with a bust of Lenin on the sideboard, he remained silent at family meals cooked by their housemaid. During a day-trip with Camilo and Maria to Laguna de la Cocha, the most stunning lake I had ever seen (sorry, New Zealand), Maria told me that the area used to be a terrorist stronghold.

She said that over fifty years before, the FARC (the Revolutionary Armed Forces of Colombia) had started off as Marxist Robin Hoods but were now like the Mafia. They make astronomical amounts from cocaine, kidnap, and murder. Many thousands have died as a result of their activity. There are links with other worldwide terrorist organisations and rumours that the US (where most of the cocaine ends up) destroys only the crops of coca that don't belong to them.

Before I left Pasto, I received some long-distance reassurance from Horizons Unlimited contacts. The reason the bike was using so much oil was because the new piston was still "bedding in." As for the spluttering, El Ray suggested adjusting the air screw as per the manual, but I'd already done that. I squatted down and stared at the carburettor that I'd taken apart so many times. I prodded the rubber manifold and revealed a large split in it. Of course! Too much air would alter the air-to-petrol mix, making the engine race and slow; it's a wonder it went at all. At a market, I found some car radiator hose the same diameter as the manifold and, after trimming with a knife, made it fit—no more spluttering.

Thrilled at my achievement, I rode off and, not noting any landmarks, got lost and almost ran into an elephant. The circus had arrived on the outskirts of town. I found my way back to the apartment, having learned to be wary of taxi drivers, of people opening car doors in front of me, and of course, elephants.

Camilo, keen for me to try another Colombia experience, took me to a restaurant for some cuy (guinea-pig). Not at all sure I could eat a distant relative of my first pet, Squeak, I was relieved when cuy was off the menu and ate seafood instead.

On the way home, we passed some musicians playing in a quiet street. Camilo explained that music is performed outside the home of the loved-one to show the man's devotion. He would be paying them to serenade his love. A minstrel with a lute might have been effective, but this music was loud and brash, hardly the food of love.

I bought copies of *Love in The Time of Cholera* and *One Hundred Years of Solitude*, by the Colombian author Gabriel Garcia Márquez, and a new notebook for my diary. As I ended the last one, I noted that it was the same way I'd started it in January on returning to New Zealand, planning a new life there with Paul. He told me in an email that he was expecting news on his bankruptcy case and the legal case against the farmer who stole his cows. So much had changed for me, but he was still in the same place—*"I am troubled both for and about him."*

With grateful thanks to the family for giving me a place to stay whilst I acclimatised, organised more funds, and sorted the bike out, I set off to ride north about 155 miles to Popayan, a Spanish colonial town destroyed by an earthquake in 1983 and completely rebuilt as it had been before. There I found a charming hotel with a courtyard and fountains, further enhancing it with an Enfield. Our stay there cost the same as a coffee would at home. In my diary I record having smiled all day.

Full of confidence in myself, the bike, and the country, I went off-road again to see the weird statues in the archaeological park of San Agustin to the south-east. It was one of those occasions when I was grateful for a well-fitting bra, as the road was so bumpy. The track took me right over the Andes, from one side to the other. It was cold, wet, and tough-going but was worth every drop of oil lost from the front forks.

As I rode over rickety bridges through the national park, the hammering rain hardly let up all day. The skies were dramatically sinister in design and palette with purples, greys, and navy blues appearing at the same time as the sun broke through to highlight the lush mountains all around. The few people I saw on the track looked sinister too. I heard later that the area had a high level of insurgency.

At Isnos I was reunited with tarmac and, whilst wallowing in relief and self-congratulation, was practically pulled off the bike and dragged into the tourist office to sign the visitors' book. The tourist officer was delighted to see a foreigner, demanding photos with me and the Enfield. The sun was as hot as a furnace and dried me and my leaking rain-gear in minutes, before I rode the short distance to San Agustin.

I stayed at a little hotel run by two women, who fussed around me. The Enfield, with its scratches and dents and old-fashioned round-the-wrong-way gear-change, was hardly a temptation to thieves, but the proprietors would not hear of it being left in the street. They were excited when I rode the bike up the steps, through the lobby, and into the pretty garden outside my room and watched, as fascinated as they might have been had I been performing brain surgery, when I replaced the brake-light bulb.

Caged birds were in the garden. I recoiled. What to do? I had vowed in Indonesia that I would check before booking in anywhere that there were no imprisoned birds. It was too late, and I'd have to accept that not everyone thinks the same way. I'd be more careful next time.

I recorded being very happy with the bike and my idyllic wandering life. I had crossed from the western side of the Andes to the east that day. But my pride turned to humility when eating at a cheap café that evening. Another diner whistled to a beggar to finish his meal when he was full. A shoeshine man came in and looked longingly at my plate. I'd eaten enough. He was so grateful to finish it off, even using my knife and fork as he tucked hungrily into the chicken and rice. I often gave food to dogs and cats, but I felt like a spoiled princess with my privileged life, literally giving the crumbs from my table to the poor.

It's not often I lose my temper, but back at the hotel a guest got the rough edge of my tongue when I found him sitting on my bike. He was completing a tick-list of countries and boasted that he'd visited over one hundred but couldn't tell me much about anywhere he'd been, even though he spoke English well. He presumed it would be my privilege to take him as pillion to the nearby statues the following day, but I found him too arrogant for good company and spent the next day happily alone amongst the mystical, squat statues from between the sixth and fourteenth centuries set in their beautiful parkland.

I left San Agustin but, instead of repeating the rough track back to Popayan, carried on towards the north-east on a much kinder road. For some time it followed the young Rio Magdalena, not just Colombia's longest river, but also one of the great rivers of South America. I'd eaten no breakfast because of an upset tummy. Could it have anything to do with a restaurant where a chicken wandered out of the kitchen and I saw the server squeezing her spots?

A handwritten sign at a farm selling yoghurt prompted me to turn in. Yoghurt should settle my stomach. At the farm a young woman, who repeatedly breathed, "Guapa ... guapa," as she circled my bike, was aghast and enthralled by my lifestyle. As I downed fresh yoghurt with pineapple, she vowed there and then to her parents that this was what she was going to do. I wonder if she did.

At Gigante, fifty miles further north, I booked in at a modern hotel with an outdoor pool. The chef noticed I had a flat tyre, so I removed the wheel and the next morning was taken by the hotel owners in the back of their truck into town, where whilst we ate ice-cream topped with grated cheese (tasting surprisingly good), a patch was ironed over the hole and the tube refitted.

The town was reminiscent of a scene from a Western, with horses and traps carrying sacks of supplies from the sort of wooden buildings you see in cowboy films. Everywhere I went, friendly people welcomed and helped me. Where were all the terrorists I'd been warned about?

So far I'd been perfectly safe. However, I was doing quite well on the self-harm front. In my attempt to save a drowning wasp in the hotel pool, it completely misunderstood my intention and stung me on the finger. It felt like a piercing red-hot needle for days. Then, on the following Sunday, at Tello, a little town with one hotel, a bar and, a church, I was invited to go swimming with a friendly local family down by the river, where showing off to the children, I hit a submerged branch as I dived in and emerged bleeding from face, hands, and arms like a monster from the swamp.

The only hotel in Tello had a huge aviary. Again, I'd broken my vow to not stay where there were captive birds, but at the end of a day's travel there was no choice. However, rather than being in small cages, the entire courtyard was netted over to roof height and filled with exotic trees, plants, and birds. Lizards darted about on the palms and banana leaves.

I sat in the courtyard embroidering yellow flowers onto Laurie's quilt, laughing at two parrots that had been taught to shout, "Clara! Clara!" comically to each other. One perched prettily on the handlebar of my bike outside my room. I approached to take a photo of it but got too close, and it gave me an unreasonably vicious nip on the nose, leaving a mark and a bruise. So there I was, gashes and bruises all over my body and a throbbing finger from an ungrateful wasp, and not a trafficker in sight.

I was at Baraya, just ten miles from Tello, when I thought trouble had finally begun. I was stopped by men in bullet-proof vests and camouflage uniforms looking like paramilitary. They were carrying guns, which they grasped at my approach. "This is it!" I thought, regretting not sticking to my promise to stay on the Pan American Highway.

Then I saw the word *Policia* and, breathing a sigh of relief, happily let them search my luggage. They soon got bored after finding nothing but a couple of tins of sardines and a bag of rice in amongst my meagre collection of cooking items, maps, diaries, ancient camera, washing stuff, books, thermals, mask, and snorkel.

If they were looking for guns or drugs, they were wasting their time. All I had was a tube of toothpaste and some evening primrose capsules.

They were interested to hear what I was doing, though, and one even smiled for a photograph. I asked about the road ahead on the edge of the Tatacoa desert. They said it was safe. I had crossed back over the Andes but at a lower altitude and rode into a magic area of beauty and complete silence.

My diary reads:

"*So off I went on this gorgeous day, happy as anything with the prospect of a great ride ahead. And so it was. One of the best I've ever had. After Baraya, there was no traffic on the narrow dirt road. Sometimes it went along the bottom of a valley, at others zig-zagging up the cliffs into the mountains some of which were bare but in other, lower places, lush with vegetation. Pink granite gorges seemed to squeeze in on the narrow road. I wore a travel-grin and no helmet. I stopped to listen to the silence. It was just gorgeous. I felt as if I was the first person ever to have seen this.*"

Not until I reached Alpujarra over an hour later did I see anyone at all. Alpujarra, like many old towns, had a church by a town square with fountains (I only saw one working once) and a tree in the middle. This tree was so massive it must have been planted by the Spanish conquistadores themselves. I found a little restaurant and sat down for the usual almuerzo of soup, meat, and rice.

A group of police came in. I should point out that they were not like our officers in blue, but like the ones who stopped me in Baraya, males and females wearing camouflage suits and carrying guns. I was invited to join them. With my limited understanding of Spanish, when they asked me to accompany them to the heavily sandbagged station, I assumed they wanted to check my documents, but they dismissed them. I was their guest.

The modern building was enshrouded in thick metal mesh. They showed me maps of the whereabouts of rebel groups and pointed out the bank next door. It had had its doors blown off by guerrillas. "Oh, are there guerrillas round here then?" I was told they would probably be watching me as I rode the twenty-five miles to Prado, the next town.

I was a bit uneasy as I rode on, scouring the hills for signs of terrorists, but arrived safely at Prado to find four police motorcyclists, who had been radioed ahead, waiting for me. They welcomed me and saw me booked safely into a hotel.

Prado, a resort on the banks of the River Magdalena, was noisy and brash. I sat in a café that evening and wrote:

> *"There is deafening music behind me, different music from the shop next door and as if that isn't enough, someone has just turned on the TV. It's a "cops and robbers" film with sirens, screaming tyres and gun-fire! Added to that, a child is wailing outside!"*

I stayed one night and went on to Bogota the next day, where I was to collect my replacement credit card from the poste restante address. It was a horrible and steep approach—three lanes of slow, heavy diesel buses and lorries belching out smoke. I would have turned and fled, had I not been trapped on the autopista.

In Bogota's Old City my preferred hostel was full, but the kind German owner offered me parking for the Enfield whilst I stayed elsewhere. The nearest place was a grim old hotel, where the owner followed the guests round turning the lights off. My mattress was covered in hard plastic and the bottom sheet so thin it was transparent. Bogota is at an altitude of 8,1661 feet, and I was cold in my cheerless room. However, things picked after I met another guest there and we went sightseeing together.

On the first day, Carlos helped me find the poste restante venue at an international bank. Never thinking it wouldn't be there, as the address was in a very recent edition of *Lonely Planet*, I was told they hadn't offered that service for three years. My post would be "returned to sender." So much for up-to-date guide books.

Carlos, a Mexican-American, had travelled a great deal, and inevitably we swapped experiences as we explored Bogota. We went to the excellent gold museum to see what pre-Columbians had made with their sacred metal before most of it was melted down and made into ingots by the Spanish conquerors. A gold breastplate had a very good likeness of Bart Simpson, and we both got the giggles. This lightheartedness continued for the rest of the day.

A cable-car takes tourists to Monserrate, the top of the mountain above the city. Gift shops surrounded the basilica, and we discovered some tacky religious memorabilia. I shrieked with shock and disbelief when I saw a gold-framed picture of a red Bogata bus and there, sprawled on the pavement in front of the bus, was a depiction of Jesus having just fallen carrying his cross. It was absurdly inappropriate. Another large picture of a Bogota bus also featured Jesus, this time with a raised hand, looking for all the world like he was hailing it. "All it needs is a clock to make it even worse," I said and there, in the corner opposite a floating Virgin Mary, was a small clock face. It was tasteless, disrespectful, and so tacky we couldn't contain ourselves.

We discovered a mutual glee of kitsch clocks we'd seen. I told him about a huge stuffed lobster wall-clock I'd seen in Vietnam with the dial in its belly and a Syrian mosque clock that played the call to prayer as the alarm. He described a Chairman Mao alarm clock he'd seen in China, where the man himself waved his arm every second. We'd had such fun, and I no longer cared about my credit card, because I had others.

When he flew back to California, I went to fetch the bike. Someone else with access to the open-air lock-up had helped themselves to one of my jerry-cans, but at least I still had one left. I continued north, having been told I mustn't miss Villa de Layva.

Half-way there, I stayed at a smart hacienda (way beyond my budget) in Fuquene, so luxurious I felt I should stay awake all night just to appreciate the room. The resident corgi also felt I didn't belong there and ran snarling beside the bike to see me off the next morning, savaging my ankle as I slowed for a cattle-grid. Its vice-like grip broke the skin through my leather jeans, and the pain lasted for days and left a nasty bruise. I'd never kicked a dog before, but I sincerely hoped I hurt that evil hound as much as it had hurt me.

I had a delightful ride up and down, round and round, on the roads to Villa de Layva. Those squiggles on my map passed by Laguna Fuquene and little villages in the mountains with their pretty gardens in front of farmhouses, stopping for empanadas and tinto (sugary black coffee). But when I arrived at my destination, I didn't fall for it at all. Fall *in* it I nearly did, as the cobblestones were like cannonballs. Perhaps it was the overpriced fruit-juice in the vast Spanish colonial square or the sight of a woman carrying a whole cow's head across it, but it just didn't feel comfortable. I felt privileged to be able to leave—the joy of having my own transport.

A bit further on I felt I'd been silly. It was late afternoon, and the sky looked heavy. Really heavy.

A few miles on was El Fossil, home of *Kronosaurus boyacensisa*, a thirty-four-foot pliosaurus crocodile from the Cretaceous Period. The skeleton was almost complete. I had a quick look but was anxious about the weather. The brewing storm developed into a spectacular sound and light show, echoing round the mountains. The whole area had an eeriness to it, reflected in a sky so dark it matched the bruise on my ankle. It was getting late, and I had nowhere to stay, having shunned the facilities of Villa de Layva. I could have gone back, but my gut feeling said to go on.

Pink piglets ran for shelter, but a warty toad emerging from under a stone seemed delighted at the heavy rain. There was an archaeological site further on, and during a lull in the rain, I made a dash for it and overshot the entrance. I'd hung my helmet on the handlebar, which stopped me making the turn, and fell ignominiously in the mud right in front of the curator, who helped to pick me up.

The site is believed to have been used to anticipate solstices and equinoxes by the Muisca people, who worshiped the sun and moon. Two parallel rows of columns, thirty feet apart, stood out dramatically against the sky. A streak of sunshine pierced through the deep purple sky and lit them up. A rainbow appeared. It was eerily sensual as I sheltered with señor the curator in a tomb with a large single slab of stone on top as the storm thundered above us.

I went on in the rain, with my lights on, ignoring the "never ride at night" rule. At nightfall, I came upon Sutamarchan, where a welcoming hotel just off the plaza had a dry garage and a good dinner. My gut feeling had guided me well.

The next day, I climbed up and up on a rough road prone to landslides, until I came to the rim of an enormous bowl with emerald green mountains on all sides. I stopped and gazed down into the bowl and across to the mountain-ranges beyond. I looked upwards at a peak some distance away. An hour later, after a steep ascent, I was looking down on it. I'd seen some scenery, but that was exquisite.

Four hours on from the state border town of Otanche, I eventually made it to Puerto Romero along a punishingly bumpy, stony, flooded, and muddy track. I hadn't found anywhere I could have rested, except when falling in a deep puddle. A local windowless bus wheezed and waddled past, like an obese person whose feet hurt, the passengers waving and smiling and giving me hope that there would be an end to the track.

As I entered the village, I was applauded and handed a bottle of beer from an outside bar. Someone led me to his house to wash the mud off the bike from my fall in the deep puddle, where water had entered the exhaust pipe.

I'd had a hard but marvellous ride those last days, so when I was invited by a rancher to stay at his hacienda, I jumped at the chance. For a few days, I swam in the outdoor pool, went horse-riding round his lush valley pastureland estate, and was almost deafened by the evening frog-chorus echoing through the valley. I felt so lucky. The puddle-water up the exhaust-pipe hadn't affected the bike whilst going uphill, but now, on the descent to Medillin, it coughed and spluttered as we left this remarkable place.

I'd felt perfectly safe in Colombia, until I was kidnapped.

On a main road I was overtaken and stopped by a young chap on a Honda, who insisted I stay with him and his friends in Medellin, Colombia's busy second largest city. I was taken to James's flat, where I parked the bike and unloaded before climbing on the back of his Vespa for a night-ride round the sights of the city with his friends.

There were statues by Fernando Botero, who made his subjects grossly overweight. In his statues and paintings, people, animals, and even buildings were depicted as being obese, including the Sphinx. Even a still-life at the museum depicted fat vases of fat flowers and fat fruit. The club members were all very good-hearted, caring people. I was able to check emails at James's flat. Claire had included tender pictures of herself with baby Laurie, making me cry with love and longing—I was certain that I was doing the right thing by going home.

My captors allowed me to leave after a few days of intensive sightseeing, drinking the local hooch, aguadienté, and eating local foods like minced beef and smoked sausage. My bike was treated to a new spark plug, and the points were adjusted at the Moto Angel workshop, where my photo was added to a gallery of fellow motorcycle travellers; testament to the assistance they have given to those who pass through. I was presented with lifelong membership of James's motorcycle club at a leaving party thrown in my honour.

Rather than kidnap and volcanoes, the foreign office website should warn of pressure to stay by friendly Colombians. So nice were the people that even when I stopped on the road later, mistakenly thinking people who were having a picnic in their garden were selling orange juice, they gave me a glass.

As I left the mountains, I knew the time had come to think about how to get to Panama and the rest of Central America. I got gloomy when I thought of it and had been putting it off. If you look at a map of Colombia, it shows a land-link to Panama. So what's the problem? Why not ride there? There must be roads, a flyover, a bridge, or a ferry. The Pan-American Highway is interrupted by an environmental gem, the Darien Gap.

The distance between where the Colombian road ends and the Panamanian road starts is about sixty-two miles. In this fifty-mile wide no-man's land lies river delta, swamp, and mountainous rainforest. Much of it is national park and home to several tribes.

Various groups and individuals have crossed on foot or with vehicles, but during the 1990s, much of it fell under the control of armed groups, who kidnapped inhabitants and travellers. FARC still controlled it. So no, I wasn't going to ride through it or fly over it. The only other way was to go round it. Other people had done it from the coastal town of Cartagena. So could I.

With the last of the Andes behind me, I reached what seemed to be an entirely different country. Suddenly, there were black people, coconut palms, incredibly loud reggaeton music, and Pentecostal churches. There were police in blue uniforms, thatched roofs, dizzyingly hot "three cold showers a day" weather (enabling me to pack away my wet weather gear), outdoor living, and "love hotels" rentable by the hour. I was in the Caribbean.

Cartagena. Traffic was busier there, with taxi-drivers seemingly determined to knock me off my bike. I shouted, "Oi!" at them, but with *hoy* meaning "today" in Spanish, it had no noticeable effect.

At the romantically decaying Hotel Doral, I had an enormous room with a door onto the enchanting courtyard with its tropical trees, parrots, and hummingbirds (the first floor was unusable due to risk of collapse). My Enfield had an open room by reception, where I changed the oil, adjusted the tappets, and gingerly tightened a loose nut holding on the leaking rocker oil pipe, loosened by all those bumpy roads. I rested in the peaceful courtyard, chatting to other visitors and making a blue butterfly for Laurie's quilt.

I explored the town whilst information-gathering about onward travel to Panama. The old walled town was founded by the Spanish as a storehouse for the gold plundered from the Indians until the galleons could ship it back to Spain, attracting other thieves, such as Francis Drake and Edward Vernon, who lurked around the Caribbean coast looting the looters. Later, pirates saved themselves the bother of going all that way and attacked Spanish ships just before they got home.

There are yacht owners who will, for about the same price as a flight from Bogota to Panama City, take passengers from Cartagena to the mainland coast of Panama. They will also take motorcycles for that much again. Someone helped me to write a plea in Spanish for a "lift" to Panama. I pinned it on the marina noticeboard with a photo. It worked almost immediately. Arrangements were made with a sailor, Jimmi, for two weeks hence. I congratulated myself at sorting things out so quickly and went to explore further up the coast. Easy-peasy. In fact, almost too good to be true.

18

Colombia to Mexico via Panama, Nicaragua, Honduras, and Guatemala

Even worse things happen at sea.

My horoscope, within a booklet called *Almanac de Bristol* (of all things) and bought in a market somewhere between Bogota and Cartagena, had this prediction for Pisces, my star-sign: "Travelling and meeting people from foreign countries will have top priority. Keep a positive mind in order to achieve your dreams, ideas and projects. You are protected by spiritual forces so nothing will hurt you."

The day I left Cartagena, the spiritual forces saved both me and the black pig that dashed from the undergrowth onto the road just in front of me. I braced myself for the impact and smacked into its rear. It squealed and ran away, while I wobbled to a halt with heart pounding.

The only other living things I'd hit were a dog in Nepal and a kangaroo in Australia, which I suppose isn't bad after six years on the road.

I'd been told I mustn't miss Tayrona National Natural Park, one of South America's most beautiful places, where the foothills of the Sierra Nevada flatten down to blend with the pristine beaches of the Caribbean Sea. 170 miles north-east of Cartagena, it was where I was heading.

It could well be the paradise I'd heard it was, but the fee would have cut deeply into my "sail to Panama" fund. I read the rules at the gates and rode on; I'd have had to carry everything to a beach-hut, a forty-five minute hike away necessitating repeated journeys with my stuff, and the bike would have to stay in an unguarded open car-park at the entrance. Impossible.

I hoped there'd be a nice place for us further on. An hour later, I was installed in my own paradise at Boca de Buritaca. The inexpensive Doña Maria hotel, run by Gloria and her family, had a concrete room for me on a flat roof that served as a balcony. The Enfield was in view outside, almost covered with bougainvillea and flame-red blooms from a tangled bush where little birds twittered as they hunted for insects. Best of all, the hotel was situated beside the wide Buritaca River.

After unpacking, I went for a walk, discovering gleefully that it was also where the river flowed lazily into the Caribbean Sea. I made friends with the children and had a beer on the balcony, happy that I had everything I needed . . . river, beach, and mountains.

As the afternoon light softened into evening, I realised I had music as well. Far from the serenity that often comes with sundown, very loud reggaeton Colombiano music boomed from the downstairs open-air bar. My room had a glassless window overlooking the outdoor billiard hut behind the hotel. Their music, sounding like a blend of oompah and country and western, competed with the music from my hotel, with both venues seemingly determined to drown each other out.

Strangely, I did not find the cacophony unpleasant and laughed at the doubly cheerful upbeat tunes. Various insects had come to join me as I read in bed, including a firefly that glowed intermittently in a dark corner by the bathroom. At a humid 86° I was grateful for the free-standing fan with a little night-light on top. I'd been reading by the light and, despite the ridiculously loud music, had started dozing.

Dropping the book and waking myself up, I opened my eyes to see a circling bat trying to catch fluttering moths lured in by the light. Afraid the bat would get chopped to bits in the fan, I reached out half-asleep to turn it off and put my hand into the unguarded fast-rotating blades. I yelled out, more alarmed than hurt, but my cries went unheard due to the surrounding din. Having more sense than me, the bat escaped unscathed. With throbbing fingers, I laughed and went back to sleep.

The next day, I stepped into the river at the bottom of the garden and floated blissfully until it became the salty sea. I was wary, though. A young Spanish woman had been swept away along that coast last week. I did not want a watery grave . . .

Entangled in seaweed on the beach was some fabric, just the right colour for robin feathers for Laurie's quilt. Once the oily smell was washed out, I started sewing. I spent days swimming, sewing, and reading. Eight hours' sleep was pretty unlikely there, but after a beer and a bit of bike maintenance, it's surprising how exhausting needlework can be. I gathered up string, ribbon, and sparkly gold thread to make a nest for the blackbird. The flora and fauna were vastly out of proportion to each other, the blackbird and nest taking up most of the tree and a smiling hedgehog the same size as one of the eggs in the nest. I hoped Laurie wouldn't mind.

One night there was a tropical storm, with accompanying sound and light displays. A power-cut silenced the sound-systems, and I wrote my diary by candle-light. All was silent, except for people laughing. Why wouldn't they? They lived in paradise.

Buritaca provided a getaway for Colombians too and was packed with throngs of happy holiday-makers on the following public holiday weekend. Beer and rum stalls sprang up with music so loud the speakers vibrated themselves off their stands.

The whole place was transformed from the quiet little riverside haven of my arrival to a scene from Brighton on a hot weekend mixed with Glastonbury Festival. Already heaving with people on the Saturday, it was bursting at the seams on Sunday and Monday. Children played like children do anywhere there is sand and water. Families with inflatable beach toys found their spot on the beach or waited for the one-man ferry across the river to the sea. I sat and ate fruit salad and watched the ferry man.

I wrote:

"Impressed almost to tears at the earnestness and hard work of the young man. He has a squarish boat with the inappropriate name "Tintorera" (little shark) without engine or oars. Instead, this strong, healthy young man pushes off as hard as he can from the river-shore once he has a boatful of fourteen passengers. He then swims behind the boat, pushing it forwards across the lazy current about 30 metres [100 feert] to the opposite beach, discharges his passengers and poles back. He must have done this a hundred times or more this weekend. Men were rocking the boat, making the girls squeal, just like they do everywhere. It was lovely to witness this experience and I thought, "We are all the same really!""

Amid this commotion sat a group of very different people with long black hair, wearing white tunics and trousers, quietly watching the scene. I was told they were Indians from the mountains and to avoid them, as they were "dangerous." It was another one of those injustices where the original people are looked at suspiciously by the invaders. Much later, I read with sadness that the 20,000 of the indigenous ethnic group called the Kogi are so distressed at the way we are destroying nature whilst they work with it that some years ago some elders came down from the mountains to warn against upsetting the "Great Mother" with our greed. A BBC documentary was made about their appeal. Having avoided colonisation from the conquistadores, they rarely interact with the modern world and wish to be left alone. I wondered why they came to the beach that day.

The public holiday over, the mayhem reduced to just the deafening music from the bar downstairs and the billiard hut. I continued to enjoy fresh fish cooked with coconut, plantain, and rice. At lunch and breakfast I ate heavenly fresh fruit. In that humid heat it was quite sufficient.

The next time I checked my emails, there was a message, not from Jimmi, but another skipper who had seen my advert, but by the time I read it I had less than an hour to get back to Cartagena, which was impossible. I had been away for ten days with no word from Jimmi. It looked unlikely that he'd take me now. It had all been too good to be true. If I wanted passage to Panama, I had to go back and start all over again.

Trying to "keep a positive mind," as instructed by my horoscope, I packed up, left my noisy paradise, and returned to Cartagena. It took a further two weeks of asking people at the marina before I was put in touch with Alberto, a sixty year-old Italian with a forty-two foot monohull yacht. He seemed reliable but bore an uncanny similarity to Marcel, the skipper of the catamaran I'd escaped from in Jakarta. He, too, declared to be a vegetarian and had a daughter of the same age and even the same name. He also lived alone on his boat.

Red danger flags were waving, but I refused to acknowledge them through my rosy determination to see the best in people and my "It'll be alright" attitude. He told me that if I could find another passenger for the trip, the Enfield would go for free. The deal also included my painting anti-fouling to the hull; a filthy, toxic, and horrible job. I was becoming uneasy about my visa expiring. My skivvying would hurry things along. It was a mystery as to whether or not trips to and from Panama on small yachts were legal; it all seemed a bit "cloak and dagger." An agent is given the passengers' passports, the fare is then paid to the boat-owner, and the stamped-out passports are returned.

Word got round that I was to sail with Alberto. Another "yacht-ferry" owner sent a message to my hotel saying it was unsafe to sail with Alberto, reporting that he was an incompetent sailor and was hostile to his passengers. I put this bad-mouthing down to professional jealousy. Then an American couple with a boat at the marina told me that they were concerned for my safety. Apparently, Alberto had been in prison for people-smuggling and had also hit his daughter publicly. I confronted him with these things but was satisfied with justifications and denial. How much more of an idiot could I be? There was a popular backpacker hostel in Cartagena, where I thought I may find another passenger, but they would not allow me to put an advert on the notice-board because of Alberto's reputation. They did not want to be responsible for any disasters and told me they warned guests against sailing with him.

I continued to ignore ALL those warnings, preferring to believe that lightening doesn't strike twice in the same place and that it couldn't possibly be as bad as the last voyage with Marcel. Alberto did have the odd outburst of temper whilst we were preparing the boat, but I put that down to Italian temperament.

The boat looked seaworthy, so I got on with the hull and waited for a departure date. Anyway, my horoscope said spiritual forces would protect me. The idyllic-sounding trip was to take four days and included snorkelling in the San Blas islands before landing on the Panama mainland, only about 250 miles south-west of Cartagena.

Meanwhile, I was enjoying life at the Hotel Doral in Half-moon Street with its interesting variety of guests. Well past its top-notch glory days, but only a short walk from the historical town, it attracted people who appreciated beauty even when it was well-faded. It was also cheap. In the nearby park one could search the trees to find the resident sloth, or for a few pesos, you could play roulette on a home-made board. Guests gathered in our hotel courtyard after a scorching day's work or sightseeing. We sat in the middle to avoid falling masonry from the balustrades.

An American woman in her forties checked in and introduced as her gigolo her much younger companion, Juan Carlos. She was absolutely plastered. It was horrifyingly tantalising watching her trying to light a cigarette that she could not get to meet the flame. My neighbours were from Ecuador and had brought with them hundreds of loofahs to sell on the buses, leaving in the mornings, hidden amongst a cloud of them with their legs sticking out. Another guest, Felipe, also made a living on the buses by playing his guitar. He sang and played Cuban ballads in the evenings as we all sat in the courtyard with a beer, the parrots roosting overhead in the palm trees. Maria, the cleaner, would sometimes join us and do palm-readings.

Brian, a quiet Englishman keeping to himself, sat apart, drinking his way through a bottle of rum. This pleasant socialising was to the echo of people shouting, "Ello? Ello?" into the mobile phone of the man hiring it out at the hotel entrance. I met Tamara, an elegant, well-travelled woman of about my age, who carried everything in a small backpack but looked like she had stepped out of a fashion magazine, floating around ethereally in some beautiful "old thing" she had picked up for a song in Cuba or Peru.

The shower-head in my room was just a cold-water pipe emerging from the wall, and the light-fittings replaced by a single bulb. One night, I awoke to the smell of burning and, on opening my eyes, saw that my ceiling fan was on fire. I ran out into the courtyard to find the manager, who extinguished the fire with a wet mop. I wrote, *"Love this 'no frills' hotel, this room, this bed."*

Someone had left behind a "started but given up" book of Sudoku puzzles, and during the wait for the boat to be ready, I became adept at them as I worked my way through it. One of the guests commented that he could almost see the air through the canvas of my rear tyre. I looked for a new one, but nineteen inch tyres aren't common, and I just wore out more rubber whilst riding around searching. Confident that the bike and I would get to Panama City without much riding, I hoped to find one there. I replaced a parking light bulb and adjusted the chain.

The beautiful old walled town of Cartagena is almost too picturesque to be real. Its sixteenth and seventeenth century Spanish architecture is little changed, with leafy plazas to settle in and people-watch. Outside the fortifications, the beach was a good place for swimming and watching pelicans diving for fish.

One day there was a carnival, and I felt someone in the crowd unzipping my backpack behind me. I had a furled umbrella with me and beat the pick-pocket off with it until his friend asked me to stop.

The boat was beginning to look finished.

I had some fantastic days on gorgeous island beaches with fellow travellers, eating fresh seafood and swimming. Corrupt police in launches tried to catch ferry-boat skippers taking people like us on trips without giving them a cut, and we got involved in a thrilling boat-chase that our skipper was winning until the engine stalled and he had to pay up. I enjoyed life in the vibrant, historic and pretty colonial city, drinking exquisite fruit juices and rum and learning to salsa.

Alberto's boat was launched.

Just as you would have curry in India, Havana cigars in Cuba, and perhaps buy a huge sombrero in Mexico, I decided to try some of the local produce in Colombia. It was a public holiday and an excuse for a fiesta. I'd gone out for a quiet beer but bumped into Evan from London and Australian Dan who were also Hotel Doral guests. They'd bought some "special" white powder. It had got damp, so rather than sniffing it through a rolled note, we put a wodge of it on our gums, taking away some of the naughtiness of it. That night the old city became a string of street parties. We stayed together and, due to the stuff we'd had, didn't get tired and danced with complete strangers all night. We got back to the hotel at six in the morning.

As I went to get my usual coffee, orange juice, and fried plantain one morning, I was halted at the door by an astonishing sight. Overnight, Half-moon Street had been transformed from a busy thoroughfare into a muffled film-set and was a sawdust-strewn street of more than a hundred years ago. Horses and carts replaced engine power. The Marquez novel *Love in The Time of Cholera* was being filmed. During a lull in shooting, I was given the signal by someone with a clapper-board that I could ride my bike (to the marina for a day's work on the boat) along the street amongst ladies dressed in more modest attire than nowadays . . . long dresses, nipped in at the waist, dainty gloves, parasols, and lovely straw hats with flowers tumbling over the brim.

One evening, Brian approached me to ask if he could come on the voyage to Panama. Alberto was agreeable, and that meant the Enfield, now aboard, could travel for free. I bought food for the four-day voyage, as that wasn't included in the price. Alberto filled up with diesel at a place selling it cheaper than at the marina, and we set off for Panama. Through Horizons Unlimited I had made contact with Steven and Karen, who lived in Panama City. They offered to meet me and help me find a tyre.

It's ironic that having spent nearly three months in what was supposedly one of the most dangerous countries in the world I should have my worst experience just after leaving it. Most of the time it is possible to laugh with hindsight at the narrow escapes one has whilst long-term motorcycling, but reliving that experience still makes me shudder.

Shortly after we set off, with the Enfield securely lashed on the foredeck, things started to go wrong. Keen to navigate with charts and a compass, I noticed that the compass needle was motionless as we left the harbour. Alberto said that he had smashed it with his fist in a fit of temper. And that was before we set off. There was an autopilot, but it was unusable, as the alternator had burnt out when Alberto's Colombian girlfriend had insisted on going as fast as possible round the harbour. Therefore, the whole electrical system was out of use.

As dusk fell and the stars appeared, I started to relax. It was a romantic scene as we sat in the cockpit sailing and steering by the same stars those ancient mariners had used. "This is the life," I thought, enchanted by the phosphorescence as the boat slid through the sea. I steered, Brian swigged rum, and Alberto tried to fix up a bailing system because the boat was leaking via the propeller shaft. The electric bailer wasn't working, and the batteries were unable to charge. We had no lights and couldn't cook in the galley. At dawn, we moored off the inhabited island of Chichime. An exhausted little bird rested on the boat in the blinding light and fierce heat. Brian cared for it by giving it shade and a dish of water.

Some islanders rowed out with live lobsters, and Brian bought three. Alberto tried to make him feel awkward when he emerged from the galley with a cooked one. He accused him of hypocrisy. "How can you rescue a bird (it had died) and then boil and eat a lobster?" He had a point, but I'd had lunch with him one day when anti-fouling the boat and had seen him devour a steak. That was hypocrisy, but whilst I couldn't help but raise an eyebrow, I thought it best to say nothing. I went snorkelling but found little of interest except that the sea-floor was like a lawn with flat weed giving little chance for the anchor to grip.

As Brian and I explored the island, we found souvenirs but no bar. Meanwhile, the weather changed with foreboding as the sky darkened and the wind blew up. I started to swim to the boat but turned back for fear of being blown away. I still did not want a watery grave.

Alberto rowed the dinghy to fetch us and said that he was worried about the anchor being too small and the wrong type, not to mention the thin and rusty anchor-chain. He dived down and attached an old battery to the chain to prevent our drifting as the storm developed. A previously upright palm tree on the island became almost horizontal within a couple of hours. I went to bed, hoping the morning would bring better conditions. Alberto was throwing tools about but wasn't speaking. Brian was his usual withdrawn self. The storm held up at thirty miles an hour, Force Seven, for three days.

The entire voyage was to have taken only four. Brian had drunk his stash of rum by the second day. Tempers were frayed; food was short. All the torch batteries were exhausted. Alberto had no girlfriend, Brian had no alcohol. I read *A Hundred Years of Solitude*, unable to keep food down. I couldn't even wash, as the water pump wasn't operating.

Alberto decided late in the afternoon of the fourth day to make a break for Porvenir Island, nearer the mainland. Unable to sail in the crazy wind, the engine had to be used. Cheap, dirty diesel clogged the fuel injector, and the engine kept cutting out. Brian was pacing, desperate for a drink. Alberto started behaving like a caged animal, snarling abusively, blaming me for bringing an alcoholic aboard. I was afraid of losing my life that night as the boat drifted towards a reef in the howling gale when the anchor wouldn't hold.

Alberto screamed abusive names at me, which I absorbed with utter disdain until he made a grave error. Eying up my bike, he threatened to throw it overboard as an anchor. I backed up against it with my arms out protectively, "OH NO YOU'RE NOT!" I was quite prepared for him to lose his boat and even put them and myself in danger, but if he went anywhere near it, I knew I would fight him. Whereas Marcel had threatened to kill me, this skipper had murderous intentions towards my bike, which at that moment, seemed even worse.

After many attempts at anchoring in the relatively sheltered bay, making other yacht-owners uneasy, the anchor held. At that stage, Brian decided his need for alcohol was more important than his life and launched the dinghy. Alberto and I watched as the wind and tide pushed him on a course that might well have taken him straight past the island, but his determination to get a drink got him to the furthermost point, where we could just see him land and pull up the dinghy before the light of the day finally went.

It was just me and Alberto then, the anchor wasn't holding, and we were constantly driven towards the other, properly moored yachts, whose owners shouted, "GO AWAY," and armed themselves with boat-hooks at our approach. Alberto was wailing with despair, alternately frozen with panic or scuttling uselessly around the deck. "Mamma mia!" he cried as night fell, "I'm going to lose the boat." I took control, because he had lost it. "We're tying up to the jetty," I announced firmly, receiving no resistance.

On the shore I could make out islanders waving torches to guide us in. Conversation was useless in the ferocious wind with the rain lashing down, hammering against the hood of my jacket, with the incessant clanging of ropes being dashed against the metal mast. He motored towards the lights, and I blessed the angels, who then threw us ropes and secured us to the jetty on that dark, stormy night. During mooring up to the jetty I had thrown him a rope that he had failed to catch. "FUCK YOU," he yelled, "YOU PIECE OF SHIT." It had taken three hours to get safely tied.

Afterwards, during the ensuing post-emergency calm, things became surreal. Back in the cabin, he showed me a maths book he had written. He tested me by presenting me with a Sudoku puzzle he had been unable to finish but which, because I had finished a book of them, I was able to complete. He was incredulous. How could a person like me complete this stinker of a puzzle when a mathematician such as he could not? His calm demeanour dissipated, and he returned to his name-calling unpleasant self. I exploded with the pent-up fury and fear I had been suppressing since he'd called me such dreadful names, and from a place I had never accessed before, came the words, "How dare you call me names when I got us to safety last night? I'm a paying passenger, not crew, you incompetent wanker."

I am quite unable to say where that language came from. I never, ever heard my parents swear, and I rarely did. I could tell he wasn't best pleased. The next morning, Brian appeared, having spent the night in a bar. A row ensued, and Alberto ordered us both off the boat. Brian decided to fly from the little island airport to Panama City. I reminded Alberto that I had paid for a trip to Panama. "This IS Panama," he retorted with a sly grin. He knew perfectly well that the arrangement had been to deliver me and the bike to the mainland, not some Panamanian island hardly within sight of it. But as I was keen to get away from him, a deal was made with some local fishermen with a sizeable boat, and an hour and thirty dollars later, the Enfield and I were unloaded at Miramar, an unfriendly fishing village on the mainland.

Once more, I promised the bike I would never put it on a small yacht again and forgave it every one of its stalling and non-starting episodes over the past six years, because it started on the second kick and ran on a teaspoon of fuel. Keeping the sea to my right, I rode joyfully and gratefully, topping up along the way from litre bottles of petrol at roadside stalls, through villages called Viento Frio and Nombre de Dios, past Portobelo, where I should have been landed, and to Colón, where I phoned Steven to tell him I was on my way, and finally to Panama City, where I almost threw my arms round him.

Steven and Karen soothed and pampered me for several gloriously comfortable, non-threatening days in their spectacular twenty-seventh storey apartment as big as a house. It included a garden balcony from where I watched ships queuing up to go through the Panama Canal. Steven took me to a tyre shop, where I found a rather flashy rear tyre. Karen took me sightseeing, and I saw huge ships squeeze with inches to spare through the entrance to the Panama Canal, guided by pilots.

When I went to register my arrival in Panama three days late, having taken a rather unorthodox sea-route I was expecting trouble at Immigration and Customs, but it took an unprecedented half an hour. Customs officials didn't even glance at the bike, but a clerk urged me to add Panamá to the list of countries painted on the air-box. Thrusting correction fluid at me, he insisted I put the accent on the final á.

There were lots of American accents. America was "in charge" of the canal for about a hundred years until recently. One Panamanian I spoke to said he'd had a well-paid job at the port in those days but now earned a fraction of that as a security guard for McDonald's. America hadn't left entirely.

I pondered the boat trip. "I must learn from this," I thought, but was too busy converting Panamanian balboa into US dollars or litres into US gallons. By then I had recovered enough equilibrium to set forth towards Costa Rica. With grateful goodbyes to my hosts, I left Panama City. Hours later, the late afternoon sky darkened, heralding a thunderstorm.

Through torrential rain, a barely visible sign pointed to "La Ponderosa Animal Sanctuary—Hammocks and Cabins." At the end of the track I was welcomed by a bouncy Jack Russell. My sleeping bag sheet had got wet, so rather than sleep in a hammock, the owners suggested staying in a cabin with dry bedding. Convalescing at the sanctuary were giant iguanas, fox cubs, toucans, little piggy creatures, a black monkey, porcupines, and birds of all colours and sizes. I awoke to sunshine and left my sheet drying over a bush whilst I went to settle up, but apart from accepting a donation for the sanctuary, the owners wouldn't let me pay.

It was a different experience at the hotel I stayed at the following night. The pompous manager had studied English. He told me I didn't have a proper English accent and corrected what he deemed a grammatical error. I checked my emails. Paul reported that he had the courts "on the run." A very close one from Claire described her life, making me feel like I was with her. She told me that all the family would be at their house for Christmas and that I was the missing piece of the jigsaw. After our conversation, I reviewed my plan. I'd imagined leaving for the UK from New York, but it would take me months to get there. So I looked at my mini atlas and decided I'd leave the Americas from Mexico City to get home quicker, but not in time for Christmas.

I'd had quite enough of the sea, so after the straightforward, two-hour border-crossing into Costa Rica, decided to go inland on the Pan American Highway again. All in one day, I went from sea level to 9,843 feet and from sunshine and warmth to rain and cold. I would have enjoyed copying Aretha Franklin in asking the way to San Jose in song, but I didn't need directions, although I couldn't rid myself of the tune all the way there. It was impossible to find a hotel with room for the bike, which kept stalling and was not enjoying the change of temperature, the rain, or the altitude.

I couldn't resist staying at the Hotel Bristol, apparently a name for quality everywhere, although this one was far from prestigious. The hotel opposite was a "love hotel" (I was confident I could identify them by then). They were happy to let the bike stay in the foyer, and I was amused that it, and not I, would be spending the night in such a place. It was election time, and there was no beer in town, so after a cup of coffee in a Chinese restaurant, I turned in. It wasn't long before I realised I, too, was staying in a "rent by the hour" hotel. The woman in the room opposite had three orgasms in the time it took me to find where I was on the map and plan my ongoing journey in the morning.

I made for Arenal Volcano at La Fortuna, fifty-six miles northwest. Happy to leave San Jose and with spirits high, I passed mile after mile of pineapple, sugar-cane, coffee, and banana plantations while making my tongue sore with glasses of pineapple juice bought at roadside stalls. Cream started to feature in meals, and for lunch I had it with red beans, rice, tortillas, and ham and eggs which was superb.

The rain lashed down, and I arrived soaked at La Fortuna, hoping to see the volcano that the guide book reported spews constantly. But it was heavy with cloud during my stay, and I couldn't even see the volcano, let alone any molten lava.

There were many tourists and cafés there, the coffee in Costa Rica the best I'd had anywhere, so I was aghast when an American tourist complained that she couldn't wait to get home for a decent cup of Starbuck's (who reportedly get their coffee from Costa Rica).

One night, the clouds separated just enough to see a red glow. Someone at the hostel said it was lava, but it might just as well have been someone nearby drawing on a cigarette. I bought a postcard and rode on. It rained constantly and heavily. I bought Wellington boots, as I was so fed up with wet feet.

The sun came out as I descended from the mountains, and I brightened up too, my travelling joy totally restored by the weather and an interaction on a forest road with a cat-sized mammal, a kind of racoon known locally as "gato solo." We each stopped in the middle of the road to look at each other. It had a kind face, a rubbery brown snout, and a long striped tail. It trotted off and seemed to float up a steep, muddy bank as if by magic.

At the border into Nicaragua, there was a fee for cursory vehicle fumigation from a man with a pathetic spray-wand. Insurance and immigration costs were added, totalling twenty-two dollars US. I rode on to León and chose a backpackers' hostel with a garage where the bike would be safe. It was parked next to an enormous BMW 1100 GS Adventure that made mine look like a toy. I really liked the towns in Central America. Most retained their original Spanish colonial plan with a central plaza, where I always started my search for accommodation. The hotels were old and generally quite cheap, richer tourists preferring to stay in modern hotels outside.

I preferred to be in the lively plaza with tempting food being cooked at stalls, where there were fresh tortillas, rice, and beans. In the warm evenings, families were out enjoying ice cream made from flavoured shaved ice and condensed milk. The town's church oversaw the activity, with its dark interior containing gory effigies of Christ, the more blood and agony the better.

As I moved north-westwards, music was changing from reggaeton to more brass and big bands, instrumentals, and romantic ballads. I was getting closer to Mexico. Men had droopy moustaches, and food was changing, too. Beans still featured, but spicy chorizo was making more of an appearance.

On the back roads, there was little traffic, apart from the odd lorry or donkey and cart. The bike was happier when not at high altitudes and tootled along as we passed between volcanoes on either side on good roads in the hot sunshine. I thanked it and, patting the much-scratched tank, asked, "Please, Bike, get me home."

My Spanish was improving. Stopping to ask directions made me prepare my vocabulary, and using my little Spanish dictionary I learnt some language necessities whilst enjoying contact with people. These exchanges were more important to me then than sightseeing.

I was moving on well and going so quickly through small countries, each with its own currency, I couldn't get my head round the noughts. At the cash machines I invariably withdrew either too little or too much, leaving me short in some countries but with a surplus in others.

Now in Honduras, at Choluteca, when looking for a bank to exchange Nicaraguan córdoba into Honduran lempira, I went into a dress shop to enquire (I have no idea why I chose a dress shop). Scrutinising clothes for Christmas was a mother with her four daughters. I followed her as she popped into the next-door bar to ask her husband. He looked alarming in a black cowboy hat, dark shirt, and jeans, with a hand-gun tucked in his belt, but he was charming, and I found myself included in the family lunch party at a smart hotel with a pool.

After being taken to the bank, I was invited to go with them to a horse-race that afternoon. A safe place was found for the bike, and I joined Juan and Victoria, and their children, Daisy, Patricia, Emma, and Isabel, in their truck, feeling uncomfortable at my scruffy appearance.

That wouldn't do for Cheltenham races, but they reassured me that I'd be fine, and on arrival at the rough field, deep into the countryside, there were no dressy hats or designer frocks. My road-weary outfit blended in well, but there was big money there with expensive-looking trucks and four-wheel-drive vehicles. The men wore cowboy hats, and everyone wore jeans.

There was no racetrack, only some roped-off lanes of about 550 yards in length. Ascot it wasn't! Small boys and small horses milled about, not the liveried stable-hands and thoroughbreds seen at racecourses in Britain. There were four races, with only two or three horses in each.

My diary reads:

"The horses were wild-looking things, not the shiny racehorses I'm used to. But even more unusual and staggering was that they were ridden by half-naked ten or eleven-year old boys with bare feet using no saddle or stirrups and just rope for reins. And boy did they go! Much gambling money changed hands. Much rum was drunk."

I stayed at the same hotel as the family and insisted on paying for breakfast in the morning. They had been so generous I hadn't been allowed to pay for anything. Everyone hugged me and wished me a good onward journey before they went. Later, while packing up to leave, I found the breakfast money folded up in my pocket. Victoria had slipped it in when we were hugging goodbye. People were astonishingly kind.

I stopped to look at the Pacific Ocean but, having been brought up in Weston-super-Mare, thought little of the brown sea and started to make the climb up towards the capital, Tegucigalpa. On the way, I was able to supply a patch and help repair a puncture for two men on bicycles, for once able to help someone else in trouble.

I'd had a few brushes with death during my trip and had come to terms with it. But not now . . . not when I was on my way home! I was riding on a three-lane road when a car-driver, blinded by the low afternoon sun, didn't see me and suddenly pulled out to overtake another car on his side of the road in the opposite direction. It was nearly curtains for me as the car passed within an inch. I stiffened. The bike wobbled, buffeted by the approaching wall of on-rushing air. Shocked, I just rode on, adrenaline pumping, knowing I'd been very lucky indeed.

Some big fuel stations had overnight accommodation with just enough space for the bike and me inside the room. I went to bed early, aware that the lorry-drivers would be setting off at dawn. I took small mountain roads and shortcuts when I could. I didn't sight-see and chose places to stay for their proximity to the road rather than their picturesque outlook.

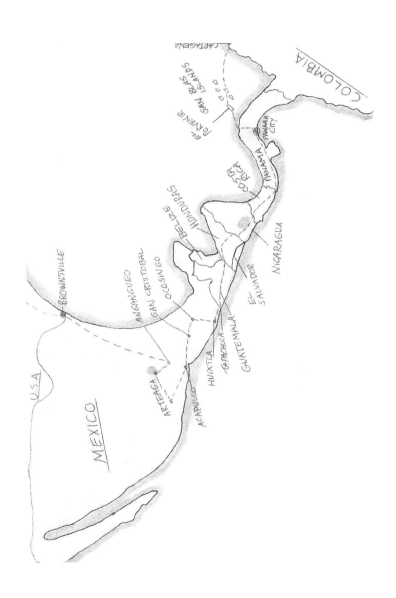

At Tutule, a mountain town, it hadn't stopped raining for so long that the woman who kindly agreed to give me a room for the night apologised that she had no clean, dry sheets. "Never mind, I have a sleeping bag," I said, but when I removed the inner sheet from its plastic bag, the acrid smell made my nostrils burn. It had been festering for two weeks after the sweet little dog at the animal sanctuary had peed on it while it was drying. I slept in just the sleeping bag.

Threatening clouds provided the mountain scenery with a dramatic backdrop. I was now on a small muddy lane heading to Gracias, the provincial capital. I fell five times within a stretch of a dozen miles that day. Sometimes the wheels got trapped in the deep, criss-crossing wheel-tracks of heavy vehicles, from which I could neither escape nor move on, or thin mud lay over hard-baked soil as slippery as ice. Five times I had to take the luggage off to lighten the bike and then, slithering about in swamps, get it upright again.

On one occasion, I'd just got everything fastened on and was waving farewell to a lorry-driver who'd helped me. I gave a hefty kick to start it, forgetting it was in first gear. It shot forward, and already covered in mud, I fell off again. He supported the bike in case this clearly incompetent woman did it again. He was right when he said the road ahead got even worse before he drove away, leaving a wash of muddy water.

It was a relief to stop for a delicious lunch at La Esperanza ("The Hope"), where the ubiquitous television was tuned into an evangelical programme showing people brought to their knees, not by mud like me, but by religious fervour.

As I'd been warned, the road to Gracias deteriorated. I rode gingerly past coffee plantations, heavily loaded horses and donkeys and oxen pulling carts. At one stage, I dropped the bike in a patch of sludge. With my back to the bike, I could find nothing to push against with my feet to right it, so I dragged a large tree-branch over so my boots would have purchase. I rode on another sixteen yards and did the same thing again. Heavy trucks, carrying materials to make the new road, had made the road even worse.

On my arrival at Gracias, I said a predictable, but heartfelt, "gracias" for my success and checked in at a cheap hotel. I cleaned up and watched the film *Pet Cemetery* dubbed into Spanish, which was amusing rather than frightening. Torrential rain in the night flooded the hotel, including my room and all my luggage. I didn't wait to dry out.

Further along a country road, a dead cow was surrounded by a funeral party of vultures. *The Jungle Book* is one of my favourite Disney films, and I was reminded of the dialogue between those cartoon vultures as they shuffled along the branches trying to relieve their boredom. "What do you want to do?" "I dunno, what do you want to do?" I imagined I could hear the same conversation amid the rustling of real feathers as these gloomy vultures flew up and hung about in the branches watching me pass beneath. They must have seen the film; they got the mannerisms just right.

There was bird-life of an altogether brighter nature in the form of tame red, blue, green, and yellow macaws in the trees surrounding the ruins of a Mayan settlement and temple complex at Copán. The birds were free but had no need to move much, as they were fed by tourists and rangers. I wondered that we seem to have learned so little from the Mayans, who despite their astounding knowledge of the universe above them, floundered from constant war-mongering and drought. There they'd had a gorgeous place to make their homes, even sleeping on jaguar skins, but they used up all their resources fighting.

Guatemala and another new currency to learn. Quetzales this time, named after the beautiful and elusive national bird. In the small city of Antigua I hardly stopped to look at anything to begin with. I was tired. More, I was jaded. I'd seen hundreds of markets on three continents, and I no longer asked about unidentifiable things on market stalls. Some of my curiosity had diminished, and I'd become a bit of a know-it-all.

Christian, a young Californian staying at my hostel, was riding his motorbike south to the tip of South America as I was going north. We were able to offer tips and recommendations to each other.

We went to the local market for breakfast. He said things like "Wow! Look at that . . . listen to that music . . . what's that smell? . . . look at those people . . . what's that fruit? . . . hey it's hot in here . . . what do you do with those? . . . look at the colour of that! . . . I gotta eat some of that . . . did you see that? . . . I'm gonna buy that stuff!"

He was so beautifully fresh and excited and enthusiastic at the start of his journey, and I'm grateful to him for opening my blasé eyes again that day. Of COURSE it was exciting. We ate delicious sausages we'd seen being stuffed into sheep intestines and barbecued. We took photos and talked about life on the road. I noticed as we talked that I had become less orientated towards sights or scenery and was more inclined to talk about the people I'd met.

Returning to the hostel to pack up and leave, I happened across a travel agency and stopped dead. It hadn't even crossed my mind, but why hadn't I thought of it before? I rushed in: "Buenos Dias; are there any flights to the UK before Christmas?" I felt excitement mixed with sudden desperation rising in my chest. My heartbeat matched the tappety tap-tap of the keys on the computer. "Si Señora, Guatemala City to Heathrow, 20th December." I didn't care about the cost and pushed my credit card at the agent, who I wanted to hug for finding me a flight. He found me a place to keep the bike too.

I tried to suppress my excitement when I emailed Claire, who was also online—"It's disappointing when you do a jigsaw and find a piece missing, isn't it?" "Huh?" It took her a while to twig, and then she was so excited. The last piece in the jigsaw was coming home.

I had one day to do my Christmas shopping, which all came from that small market in Antigua. A charming pottery angel for Laurie, some cheap T-shirts for Claire and Abby with a meaningless logo about sisters, a bottle of Caribbean rum, the CD I'd bought of the heart-breaking songs by Mario Antonio Solis that I'd heard all over Central America and which captured the essence of my travels since landing in Ecuador months before.

Aboard the British Airways flight home I wallowed in tea and British accents. Then, after warm and welcome hugs with Claire at Heathrow, we missed the turning off the motorway three times as I regaled her with the story of the voyage. I finally met little Laurie and spent her first Christmas with her. She was eight months old, crawling, lovable, and charming. I had to combine my old health visitor role with a new grandmother role whilst trying to resume my mother role amongst comments about "popping in and out of our lives" and "going on" about my travel experiences. I didn't know how or who to be.

I helped around the house with the mountains of laundry. It was a lovely family Christmas, and the following week, I felt it my duty to perpetuate my own mother's tradition of seeing in the New Year. It was magical to rouse sleepy Laurie and take her to the back door to let the old year out and then to the front door to let in 2007, her first New Year. She was too big for her baby-cot, so the quilt became a wall-hanging instead.

My mother was much the same, only even smaller. She was well and still singing hymns. My friend that I'd helped set up the Bristol backpacker hostel in 2000 had bought a forty-foot Dutch barge in Bristol harbour. I stayed with him, happy to help convert it into a floating hotel. This boat didn't go anywhere, and he didn't want to kill me or throw my possessions overboard.

Then I had a phone call from Paul, who tearfully told me he could not bear to keep in touch. He wanted to cease contact. We hadn't known where our relationship might go when we'd parted in New Zealand, but his situation, if not hopeless, then still a long way from success, meant it was wise to accept that. Whilst we felt we'd shared something very special, it was pointless to hope we'd ever meet again. He wanted to meet "another lady." I still cared and asked that when, if he ever, won his case, would he please let me know?

Three short weeks later I had to catch my return flight to Guatemala, and so it was time for more goodbyes.

Reunited with my Enfield, I continued my journey home for good, only slowing down if something enticed me to investigate. So it was that, before I left Guatemala, I took time to see an active volcano and was guided to within a few yards of molten lava during a night hike at Pacaya. I soon resumed my normal travelling mode, taking interest in my surroundings as if I'd never been away.

During an evening walk in lakeside San Lucas, an elderly woman dressed in a traditional long skirt and shawl gave me a friendly nod and a "Buenos noches, Señora." She entered a small, dark old building with a bowl of maize. Five minutes later she came out with her bowl, then filled with yellow paste. I went in and found it to be a traditional village facility, a mill operated by a boy of about ten, where people brought their own maize and corn ground to be made ready for making tortillas. As the kernels were pushed into a screw-grinder, a narrow hose played into the machine, thus making a paste that was collected underneath by a little girl.

I awoke before dawn and watched as the morning showed me Lago de Atitlán, where at first light, women went down to the water's edge to do the laundry while men were spreading nets on the lake. It was an ancient and mellow country scene, but if I thought the bizarre madness was over, I had a surprise coming with my arrival in Mexico.

19

MEXICO ONWARDS, THE USA AND CANADA

PLAN? WHAT PLAN?

I crossed the border out of Guatemala at a place called Carmen but, strangely, didn't find a Mexican border post until sixteen miles further on at Tapachula. I knew I'd like Mexico if it was that laid-back, so I immersed myself whole-heartedly by immediately diving off the main road.

I spent the night in a little village too small for a hotel, but was directed to the home of a sprightly woman, whose daughter and granddaughter lived with her. She also found room for me. I was taken, with great pride, by her granddaughter to see the village miracle. To my eye, it was a water-stain from a broken gutter; to them, it was the Virgin Mary—obvious, once pointed out.

Back at the house, Señora Carmen baked a treat called tamal, made from meat and dried fruit wrapped in pastry. I ate one with some coffee under a tree in her peaceful garden, wondering what it would be like to live there. A religious belief, family, community, and living modestly seemed to bring contentment. She looked happy, and everyone loved her.

I didn't need a hotel the next night either. The Enfield developed a leak at the point where the oil supply is taken to the top of the engine by a delicate, externally mounted, Y-shaped metal tube. I was apprehensive about re-tightening it—if I damaged it, I'd be stranded. I parked in the town plaza at Huixtla and sat beside the bike on the kerb sharing my fresh apricots with a guard who had kept an eye on the bike whilst I went into the bank for Mexican pesos. From across the road someone yelled, "Hey there, you tramp!" I looked up and smiled at the American voice. A large man strode across to talk. Bob, a Guatemalan-American, also owned a motorbike, and before long I was tinkering with my spanners on the Enfield in the garage of the house where he and his Mexican wife lived. By gingerly tightening the nut, the leak stopped. I was invited to stay.

Now by that time, I had slept in some odd places: flooded rooms in India, beneath tress, up trees, in hammocks, in a public toilet in Australia, at roadsides, on people's floors and sofas, on a flat rock in the desert, on various boats, in the cab of an Australian road-train, in tents, and on a pavement in Calcutta. I'd slept alone and with another person, but never, ever, had I slept three in a bed. I looked around for a sleeping space, but their home was tiny, and in the bedroom there was room only for the bed and a cupboard. Apart from a small shower and kitchen, that was it. Nothing else. Nada. And so, with Rosalinda in the middle, I slept for two nights with them on their enormous water-bed, as if this was an entirely normal thing to do in Mexico. As a "when in Rome" person, I was grateful for somewhere to stay for a couple of nights, and if that's how it goes in Mexico, I'd go with it.

Bob made a living by delivering sterilised water to factories around the town on a pedal tricycle and took me with him the next morning so I could see the town. I paid for meals out with the couple, a treat for them. We went on our motorbikes to local beauty spots they wanted to show me. There was a danger I would never leave, so ignoring the inner voice tempting, "One more day wouldn't hurt," I left amongst hugs and "come back soon's." Only later did the sleeping arrangement seem odd, but why should I be bothered? They weren't.

Going to Agua Azul, famous for its clear blue waterfalls and lagoons, was only a minor diversion from the onward route. I got caught in a heavy shower in the early evening and sheltered under the thatched eaves of a wooden hut at Nahilte, near the town of Ocosingo. The door opened, and I was beckoned in by a tall indigenous woman, possibly from the Tzeltal people, whom I'd observed on the way up the mountain road. They dressed differently and carried heavy loads supported by straps on their foreheads, as in Nepal. She wore a white blouse, heavily embroidered with pink and blue flowers, with a long skirt with rows of coloured ribbons sewn on it. Her husband wheeled the Enfield in, and it was clear I was expected to stay.

The family used their local language and didn't understand my poor, basic Spanish, so instead I "spoke" with my international language—the small collection of family photographs I'd been travelling with since starting backpacking in 1998: my mother holding a glass of sherry (surely what had kept her alive for so long), Claire at her graduation, Abby with our family dog, my brother with our cousin in a pretty English garden. I'd shown those pictures to people all over the world. How strange for them to see inside my mother's room with its golden clock on a marble fireplace or Claire wearing a mortar-board or Abby cuddling a dog. I'll never know what they made of it all.

There I was again, still incredulous that people welcomed, fed, and gave accommodation to a scruffy stranger on a dinosaur motorbike. I was shown around the earth-floored house, where chickens, children, and neighbours kept coming in and out. Turkeys gobbled about outside, and two pigs were growing too porky for their sty next to the toilet. The family, comprising twin girls of eleven, their parents, and grandparents, grew maize, coffee, and oranges. There were five rooms, but the kitchen was a separate building with an open fire on a plinth like an altar. The smoke left via an opening between the wall behind the fire and the apex of the roof. When the electricity went off, nobody seemed surprised.

We sang songs. Their language was guttural but pleasant to the ear. Put on the spot, I could think only of the unlilting *How Much Is that Doggy in the Window?* but following their beautiful rendition of *La Mariposa Blanca*. I remembered *Hey, That's No Way to Say Goodbye*. Paul and I had sung it tenderly to each other, and I knew every word. I slept in my sleeping bag on a wooden platform with the twins—three in a bed again. Before they went to school in the morning, I gave them a necklace and a ring, jewellery acquired along the way. Breakfast, eggs with spring onions decorated with an edible cactus flower and tortillas made from their own maize, was delicious and accompanied by their own coffee and orange juice.

Further up the mountain, in the town of Ocosingo, I met some men from the Zapatista Army of National Liberation. Formed in 1994 to gain indigenous control over local land, the local tribes had united and declared war against the Mexican state. Dozens of rebels, soldiers, and civilians died there, and it had a whiff of ill-feeling that I witnessed when I went into a café at Tenejapa.

I was questioned by two men in traditional dress and full of their own importance: "What you doing here? This is dangerous place." They wore black woolly vest-tops with large silver coins on a necklace to waist level. With their red shirts to the knee, decorated with embroidery here and there, long black socks, and ordinary shoes, they looked anything but menacing. They asked me to buy them some fizzy drinks and, when swaggering out of the shop with their bottles of pop, looked less frightening than perhaps they would have liked.

Just as I'd bought a postcard of the volcano at El Fortuna because I hadn't seen it, I bought a postcard of Agua Azul, learning too late that it is azul for only two months of the year and was "agua café" the rest of the time.

Moving west, and nearer to the United States of America, I encountered Canadians who'd fled the cold to over-winter there in Mexico. At San Cristobal, whilst admiring the beautiful cathedral, I bumped into Felice, a Canadian who I'd already met in Leon, Nicaragua. As we talked next to the bike about where we'd been in the intervening weeks, we were spotted, swept up, and taken home by Sergio, an enthusiastic Mexican member of the Horizons Unlimited community. Felice had spent a year riding an Enfield in India so was equally familiar with this sort of encounter. Neither of us thought twice about accepting his invitation to stay at his home. With Felice as pillion, Sergio took us through some hilly national parkland to El Chorreadero, a waterfall with pools where we swam.

We rode over a lofty bridge and saw a section of the vast Cañón del Sumidero, plunging hundreds of feet below that would give anyone scared of heights the heebie-jeebies.

Our ways parted. I felt incredibly lonely as I left both them and Chiapas state to enter the much warned about Oaxaca state. But if I'd heeded all the warnings I'd been offered over the years, I'd not have gone anywhere. The only place I hadn't been warned about was Australia, where I was robbed.

Mexican towns and villages seemed desperate to slow down the little traffic there was. Various devices called topes were used, the worst type being a large concrete-covered pipe across the road. They were unsigned, steep, and almost invisible. My eyes should have been on the road all the time instead of admiring white-flowering yucca plants, donkeys, and weird giant cactus. Even at the slow speed I was doing I saw the topes too late, suffering the awful jolt and dislodging of my luggage, sending tins of sardines, spare inner tubes, and my precious diaries flying onto the road, thus amusing the food vendors clustered there. Sometimes, those wretched things nearly had me off the bike.

I found a hotel in Tuxtla and went by bus to the tranquil hillside zoo, the life's work of scientific researcher Miguel Alvarez del Toro. In despair for the wellbeing of the creatures of Oaxaca, he founded the refuge habitat in 1942 to protect them. The zoo had streams running through it. Uncaged yellow birds hopped along branches. Monkeys swung by their tails in the trees. I sat quietly on a bench set in undergrowth watching them. An agouti was snuffling about, disturbing butterflies that fluttered around me.

I walked around with the zoo map and at last saw armadillos alive and well, instead of squashed at the roadside. Within a shaded cage, a pair of the elusive quetzals looked miserable, despite their spectacular plumage. It doesn't matter how beautiful you are if you are captive. Amongst dozens of species of indigenous wildlife were snakes, bats, frogs, three different types of alligator, turtles, fish, and a puma which purred as it walked round its enclosure. My favourite were the peccaries, looking like a cross between a rodent and a pig but unrelated to either. One had a tiny baby, so endearing it made me beam.

Travelling further westwards, I reached the coast. It was unbelievably windy as I rode alongside the Gulf of Tehuantepec.

I counted one hundred wind turbines at the bottom of the Istmo de Tehuantepec, where I had to lean at forty-five degrees into the vortex as it was funnelled down the valley from the Gulf of Mexico in the north. Fearful that it may blow me into the Pacific Ocean in the south, I didn't dare stop.

I was approaching Mexico City, but before arranging the journey home, I wanted to see the cliff-divers of nearby Acapulco and the migrating monarch butterflies. A squiggle on the map illustrated a shortcut via the mountains saving miles of coast road, so I turned up the un-tarmacked road. People waved at me and I waved back cheerfully. How friendly they all were.

I carried on for mile after mile, eventually coming to a tiny village where, it being that time of day, I started looking for somewhere to sleep. A woman was by her little house. I asked where I could sleep in the village. She went inside and brought out a wooden camp-bed with a sacking mattress. "Aqui!" She pointed to the bed, now under the canopy of the house. She asked me where I was from but had never heard of Inglaterra, Britain, The British Isles, England, or the UK. I smiled to think that my birthplace had absolutely no significance there and yet we feel we are so pivotal in the world. She hadn't heard of Queen Elizabeth or even David Beckham.

We ate together; tortillas and tomato salsa that she'd cooked on a skillet on the fire outside. I shared my bottle of mezcal, a spirit made from the baked heart of cactus fermented with various herbs and fruit. From the camp-bed, I watched the moon come up and light the streaky clouds from underneath before drifting off to sleep to the sound of donkeys braying and dogs barking and the smell of a day's hot sun on dusty ground.

In the morning, I saw the sun come up, lighting the clouds from underneath with red and purple, instead of the monochrome of moonlight. After tortillas and eggs, I paid Rosa and asked for directions to the onward road. She told me there was no onward road because of a rock fall. I thought back to Pakistan, where the avalanche had been cleared in three days, and imagined this one would also be soon shifted, but when I asked how long it had been there, she replied, "Fifteen years!" This was the end of the squiggle on the map. Shamefaced, I rode back past all the people who had tried to warn me with their waves the day before. So much for my shortcut.

I slept on beaches by my bike for the next week. One night I awoke thinking that someone was shining a powerful torch on me, but it was only my friend the moon. I relished sleeping outside whenever I could after a day of riding. Anxious to get home, yet not quite believing my journey was all over, I tried to prepare myself, but things kept happening to delight me.

Another night in the open was beside a bird sanctuary. Brown pelicans went "sploosh" into the water for their breakfast. Circling vultures in the mountains looked like a slow-motion tornado. The next night I slept twenty feet from the sea at Point Maldonado.

My diary entry for that night reads like an unimaginative travel brochure with such phrases as:

"Undiscovered authentic fishing village," "Beach front, thatched restaurants serving fresh fish, prawns and langoustines."

I found that if I bought food and beer at the restaurants, I was welcome to sleep next to them.

The gaudy colours of Mexico were impossible to capture on my old film camera. I stopped trying when I realised my pictures of glorious sunsets looked like a faded orange pea in a grey mist. I needed a rest day and enjoyed the beach watching pelicans, frigate birds, and white herons whilst working on Laurie's quilt-picture. Something big, black, shiny, and rubbery, possibly a whale, was looping about in the sea, just offshore. I had freshly-caught red snapper and beer for dinner.

The eighth night in a row sleeping outside by the bike was spent wedged amongst more migrating Canadians in camper-vans in a parking area next to an alligator sanctuary at Ixtapa. I was given coffee in the morning by a woman who walked with me to the harbour and with whom I'd exchanged life histories within half an hour. We watched fishermen casting their nets and freeing ensnared pelicans. When we returned, her husband pointed out an alligator-sized gap in the wire netting fence of the sanctuary near where I'd been sleeping. These (thankfully) well-fed creatures were roaming free. I would have been cross to have been gobbled up at that stage of my homeward journey.

Diary Saturday 10th February 2007. Acapulco:

"I'm writing this at the Hotel Miramar's balcony bar to see the world-famous divers launch themselves headfirst into

*the narrow gash forty metres into the sea below. I am so
excited I can hardly write! I have splashed out! For about
£7 (a comparative fortune) I am in the best viewing spot.
The price includes two drinks or one drink and a light lunch.
I opted for two drinks! I am such a lucky lady. I feel a lady
as I am wearing my dress (a change from jeans and long-
sleeved shirt) and am sipping iced grapefruit tequila with
salt around the rim of the glass. However, I am not quite
a lady as I am sleeping on a beach again! The owner of the
bar where I'm sleeping is keeping an eye on the bike. Have
now had two tequilas! Earlier I talked to and shook hands
with one of the divers. Two have just dived down together
and somersaulted half way!"*

I was thrilled at the attraction I'd paid to see, the crowd of
Americans from a cruise ship proving how popular it was. My joy
was similar to the warm glow I had from having my hand held by
the little girl who showed me the Virgin Mary miracle in her village.
It was a revealing, significant, and timely insight. I realised that I
got as much pleasure from experiencing humble things as I did the
spectacular. Every day brought such joy. I always had enough.

Turquoise sea and white sandy beaches had been lovely, but
the mountains were beckoning. There was a pretty little mountain
town called Arteaga, where I found a hotel, washed off the sea-
salt, and slept in a bed. I was just about to leave the next morning
when I saw two shiny Harleys with Canadian plates parked outside
a restaurant. I would have liked to talk with them but didn't seek
them out, as previous encounters with Harley riders had revealed
their reluctance to talk to me.

After parking the Enfield, I shopped for a few supplies. When
I returned, two middle-aged men in fringed leathers were looking
at my bike. We started chatting. Quint and Gil had been touring
Mexico for a few weeks and were heading back to their home in
Canada. I told them my plan to ship home from Mexico City. They
were amazed that I slept out and, seemingly impressed with my way
of travel, asked if they could come with me to the monarch butterfly
holiday spot in Angangueo. I said they wouldn't want to travel with
me at my speed, as I didn't go much over fifty on those roads. "That's
OK, we only do fifty too." For once, I had companions who wanted
to jump into my life instead of me jumping into theirs. I felt quite

responsible for them and their motorcycles that had never been off-road and looked as if they'd just left the showroom.

They wanted to travel how I travelled, so I told them there would be no more five-star hotels on the outskirts of town . . . we'd be sleeping wild or in cheap hotels by the central plaza. Off we went after filling the tanks (or "gassing up"), but they roared off, leaving me behind. When they stopped for more fuel (those Harleys used a lot of fuel), we realised that whilst I'd been talking about speed in kilometres per hour, they'd been talking in miles. We laughed and settled for somewhere in between. Caught out by a surprise tope, Quint came a cropper and fell, scraping several parts of his bike. "That'll be a few hundred dollars," he exclaimed.

According to my map, there was a lake ahead—perfect for our first sleep-out. I went for a swim whilst the boys were taken out in a boat by some fishermen. Later, we cooked what they had caught over a campfire and bought some beers at a local tienda, where the owners lent us hammocks. The Canadians had never done that before and, judging by the amount of snoring, slept very well.

After the first day's riding, they put it to me that, instead of shipping home from Mexico City, I could travel back to Canada with them and ship from Toronto, probably saving time in the end. They calculated there was room for the Enfield on their trailer, left with Gil's car at a friend's in Texas. They were such good fun, and my mother had always wanted to see Niagara Falls, where they lived. Although she would be oblivious of it, I felt I should fulfil one of her dreams for her and agreed. So much for my plan.

Only the fourth generation monarch butterflies migrate to where we went to see them at Angangueo. If you're born a first, second, or third generation monarch, then once fully emerged, you get to live for about ten days, but millions of the fourth generation flutter down to Mexico (like lots of other Canadians) and stay for five or six months before they fly back and start all over again. It's still chilly at night up in the Sierra Madre Oriental mountains, so they cosy up to sleep, sometimes bending, or even breaking, the branches they are huddling on.

On our way northwards to meet them, we wove up and down mountains and through small towns and villages. I found that, whereas the boys raced ahead on the straight bits of the winding roads we were on, I cruised past on bends too tight for Harleys. We spent the day walking through woodland, where butterflies fluttered down from the treetops like large falling snowflakes, landing on the branches and gently raising and lowering their wings. We stayed in cheap hotels (commonly finding rooms with three beds) in town centres, enjoying street food at the loud evening markets in the plazas where Mexican music blared.

We rode through a hilly national park where the road had disappeared but, with care, managed to squeeze along the inside edge. The scenery was so dramatic we stopped often to look down at soaring eagles and the valleys and gorges we'd just climbed. Riding past pink cliffs on our left, we posed for photos by our bikes with an enormous cactus behind us. If I were to grade my favourites, this was one of the top five rides of my entire trip. Had I stuck to my plan, I'd have missed it.

Sometimes we'd just stop and laugh for joy. In fact, I laughed nearly all the time. We ate home-made ice cream and goat tacos sold at a stall run by a stereotypical Mexican man, complete with moustache and white sombrero. Dropping down from the magnificent mountains as we neared the US border, I saw the vast landscapes of prairie I'd imagined from reading *All the Pretty Horses*. I could almost see the cattle-droving and cowboys of the past.

My Mexico experience had been a final round-up of all the things I liked best about travelling. Firstly, of course, riding my beloved Enfield. I'd encountered cultural contrasts and been just as wonder-struck as when I'd started out in India, almost seven years before. There was the spontaneity, warmth, sleeping out opportunities, variety, fun, and the promise of the unusual and unexpected to which I had become addicted.

We made the Matamoro/Brownsville border near the south-east coast on the 21st of February. I'd experienced US security at airports and imagined worse harassment coming in from Mexico on a motorbike. The stress began.

I expected every nut and bolt to be examined, my passport found wanting, to be strip-searched, and have my luggage gone through. I walked into the aliens' immigration room. They were extremely interested in my passport, quizzing me about why I had been to Pakistan and Syria. What was I doing all that travelling for?

It's difficult to explain to an expressionless immigration officer that I just like seeing places and meeting people. How could I explain the joy of travelling by motorbike, riding it in the warm sunshine past massive mountains or volcanoes with the sea at my side, when I'm feeling snackish or thirsty and wonder what the next gastronomic treat will be? Taking life at a slower pace is practically stress-free, with a growing trust and feeling of wellbeing with the world, anticipation of new things to come, and the joy of recalling the people I'd met, places I'd seen, and times I'd shared. But how do you explain all that to someone who is holding onto your passport and seems to think you're either mad or want to cause trouble in their country?

After a long wait, I was allowed to go and went back to the bike, expecting the customs stage to be even worse. But there wasn't a next stage. I was waved through and, despite asking several times about customs approval for the bike, was told to go. Didn't I need a permit or something? I caught up with the boys and rode for forty-eight ecstatic kilometres without a helmet on the roads of Texas.

We put all three bikes on their trailer behind the car in Harlingen and spent the next thirty-six hours or so batting it up through the US from the deep south (where I was delighted to find that I could have grits served by a woman who said "Hi Y'all!") to Niagara. I even got to like the country and western music they played constantly. There was a sprinkling of Italian songs, as they were both Italian-Canadians. I heard well-known songs and some new ones, such as one about "a plastic Jesus on the dashboard of my car." It tickled me, even though I wasn't sure it was supposed to be funny.

Now the norm, we shared rooms in motels. My days were spent in the back seat, often looking back fondly at my Enfield on the trailer, feeling so proud of it and the life it had given me, as we raced through Texas, Louisiana, Mississippi, Alabama, Tennessee, Kentucky, West Virginia, Pennsylvania, and New York.

Unlike at the US border, the Enfield had a thorough examination at the border into Canada. It and the luggage were X-rayed. I was told, "You're a bit of a gypsy, aren't you?" by two concerned female immigration officers assigned to talk to me about being "picked up by those two men." Was I safe? I was given a telephone number to ring in case I felt worried. Quint and Gil laughed about that.

We arrived at Toronto, where I was able to arrange shipping for the bike and me on the same flight. It was snow-covered and fourteen degrees, but it didn't feel cold as there was no wind or damp. I saw Niagara Falls, so impressive and important to my mother. I didn't have time to explore Canada much but did go skiing, visited some old friends from our teenage years, saw maple syrup being drained from trees, and used Quint's outside hot-tub. What a fantastic end to my seven years on the road.

Then I started to get worried about the procedure to get the bike off the plane at Gatwick.

20
COMING HOME

"THEY STILL MAKE THESE IN INDIA, YOU KNOW!"

Half excited, half full of dread for the bureaucracy to come, I touched down at Gatwick airport and carried my backpack of now inappropriate possessions (no need for a mosquito net, Spanish dictionary, or maps of the Americas) to the freight shed where the bike was waiting.

As bureaucratic procedures go, it was nowhere near as bad as I'd feared, and apart from signing a receipt, it was completed over the phone from a distant office, once they knew I needed the bike in order to ride away. Apparently, it was below the value at which duty had to be paid. I had arranged bike insurance before leaving Canada, having to grapple with logic and emotion to assess its value. It was priceless to me but, realistically, had cost only £1,000 new. Seven years later it was a battered and scratched heap of metal. I valued it at £25 and rode off thinking, "That was easy!"

The journey to Claire's home in Oxfordshire took hours. On the motorways, in heavy midweek traffic, I noticed that hauliers weren't called hauliers anymore—now they offered "solutions" and "logistics." I talked to the bike, telling it where we were as we travelled through Guildford, Woking, Bracknell, Oxford, and Banbury. It was dark by the time we arrived on the 22nd March 2007, seven years, almost to the day, since I'd left to meet Hendrikus in India to buy the Enfield.

I stayed with the family for two weeks, helping around the house and getting to know my granddaughter before returning to Bristol, where I would deal with making the bike officially British, its third nationality. Born Indian, later adopting New Zealand registration, it would soon have a British plate. The seven-year mileage, allowing for a new odometer in New Zealand and many kilometres lost between Nepal and India, where the speedometer hub broke during a spill, came to 40,700 miles (65,500 kilometres). I lived on Bristol Harbour on the *Kyle Blue*, the boat owned by my friend, Martin. This 118-foot Dutch barge was suitable for conversion into floating hostel accommodation.

Then, disaster. The bike had to undergo a harrowing test for vehicles entering the UK called the Motorcycle Single Vehicle Approval test. I rode to the testing centre just outside Bristol and held my breath. Looking at the bike I could see that it would be nothing short of a miracle if it passed, my greatest fear being that it wouldn't meet emission standards and that the engine would have to be rebuilt or the bike would be refused entry or, heaven forbid, have to be scrapped. Carrying a tape-measure and clip-board, the inspector, a motorcyclist himself, showed great interest in the bike, making me think it had a chance.

"Hmm . . . the front tyre needs replacing. It's not a regulation tread, and these luggage racks are too narrow by 2mm." He asked me to start the engine as he held a meter near the exhaust pipe. He told me to rev it to 4,000 revs. It doesn't have a rev counter. "More," he kept shouting, "More revs." I was wincing with discomfort. I'd never abused the engine like that. Suddenly, it shot forward and stalled. The intense revs had shocked the poor bike so much, it jumped out of neutral and into first gear. "That seems to be OK," said the torturer. "Come back with a new tyre and do something with those luggage racks and I'll pass it." But I couldn't get into neutral to start the engine. It was stuck. Nothing would make it shift. I was not pleased and let the horrid examiner know he had broken my bike. With an "Only doing my job . . . " he walked off, leaving me to make arrangements for its removal. For the first time EVER, it had to be taken away on a breakdown truck.

Over the next few days I helped Martin, an engineer, to strip the gearbox. Then, equalling the force it had taken to jam the cogs into each other on the spline, he reversed the process by tapping heavily to free them. I smoothed off the roughened edges with a rasp, and we reassembled the gearbox—a lasting repair as it turned out, still perfect ten years later. I bought a new tyre, took the luggage racks off, and arranged for another test, almost snatching the Certificate of Conformity out of the (different) inspector's hand when he passed the bike. A "MOT" roadworthiness test could then be arranged. Then it could be taxed and registered and have an ugly yellow UK rear registration plate made. It still sports its proper original Indian Tamil Nadu front plate on the front, though. It passed the MOT and was legal. It was British.

So was I, but I may just as well have been asleep for seven years. As on previous visits back to the UK, I was shocked at the prices of everything, as well as the variety of things to buy. I was so used to being frugal in countries where it was hard enough to buy necessities, let alone luxury items. I was also used to stopping for food whenever I felt hungry or the smell of something irresistible assailed my nostrils. Suddenly, I had to shop, cook, and wash up.

Three months after my return, I attended the UK Horizons Unlimited meeting in Derbyshire. Massive adventure bikes carrying huge aluminium boxes parked alongside my Enfield, with its rusting luggage racks and ex-army bags, made me feel like a time traveller from a previous era. But it was like balm; like going home. I was amongst others like me. They knew. They understood. I wasn't so strange after all. It didn't sound at all pretentious when someone yelled across the bike park to someone they knew, "Hello there– haven't seen you since Quito!" People were interested in my bike and listened to my presentation. One attendee gave up his job the following week and set off on his own travels.

I lived on the *Kyle Blue* as caretaker and labourer, wielding a sledgehammer to knock it to bits inside, ready for making it into the luxury hostel boat it now is. It was a good transition between travelling and settling down, as it didn't feel permanent. The bike lived with me on the unheated boat, the gangplank just wide enough to get it on and off. Going down to the boat was easy, but going up to the harbourside meant asking assistance from kind bikers at the nearby motorbike-friendly Brunel's Buttery café. I was living on a cold, bare boat and could offer little in the way of hospitality.

Without any heating or washing facilities on board, a nearby harbour shower was the only water, apart from a cold tap in the ship's toilet. I couldn't expect anyone to come and stay. A harsh winter, when water in the kettle froze overnight, helped me acclimatise to British temperatures. I spent my days at the centrally heated library or the Crown Court, wrote a few articles for motorcycle magazines, and gave talks at motorcycle events.

At one such event I met Jerry. He lived in north Wales, and we visited each other at weekends. One dreary, cold, and drizzly December Sunday, eight months after I'd returned to the UK, when the clocks had gone back and it was dark at 4PM, I was staying there, and we went for a ride around the hills and towns. I was in thermals and thick clothing with gauntlets, instead of fingerless gloves, and a full-face helmet, instead of my usual open-face helmet, if helmet at all. We stopped for a cup of tea, making sure our bikes were parked safely within sight and not on double yellow lines. Used to stopping wherever suited me, I could hardly bear the stifling rules and precautions there were to everything.

Sitting in the café, warming my hands round a mug of hot tea, something happened to me. I had the most desperate feeling of loss and an overwhelming wave of gloom matching the heavy cloud outside. My trip was OVER. I was no longer free. It struck me that no matter how much I wanted to be back, I was no longer doing what I'd been good at and would have to learn not to be a traveller now. I'd loved my slow-motion life, and this is what it had come to . . . going for a ride in the drizzly cold, stopping to thaw out in a café, and riding back to where I'd started from. It affected me severely.

I thought I was ready. I wanted to come home. I'd had months to prepare. After all, this wasn't new to me, as I'd been home on many occasions for weeks or even months at a time. But this time it was permanent. As I groped around in my personal fog of rehabilitation, people around me helped as much as they could, given the restrictions they had with their own problems, careers, and families. Not for them the life of whim and circumstance.

My fingernails were no longer dirty; grease and engine-oil no longer lodged there. My hair did not have dirt and diesel from the road clinging to it, making it smell of road dust and feeling like wiry hay, but half of me was still travelling. I'd bought some reasonably smart clothes from a charity shop in Toronto before coming home but still wore "on the road" clothing, viewing with disinterest anything not suitable for motorcycling. I wanted to adapt but couldn't. For seven years, I'd discovered an identity for myself that I liked. It came with a sort of uniform. It was hard to jettison serviceable black jeans, boots I'd bought in Mexico, a black sweat-shirt, and my rucksack.

I lost confidence. It had been easy to drop out of this life but much harder to ease back in than I'd thought. I also found that, yes, you can run away from difficult situations and relationship problems and spend seven years overcoming other obstacles, but you've still got to face the problems, accusations, and shattering admonishments when you come back. So used to having no plan, I found making arrangements for anything more than a week in advance brought on great anxiety. For the best part of ten years I'd been living a life of making day-to-day, minute-to-minute decisions, coping with situations as they occurred. A spontaneous life suited me.

I now panicked about putting dates in a diary and was told by my family that my reluctance to be pinned down to anything was because I was hoping for a better offer elsewhere. It must have been hurtful but was not like that. For years, I hadn't had any appointments, open to what the day brought. Having a plan was alien.

My "planning ahead" head has taken years to redevelop. It was as if I'd had a stroke and that the planning part of my brain had to be retrained. But oh, how long it has taken. At first, the thought of living anywhere permanent was frightening. I was quite lost. My life was "all change" again. Settling, for me, bears connotations of settling for second best, a negativity of accepting restriction, of being bound.

Riding my bike still always makes me smile, but it just isn't the same as riding it in hotter climes without the need for so much clothing. As I ride it to the supermarket, I look at it with wonder. How can this be the same machine I was astride when riding between volcanoes in Guatemala, in deserts in India, and riding along planks onto wooden canoes in South East Asia? Did I really sleep beside it all over the world and have it with me on those two frightening voyages? Am I the same person who took off with a Dutchman I hardly knew, bought this motorbike in India, and saw the world?

I am now one of those people I used to envy, with photos of foreign places and wooden masks on display in their homes. My aboriginal paintings and boars' tusk necklaces hang on my walls. I have age-spots from the sun, and I don't care, because each one reminds me of eyeball-melting heat in the Indian desert when I first met Hendrikus and the adventure began. I knew the risks I was taking with my skin and health and, totally content with the present, decided to accept my fate.

Now I wear proper clothes but remain an unenthusiastic cook. I still hand-wash my clothes, rather than using the washing machine, finding that if they drip-dry, they don't need ironing—I don't have an iron. I don't have a television, either, finding more than enough to do in the sociable city of Bristol.

I have no car. My Enfield remains my only means of transport and lives in the bin-store of the flat I now call home. I lived on Bristol harbour as a boat-dweller for almost three years. Home is a different concept now. On the road, wherever I slept that night was home, be it on a beach in Mexico, beside a gum tree in the Australian Outback, or in someone's luxury home in Pakistan. I enjoy where I live but am happy to leave it, without the urge to go back. I feel at home anywhere. I am my own home. I choose the ways of Buddhism and try to be complete.

That doesn't mean I don't suffer from nostalgia, though. In the early days of learning how to travel with Hendrikus and the Enfield in Tamil Nadu, I'd eaten a masala dosa every day. Recently, I ate one in Lewisham, London, and found tears streaming down my face in the restaurant. Accompanied by south Indian music, all it needed was a stainless steel "glass" and plate to complete the nostalgic experience.

Some updates:

Claire had another baby in January 2008. Laurie has a brother, Edgar. This time I was there to help. I held her son shortly after his birth and was there during his early months.

My mother died from "extreme old age" when she was 105. All the close family said their farewells the day before she slipped away. I told her about the Taj Mahal and Niagara Falls, but she'd travelled too deeply into her own foreign land inside herself to understand. I went through a period of ranting about my upbringing, blaming my own shortcomings on my parents. They were great parents to have. Neither of them tried to gender stereotype me, my mother giving up on ever getting me into pretty dresses and my father teaching me how to use an axe, saw, and carpentry tools and teaching me to view the world fearlessly and with wonder. I miss them and thank them for the freedom I had as a child to run wild with my big brother, who shared his world with me until I could make my own way. He was already in place in my world as I arrived into it, and I feel privileged to have recently spent his last few weeks looking after him as he left it.

Hendrikus lives in Perth, Australia, with his third wife. I contacted him to thank him for changing my life, and although Facebook "friends," we rarely contact each other. I asked if he still had his Enfield but received a vague reply. He has a beautiful home and lots of shiny new things. I will be forever grateful to him.

Quint died in an accident on his Harley in Mexico during another winter trip. He'd had a pleasant evening dining with friends.

Stuart Owen Fox, the photographer I stayed with in Canberra, died in 2009.

I watched the film *Love in The Time of Cholera*, but there was no sign of a battered old Enfield in the street scene in Cartagena, Colombia, where I rode onto the set.

Laurie's quilt-picture is finished and framed on her bedroom wall. She is now eleven. Edgar is nine.

My ex-husband and I are able to tolerate each other and take the grandchildren camping and spend family events and holidays together. He was big enough to tell me that he accepted he, too, was at fault for the end of our marriage by putting too much of his time and energy into work and hobbies. He said he regretted it now.

I've had a couple of initially promising, but ultimately "wrong," relationships. Paul's bankruptcy order came to an end, and he left

New Zealand to come and visit me, ten years after we'd parted. Sadly, the years did not preserve our feelings for each other, and although we had an enjoyable time during his visit, the magic had gone.

I had an operation to straighten my Pakistani-repaired leg and now walk with my foot and knee facing the right way

EPILOGUE

When I leave the bike parked somewhere, someone will inevitably talk to me and say they (or their dad) used to have one. I am often told, "They still make these in India you know!" This makes me laugh, and sometimes I play with them for a while before telling them where it came from and how it got here. It has just completed exactly. 62,137 miles (100,000 km).

I have pondered much on the subject but still don't know if it's right or wrong to give to beggars.

Many people all over the world invited me into their homes. They probably didn't have any idea of what it meant to me. I apologise to people who gave me shelter who I offended by offering to pay and to those expecting payment who were offended when I didn't. I usually left gifts or bought meals and treats. It was often difficult to know what to do. I welcome travellers to my own home whenever I can.

The Enfield and I have had many enjoyable trips since our return, and now there's a list of European countries and Morocco painted on the bike.

You could say I've had it all: freedom in my childhood, a reasonable education, a career in nursing, a happy marriage, two outstanding daughters, and then meeting a man who entirely changed my life. But I haven't finished yet and wonder what's around the corner.

I love my life. I have been re-educated into British society and have good, loving family relationships and hope I am now the mother I was asked to come home to be. I have excellent friends. I still travel, but not always on the bike. Wherever I am, I'm where I want to be, and that's a good place to be.

Shortly after my return I was having lunch with Claire and Abby, when Claire turned to me and asked, "So—what have you learned on your travels then, Mum?" Aware that journeys rarely disclose their true meanings until long after they're over, I had a think. My mind took me back to when I'd watched the cave-divers in Acapulco and afterwards had thought about how nice it was to see such things, but that what really mattered was ordinary human contact and kindness. I took a breath and replied:

"After a while, when you've seen the highest mountains, the clearest rivers, the whitest sandy beaches fringed with palm trees and turquoise sea, the most beautiful forests and the widest deserts, you realise that the people you encounter are most important; the stories they have to tell and the way they live their lives. Beauty lies in the ugliest of places. Love is universal and under our noses."

It was love that made me complete my wandering life. Most people in the twenty countries I had travelled through had been kind. That's what I learned.

My relationship with the bike (which still has no name other than Bike) has grown deeper as I realise the significance of our journey. Recently, I was attending to a rare oil leak and, having finished the job, patted the bike and asked it, "Would you like me to treat you to a nice new battery?" It didn't reply, of course. Well, not in so many words . . .

Other Books from Road Dog Publications

In Search of Greener Grass¹ by Graham Field
With game show winnings and his KLR 650, Graham sets out solo for Mongolia and beyond. Foreword by Ted Simon

Eureka¹ by Graham Field
Graham sets out on a journey to Kazahkstan only to realize his contrived goal is not making him happy. He has a "Eureka!" moment and turns around and begins to enjoy the ride as the ride itself becomes the destination.

Different Natures¹ by Graham Field
The story of two early journeys Graham made while living in the US, one north to Alaska and the other south through Mexico. Follow along as Graham tells the stories in his own unique way.

Motorcycles, Life, and . . . ¹ ² by Brent Allen
Sit down at a table and talk motorcycles, life and . . . (fill in the blank) with award winning riding instructor and creator of the popular "Howzit Done?" video series, Brent "Capt. Crash" Allen. Here are his thoughts about riding and life and how they combine told in a lighthearted tone.

The Elemental Motorcyclist¹ ² by Brent Allen
Brent's second book offers more insights into life and riding and how they go together. This volume, while still told in the author's typical easy-going tone, gets down to more specifics about being a better rider.

A Tale of Two Dusters & Other Stories¹ ² by Kirk Swanick
In this collection of tales, Kirk Swanick tells of growing up a gear head behind both the wheels of muscle cars and the handlebars of motorcycles and describes the joys and trials of riding

Bonneville Go or Bust¹ ² by Zoë Cano
A true story with a difference. Zoe had no experience for such a mammoth adventure of a lifetime but goes all out to make her dream come true to travel solo across the lesser known roads of the American continent on a classic motorcycle.
I loved reading this book. She has a way of putting you right into the scene. It was like riding on the back seat and experiencing this adventure along with Zoe.—(★★★★★ Amazon Review)

Southern Escapades¹ ² by Zoë Cano
As an encore to her cross country trip, Zoë rides along the tropical Gulf of Mexico & Atlantic Coast in Florida, through the forgotten back roads of Alabama and Georgia. This adventure uncovers the many hidden gems of lesser known places in these beautiful Southern states.
...Zoe has once again interested and entertained me with her American adventures. Her insightful prose is a delight to read and makes me want to visit the same places.—(★★★★★ Amazon Review).

Chilli, Skulls & Tequila¹ ² by Zoë Cano
Zoë takes to four wheels this time for an adventure south of the border in Baja. The extra set of wheels does nothing to dimiunish the "adventure" of this journey as Zoë travels to unique, out-of-the-way places tucked into Baja's forgotten corners.

Thoughts on the Road¹ ² by Michael Fitterling
The founder of Road Dog Publications and Editor of *Vintage Japanese Motorcycle Magazine*, ponders his experiences with motorcycles & riding, and how those two things intersect and influence his life.

Northeast by Northwest¹ ² by Michael Fitterling
The author finds two motorcycle journeys of immense help staving off depression and the other effects of stress. Along the way, he discovers the beauty of North America and the kindness of its people.
... one of the most captivating stories I have read in a long time. Truly a MUST read!!—(★★★★★ Amazon Review)

Beads in the Headlight¹ by Isabel Dyson
A British couple tackle riding from Alaska to Tierra del Fuego two-up on a 31 year-old BMW "airhead." Join them on this epic journey across two continents.
A great blend of travel, motorcycling, determination, and humor.—(★★★★★ Amazon Review)

A Short Ride in the Jungle¹ ² by Antonia Bolingbroke-Kent
A young woman tackles the famed Ho Chi Minh Trail alone on a diminutive pink Honda Cub armed only with her love of Southeast Asia and its people, and her wits.

Asphalt & Dirt ¹ ² by Aaron Heinrich
A compilation of profiles of both famous figures in the motorcycle industry and relatively unknown people who ride, dispelling the myth of the stereotypical "biker" image.

Man in the Saddle¹² by Paul van Hoof
Aboard an old 1975 Moto Guzzi V7 Paul starts out from Alaska for Ushaia. Along the way there are many twists and turns, some which change his life forever. English translation from the original Dutch.

Chasing America ¹ ² by Tracy Farr
Tracy Farr sets off on multiple legs of a motorcycle ride to the four corners of America in search of the essence of the land and its people.

ECUADOR
COLOMBIA
PANAMÁ
COSTA RICA
NICARAGUA
HONDURAS
GUATEMALA
MEXICO
(U.S.
CAN) BRISTOL